"*OUR GOD IS YOUR GOD TOO, BUT HE HAS CHOSEN US*"

Essays on Jewish Power

Laurent Guyénot

ISBN : 978-2-9571704-0-1

CONTENT

INTRODUCTION   1

1 - THE CYRUS SYNDROME:
How Yahweh Grasps the Emperor's Right Hand   3

ZION IS A BIBLICAL PROGRAM   4
JEREMIAH, BABYLON AND PERSIA   7
EZRA AND NEHEMIAH   8
DISRAELI, HERZL, AND THE SULTAN   10
LORD BALFOUR'S LETTER TO LORD ROTHSCHILD   12
"AN OLD ZIONIST LIKE ME" (WINSTON CHURCHILL)   14
"I AM CYRUS" (HARRY TRUMAN)   16
ZION AND THE NEW WORLD ORDER   19
THE SOLOMON HOAX   20

2 - CRYPTIC JEWISHNESS:
Zionism, Marranism, and the Biblical Hoax   23

WHAT'S A NEOCON, DAD?   23
TARGET SEVEN NATIONS   26
FROM CRYPTO-JUDAISM TO CRYPTO-ZIONISM   27
THE MASK OF RELIGION   30
FAKE UNIVERSALISM   33
ISRAEL AND THE DIASPORA   34
THE NATIONAL GOD WHO CLAIMED TO BE GOD   36
THE BOOK OF EZRA AND THE PROSTITUTE OF JERICHO   38

3 - ISRAEL AS ONE MAN:
Blood Covenant and Jewish Power   43

IS THE HEBREW BIBLE MATERIALISTIC?   43
JEWISHNESS AS RACIAL SOUL   46
THE PARASITIC NATION   51
CONSPIRATORIAL NETWORKING   53
THE PROBLEM OF CHRISTIAN INDIVIDUALISM   57
GERMAN HOLISTIC REACTION   60

4 - THE HOLY HOOK:
Yahweh's Trojan Horse in the Gentile City   65

IS THE CHURCH THE WHORE OF YAHWEH?   65
THE OLD TESTAMENT AS ISRAEL'S TROJAN HORSE   68
CHRISTIANS' LEARNED HELPLESSNESS   72
HOW CHRISTIANITY REINFORCED JEWISH ALIENATION   75
CHRISTIANITY AS "CONTROLLED OPPOSITION"   77
CHRISTIANITY WITHOUT THE OLD TESTAMENT?   81

5 - THE VOLCANO GOD:
The Arabian Cradle of Judaism   85

WHEN YAHWEH RESIDED IN AN ARABIAN VOLCANO   85
NEOM AND THE SAUDI-ISRAELI SECRET DEAL   88
THE ARABIAN ORIGIN OF JUDAISM   92
OTHER ABRAHAMIC PEOPLES   95
THE JUDAIC CRADLE OF ISLAM   98
WHAT DID THE MUSLIMS DO FOR THE JEWS?   103

6 - THE CRUCIFIED GODDESS:
The Rise and Fall of Western Romanticism   107

32,000 SHIKSES AND OTHER BIBLICAL STORIES   108
THE QUEEN OF HEAVEN   112
THE VIRGIN MOTHER MARY   115
THE COURTLY TRADITION OF FIN'AMOR   117
DANTE AND THE FEDELI D'AMORE   119
ROMANTICISM AND THE DIVINE SOPHIA   122
THE JEWISH ASSAULT ON LOVE   124

7 - THE LEVITICAL TERROR:
Is Yahweh an Anti-Semite?   129

JEWISH BLOOD FOR ZION   129
HOW HITLER WAS TRAPPED BY HIS OWN PROPHECY   131
THE NAZIS' GOOD JEWS   135
THE LEVITES' RULE OF TERROR   138
THE PSYCHOPATHIC BIBLICAL PARADIGM   141
THE HOLOCAUST CULT   143

8 - THE DEVIL'S TRICK:
Unmasking the Psychopathic God of Israel — 147

THE COVENANT WITH THE PRINCE OF THIS WORLD	148
THE PROHIBITION OF THE KNOWLEDGE OF GOOD AND EVIL	151
THE JEALOUS AND MURDEROUS GOD	154
ACCUSATORY INVERSION	157
YAHWEH MOLECH	159
THE LORD OF FORESKINS	161

9 - THE FREUDIAN COMPLEX:
Sigmund Freud, Sexual Abuse, and Cover-Up — 165

FREUD'S ASSAULT ON TRUTH	166
THE HIDDEN FAULT OF THE FATHER	169
THE "DARK, EMOTIONAL POWERS" OF JEWISHNESS	172
DENIAL, PROJECTION, INVERSION	176
B'NAI B'RITH AND THE ROAD TO FAME	178
THE ISAAC COMPLEX	181
FREUD ON CIRCUMCISION	184

10 - THE MARXIAN COVENANT:
Karl Marx in Yahweh's Plan for Mankind — 187

MARX'S PROPHECY AND BAKUNIN'S FORESIGHT	188
THE JEWISH QUESTION IN NINETEENTH-CENTURY GERMANY	191
MARX'S RESPONSE TO BRUNO BAUER	193
PROUDHON AND THE SOCIALIST MOVEMENT BEFORE MARX	198
MARX'S HIJACKING OF THE PROUDHONIAN LEGACY	199
THE COMMUNIST MANIFESTO, A MONOPOLIST'S DREAM	202
MARXISM VS. ZIONISM: THE DIALECTICAL PLIERS	205

INTRODUCTION

This is a collection of ten essays, originally published as feature articles on the Unz Review. I am grateful to Ron Unz for their online publication, and to all the commenters for their useful feedback, from which these essays have now benefitted.

Some of them synthetize and complement parts of my earlier and much longer book, *From Yahweh to Zion,* while others explore new ground. In particular, I have delved deeper into the causes of Christendom's vulnerability to Jewish power. The last two essays are case-studies on Freud and Marx, whose intellectual biographies provide windows into the Jewish mind, while their profound impact informs us on the workings of Jewish cultural power.

Gilad Atzmon, a great source of inspiration for me—both intellectually and morally—once wrote: "Israel defines itself as the Jewish state. In order to grasp Israel, its politics, its policies and the intrusive nature of its lobby, we must understand the nature of *Jewishness.*"[1] My own research has led me to the conclusion that Jewishness is essentially the internalized ideology of the Hebrew Bible. The Tanakh is the single ultimate root connecting all expressions of Jewishness, whether religious or secular—for what that distinction is worth. Therefore, in order to understand the nature of Jewishness, we must analyze the core message of the Tanakh.

Because it is a manifestation of Jewishness, Zionism is thoroughly biblical, as Israeli leaders, to this day, insist. David Ben-Gurion declared that, "There can be no worthwhile political or military education about Israel without profound knowledge of the Bible."[2] That statement should be taken seriously. If it is true for the Israeli leadership—and Benjamin Netanyahu would certainly not contradict it—, then it is also true for all serious analysts: there can be no real understanding of Israel and its agenda, without profound knowledge of the Bible.

The Mosaic Covenant is the original mold of Jewishness. Its basic terms are separateness, on one hand, and supremacy, on the other. If the Israelites refrain from assimilating and intermarrying

---

1. Gilad Atzmon, "Netanyahu Is Not the Disease, He Is a Symptom," March 25, 2019 on unz.com

2. Dan Kurzman, *Ben-Gurion, Prophet of Fire*, Touchstone, 1983, p. 26.

with the nations, Yahweh will make them dominate those nations. This is the leitmotiv of the Torah: "I shall set you apart from all these peoples, for you to be mine" (Leviticus 20:26), and "Yahweh your god will raise you higher than every other nation in the world" (Deuteronomy 28:1). Separateness can be seen as a form of self-alienation from the rest of humankind. But it is originally a means of oppression imposed on the Jewish people by the Levites, the elites of biblical times, who created Yahweh in their own image as a cover for their tyranny. To this day, alienation and domination go hand in hand, but are not shared by the same: to the Jewish masses, the curse of alienation, sometimes destruction; to their elites the blessing of domination. This book, therefore, is aimed at the emancipation of the Jews and Gentiles alike from the biblical matrix. For as Samuel Roth wrote in *Jews Must Live*:

> "Beginning with the Lord God of Israel Himself, it was the successive leaders of Israel who one by one foregathered and guided the tragic career of the Jews—tragic to the Jews and no less tragic to the neighboring nations who have suffered them."[3]

I will quote the Tanakh from the New Jerusalem Bible (NJB), the English adaptation of the French scholarly translation by the Dominicans of the École Biblique de Jérusalem, which I value for its scholarly standard, and for breaking with the old custom, inherited from Judaism, of replacing the tetragram YHWH by "the Lord". The god of Israel has a name, and that name is Yahweh. That is the name by which he first introduced himself to Moses, and by which he insisted on being called: "I am Yahweh, that is my name!" (Isaiah 42:8). Calling Yahweh by his name when quoting the Bible is important because it helps to understand that the god of Israel is originally a national god who only impersonated the Supreme God long after his first appearance in the crater of an Arabic volcano.

I make only one alteration to the NJB translation: since capitalization is a convention of modern translators, I usually write "god" rather than "God" when the word is used as a noun rather than a name, as in "the god of Israel." For example, where the NJB arbitrarily differentiates "Chemosh, your god" from "Yahweh, our God" in Judges 11:24, I do not.

---

3. Samuel Roth, *Jews Must Live: An Account of the Persecution of the World by Israel on All the Frontiers of Civilization,* 1934 (archive.org).

1 - THE CYRUS SYNDROME
How Yahweh Grasps the Emperor's Right Hand

When Donald Trump kept his promise to AIPAC to "move the American embassy to the eternal capital of the Jewish people, Jerusalem," that decision gave a timely support to Benjamin Netanyahu, whose popularity in Israel is largely based on his capacity to manipulate the United States, of which he occasionally brags.[1] Commenting in May 2018 on Trump's decision, Netanyahu paid him this compliment: "This will be remembered the way we remember the Cyrus declaration of 2500 years ago, when he told the exiles of Babylon, 'you can go back and rebuild the temple in Jerusalem.'"[2]

Cyrus is that Persian king whose spirit "Yahweh roused [...] to issue a proclamation" and "build him a temple in Jerusalem," according to the Book of Ezra (1:1-2) A successor to Cyrus later appointed Ezra to oversee the building. For his decree, Cyrus is bestowed the title of Yahweh's "Anointed" (*Mashiah*) by the prophet Isaiah:

> "Thus says Yahweh to his anointed one, to Cyrus whom, he says, I have grasped by his right hand, to make the nations bow before him and to disarm kings: [...] It is for the sake of my servant Jacob and of Israel my chosen one, that I have called you by your name, have given you a title though you do not know me." (Isaiah 45:1-5)

Yahweh, who "roused Cyrus' spirit" and "grasped him by his right hand," stands, of course, for "Jewish Power"—a name so holy it can only be uttered at your own risk.

Netanyahu's enthusiasm was echoed on Fox News, when Jeanine Pirro declared: "Donald Trump recognizes history. He, like king Cyrus before him, fulfills the biblical prophecy..."[3] Trump was like Cyrus again in March 2019, when he signed a decree recognizing Israel's sovereignty over the Golan Heights. It

---

1. "Netanyahu In 2001: 'America Is A Thing You Can Move Very Easily'," July 16, 2010 on www.huffpost.com

2. "Jeanine Pirro's exclusive interview with Netanyahu" on YouTube.

3. "Fox News Host Claims Trump Fulfilled 'Biblical Prophecy' By Moving U.S. Embassy To Jerusalem" on YouTube.

inspired Miriam Adelson, wife of Trump's biggest donor, to comment that the President deserves his "Book of Trump" in the Bible.[4] Israel's history is always biblical, one way or another.

Of course, moving the American embassy to Jerusalem is not exactly like rebuilding the temple. But Trump's announcement boosted messianic yearnings for the Third Temple. Confident that Trump is the new Cyrus, the Mikdash Educational Center has minted medals with Trump's and Cyrus' portraits superimposed on one side, and the future temple on the other.[5] Of course, ecstatic Jews and Evangelicals have no clue that the so-called Temple Mount never supported a temple at all: what they take for the walls of Herod's Temple is actually the remains of the Roman fort housing the legion that destroyed the Temple (as demonstrated archeologically in the documentary "The Coming Temple").

It is not the first time that a Christian statesman is compared to Persian king Cyrus. It was said before of Lord Balfour and Harry Truman. Netanyahu actually referred to them when meeting Trump in the Oval Office in March 2018:

> "I want to tell you that the Jewish people have a long memory, so we remember the proclamation of the great king, Cyrus the Great, the Persian king 2,500 years ago. He proclaimed that the Jewish exiles in Babylon could come back and rebuild our Temple in Jerusalem. We remember a hundred years ago, Lord Balfour, who issued the Balfour Proclamation that recognized the rights of the Jewish people in our ancestral homeland. We remember 70 years ago, President Harry S. Truman was the first leader to recognize the Jewish state. And we remember how a few weeks ago, President Donald J. Trump recognized Jerusalem as Israel's capital. Mr. President, this will be remembered by our people through the ages."[6]

Zion is a biblical program

Netanyahu's declaration provides a good opportunity for reflecting on the importance of biblical narratives in Israel's national consciousness, propaganda, diplomacy, and geopolitical

---

4. "A Time of Miracles," July 6, 2019, on www.reviewjournal.com

5. "Israeli group mints Trump coin to honor Jerusalem recognition," February 28, 2018, on www.timesofisrael.com

6. Andrew Silow-Carroll, "Who is King Cyrus, and why did Netanyahu compare him to Trump?" March 8, 2018, on www.timesofisrael.com

strategy, and to analyze the Cyrus pattern in the history of the relationship between Israel and imperial powers.

Netanyahu is certainly typical of Israeli leaders' tendency to see history as a perpetual reenactment of Bible stories. In 2015, he dramatized his phobia of Iran by referring to the Book of Esther, in an allocution to the American Congress that he managed to program on the eve of Purim, which celebrates the happy ending of the Book of Esther—the slaughter of 75,000 Persians.[7]

Esther's story is not unlike Ezra's: through her, Yahweh "roused the spirit" of another Persian king, Ahasuerus, to protect the Jews and hang their persecutors. In December 2019, Trump became a modern-day Ahasuerus when he signed an executive order against anti-Semitism and Israel-boycott in university campuses.

Actually, the Book of Esther is the only book in the Tanakh that makes no mention of God, which proves that "biblical" does not necessarily mean "religious". This is a point sadly misunderstood in the Christian world.

The biblical foundation of secular Zionism is ignored or denied by critics of Zionism, even when it is affirmed by the Zionists themselves. It is true that Theodor Herzl did not argue in biblical terms for his 1896 program, *The Jewish State*. Yet he named his movement after the Bible: Zion, originally a Canaanite fortress conquered by David, is used by biblical prophets, especially Isaiah, as a metonymic designation for Jerusalem.

The pioneers of the Yishuv and the founders of the Jewish State were steeped in the Bible. David Ben-Gurion was not religious; he never attended a synagogue and ate pork for breakfast. Yet he was intensely biblical. Dan Kurzman, who calls him "the personification of the Zionist dream," titles each chapter of his biography (*Ben-Gurion, Prophet of Fire*, 1983) with a Bible quote. The preface begins like this:

> "The life of David Ben-Gurion is more than the story of an extraordinary man. It is the story of a biblical prophecy, an eternal dream. [...] Ben-Gurion was, in a modern sense, Moses, Joshua, Isaiah, a messiah who felt he was destined to create an exemplary Jewish state, a 'light unto the nations' that would help to redeem all mankind."

---

7. "Benjamin Netanyahu Speech to Congress 2015" on YouTube.

For Ben-Gurion, writes Kurzman, the rebirth of Israel in 1948 "paralleled the Exodus from Egypt, the conquest of the land by Joshua, the Maccabean revolt."[8] Ten days after declaring Israel's independence, he wrote in his diary: "We will break Transjordan [Jordan], bomb Amman and destroy its army, and then Syria falls, and if Egypt will still continue to fight—we will bombard Port Said, Alexandria and Cairo." Then he adds: "This will be in revenge for what they (the Egyptians, the Aramis and Assyrians) did to our forefathers during biblical times."[9] Can you be more biblical than that? Ben-Gurion was in no way a special case. His infatuation with the Bible was shared by almost every Zionist leader of his generation and the next. Moshe Dayan, the military hero of the 1967 Six-Day War, justified his annexation of new territory in a book titled *Living with the Bible* (1978). Naftali Bennett, Israeli minister of Education, has also recently justified the annexation of the West Bank by the Bible.[10]

It is certainly helpful for understanding the Israeli treatment of the Palestinians to know that the Book of Joshua is considered a glorious chapter of Israel's national narrative. As wrote Avigail Abarbanel in "Why I left the Cult," the Zionist conquerors of Palestine "have been following quite closely the biblical dictate to Joshua to just walk in and take everything. [...] For a supposedly non-religious movement it's extraordinary how closely Zionism [...] has followed the Bible."[11] Kim Chernin, another Israeli dissident, wrote in "The Seven Pillars of Jewish Denial": "I can't count the number of times I read the story of Joshua as a tale of our people coming into their rightful possession of their promised land without stopping to say to myself, 'but this is a history of rape, plunder, slaughter, invasion, and destruction of other peoples.'"[12]

If the Book of Joshua, possibly written before the Exile, is the alpha of Zionism, the Book of Ezra is the omega. Cyrus' edict reproduced in the Book of Ezra, whether genuine or fake, is the blueprint for Zion's exploitation of the Empire's foreign policy in

---

8. Dan Kurzman, *Ben-Gurion, Prophet of Fire*, Touchstone, 1983, pp. 17-28.

9. Ilan Pappe, *The Ethnic Cleansing of Palestine,* Oneworld Publications, 2007, p. 144.

10. "Israeli minister: The Bible says West Bank is ours" on YouTube.

11. Avigail Abarbanel, "Why I left the Cult," Oct 8, 2016, on mondoweiss.net

12. Kim Chernin, "The Seven Pillars of Jewish Denial," *Tikkun*, Sept. 2002, quoted in Kevin MacDonald, *Cultural Insurrections: Essays on Western Civilization, Jewish Influence, and Anti-Semitism,* Occidental Press, 2007, pp. 27-28.

modern times. Transforming Gentile leaders into Cyrus-like figures is the rule of the game.

Jeremiah, Babylon and Persia

Before we recall how the proto-Zionists Ezra and Nehemiah convinced the Persian administration to give them control over Jerusalem, let's go back one century earlier. In 588 BC, to subdue the rebellious Judeans, Babylonian king Nebuchadnezzar II besieged and finally burned Jerusalem, then deported some of its elites (Jeremiah 52:30 gives the plausible figure of 4,600 people). The exiles enjoyed broad autonomy in Babylon, and some acquired wealth and influence. Speaking on behalf of Yahweh, Jeremiah wrote to them, from Egypt: "Work for the good of the city to which I have exiled you; pray to Yahweh on its behalf, since on its welfare yours depends" (Jeremiah 29:7). Yahweh even asked Jeremiah to convey the following message to the kings of Syria-Palestine:

> "For the present, I have handed all these countries over to Nebuchadnezzar king of Babylon, my servant. [...] Any nation or kingdom that will not serve Nebuchadnezzar king of Babylon and will not bow its neck to the yoke of the king of Babylon, I shall punish that nation with sword, famine and plague, Yahweh declares, until I have destroyed it by his hand." (Jeremiah 27:6-8)

But twenty chapters later, Jeremiah announced the "vengeance of the Lord" on the Babylonians and called on their Persian enemies to "slaughter and curse with destruction every last one of them" (50:21). In the same spirit, the author of Psalm 137 wrote: "Daughter of Babel, doomed to destruction, [...] a blessing on anyone who seizes your babies and shatters them against a rock!" The reason for this violent shift in Yahweh's sentiment was that the situation had changed: in 555 BC, a prince named Nabonad seized power in Babylon. He made war against the Persian king Cyrus. It is believed, by Jewish historian Heinrich Graetz in particular, that the Judean exiles in Babylon sided with the Persians, and perhaps "opened secret negotiations with Cyrus." That would explain "the kindness shown later on to the Judeans by the Persian warrior, and their persecution by Nabonad."[13]

---

13. Heinrich Graetz, *History of the Jews,* Jewish Publication Society of America, 1891 (archive.org), vol. 1, p. 343.

In Babylon, the Jews had gained positions of economic influence, by specializing, perhaps, in usury and tax collecting. Their influence was turned into political power under the Persians. They were rewarded for their support by high offices at the Persian court. It is believed by modern biblical scholars that the writing of the legendary stories of Joseph (Genesis 37-50), Daniel, and Esther date from this period. All are Jews who attain positions of influence in the royal court thanks to their practical intelligence or their charm, and use their power for the benefit of their people. Joseph advises the King of Egypt; Daniel, the King of Babylon; and Esther, the King of Persia.

As the king's highest official, Joseph makes his brothers wealthy (even though they have conspired against him) at the expense of the Gentile people he is supposed to serve, but really enslaves by debt. (Modern equivalents are not hard to find, and Bible worshippers shouldn't blame them for emulating the great biblical hero.)

Although placed in Egypt, the story of Joseph's ascension from slave to vizier seems to fit the Babylonian situation. The persecution of the Jews by Nabonad is perhaps reflected in the Exodus story that follows immediately Joseph's story in Genesis, where a new Pharaoh, seeing that the Israelites had become "more numerous and stronger than we are," decided to take measures "to stop them from increasing any further, or if war should break out, they might join the ranks of our enemies" (Exodus 1:9-10). Babylonian Jews, having increased in number and influence, did join Babylon's enemy.

Interestingly, the situation would be repeated in the seventh century AD, when Jews took advantage of the Byzantine-Sasanian wars to conspire against the Byzantine Empire. When in 614 the Persians besieged Jerusalem, they were assisted from within by the Jews, who then received governorship over the city and permission to build a temple. The Jews then committed one of the largest massacres of Christians in history.[14] The Persians changed their policy within three months and expelled the Jews from Jerusalem.

Ezra and Nehemiah

In exchange for their crucial support, Judeans (or Jews, the same word in Antiquity) were granted the right to return to Judea,

---

14. Read Israel Shamir, "Mamilla Pool," April 26, 2001 on unz.com

rebuild their temple, and usurp the name of Israel. Under King Cyrus' protection, some of the exiles' descendants (42,360 people with their 7,337 servants and 200 male and female singers, according to Ezra 2:64-67) returned to Jerusalem.

Under the next emperor Xerxes, the Palestinian locals tried to warn Persian authorities that the returned exiles are not just building a temple, but the city walls: "now the king should be informed that once this city is rebuilt and the walls are restored, they will refuse to pay tribute, tax or toll" (4:13). The emperor realized the abuse and put an end to the rebuilding of the walls. But Jewish Power suffered no reprisals, and their right to build the temple was confirmed by the next emperor Darius, who even ordered gigantic burnt offerings paid by "the royal revenue." If anyone resists the new theocratic power backed by Persia, Darius allegedly decreed, "a beam is to be torn from his house, he is to be impaled on it and his house is to be reduced to a rubbish-heap for his offense" (Ezra 6:11).

Then another Persian king, Artaxerxes, is said to have granted Ezra authority to lead "all members of the people of Israel in my kingdom, including their priests and Levites, who freely choose to go to Jerusalem," and to rule over "the whole people of Trans-Euphrates [district encompassing all territories West to the Euphrates]" (7:11-26). In 458 BC, eighty years after the first return of exiles, Ezra, proud descendant of Aaron, went from Babylon to Jerusalem, accompanied by some 1,500 followers. He was soon joined by Nehemiah, a Persian court official of Judean origin, whose actions are told in the Book of Nehemiah, a sequel to the Book of Ezra.

The edicts of Cyrus, Darius and Artaxerxes, as they are quoted in the Book of Ezra, are certainly not authentic. But the notion that Persian kings granted to a clan of wealthy Levites legal authority for establishing a theocratic semi-autonomous state in Palestine is probably historical. The manner by which these Judeo-Babylonian Levites maneuvered the Persians' imperial policy in support of their theocratic project for Palestine is not explained in the Bible, but we can imagine that it was not very different from the way the Zionists hijacked the Anglo-American empire's foreign policy in modern times; the edict of Cyrus the Great is comparable to the Balfour Declaration.

Calling himself the "Secretary of the Law of the God of Heaven" (Ezra 7:21), Ezra carried with him the newly redacted

Torah. Spinoza plausibly suggested in 1670 that Ezra was the head of the scribal school that had compiled and edited most of the Tanakh.[15] The greatest part of the Tanakh, including the historical books, was edited during the exilic period, and reached its near-final form after Babylon had fallen under Persian rule in 539 BC. That thesis has always met with fierce opposition from the Christian world, but it was accepted by the great British historian of civilizations Arnold J. Toynbee,[16] and it is now getting the high ground.[17] Biblical historian Philip Davies wrote that "the *ideological structure* of the biblical literature can only be explained in the last analysis as a product of the Persian period."[18]

There is an important lesson to be drawn from the books of Ezra and Nehemiah: the capacity of Israel to hijack the Empire's foreign and military policy requires that a substantial Jewish elite remain in the Diaspora. Ezra went back and forth from Babylon to Palestine, and has his tomb in today's Iraq. Nehemiah retained his principal residence in Babylon. For centuries, the kingdom of Israel was virtually ruled by the Babylonian exiles, and after the destruction of Jerusalem by the Romans, Babylon remained the center of world Jewry. Likewise today, Israel's survival is entirely dependent on the influence of the Zionist power complex in the United States (euphemistically called the "pro-Israel lobby"). The comparison was made by Jacob Neusner in *A History of the Jews in Babylonia* (1965), and by Max Dimont in *Jews, God and History* (1962). The American Jews who prefer to remain in the United States rather than emigrating to Israel are, Dimont argued, as essential to the community as were the Babylonian Jews who declined the invitation to return to Palestine in the Persian era.[19]

Disraeli, Herzl, and the Sultan

The way the wealthy and influential Judean exiles manipulated Persian foreign policy is the blueprint used for later Jewish attempts to recolonize Palestine. In the Middle Ages, there were already attempts at exploiting the holy wars waged by the imperial Roman Church in the Levant. Rabbi Moses Nachmanides declared

15. Spinoza, *Theological-political treatise,* 8.11, Cambridge UP, 2007, pp. 126-128.

16. Arnold Toynbee, *A Study of History,* vol. 12, *Reconsiderations,* Oxford UP, 1961, p. 486, quoted on mailstar.net/toynbee.html

17. Thomas Römer, *The Invention of God,* Harvard UP, 2016.

18. Philip Davies, *In Search of "Ancient Israel",* J.S.O.T., 1992, p. 94.

19. Michael Collins Piper, *The New Babylon,* American Free Press, 2009, p. 27.

in 1263: "When the end of times approaches, the Messiah will come to the Pope and will ask from him the liberation of his people" (liberation meaning the end of the dispersion). With this in mind, seventeen years later, Abraham Abulafia proclaimed himself Messiah and travelled to Rome in the hope of meeting Pope Nicholas III. A last attempt was made by Solomon Molcho (1500-1532) who, with the support of several bishops, tried to convince the Pope to raise an army of Marrano Jews to liberate Palestine.[20]

Jewish interest soon shifted away from the Catholic Empire to its British enemy. Marrano Jews in Antwerp and Amsterdam supported the anti-Spanish Calvinist uprisings in 1566, and, under Cromwell, gained unprecedented influence in British political affairs. During the reign of Queen Elizabeth (1558-1603), although the Jews remained officially banned from the kingdom, many of them penetrated into the higher spheres of the state under an (often perfunctory) Anglican or Calvinist disguise.

From then on, Jewish diplomacy focused simultaneously on the British Empire and the Ottoman Empire, which controlled Jerusalem. British Prime Minister Benjamin Disraeli (1804–1881) failed to convince the Ottoman Sultan to concede Palestine as an autonomous Jewish province at the Berlin Congress, but master-minded a successful strategy to tie British interests to the Middle East. He orchestrated the British takeover of the Suez Canal in 1875, thanks to funding from his friend Lionel Rothschild (an operation that also consolidated the Rothschilds' control over the Bank of England). Disraeli was a modern-day Ezra, capable of steering the Empire's policy according to the Jewish agenda of seizing Palestine, a dream that he had cherished ever since his first trip to the Holy Land in 1830 (at the age of 26), and that he had expressed through the hero of his novel, *The Wondrous Tale of Alroy*. It has been said that Disraeli actually invented the British Empire, for it was under his initiative that Queen Victoria was proclaimed Empress of India in 1876.

A quarter of a century after Disraeli, Theodor Herzl also turned first to the Ottoman Empire. He proposed to Sultan Abdul Hamid to use his Rothschild connections to set straight the bankrupt Turkish finances: "If His Majesty the Sultan were to give us Palestine, we could in return undertake to regulate the whole

---

20. Youssef Hindi, *Occident et Islam*, Sigest, 2015, pp. 32-36, 137-142.

finances of Turkey" (*The Jewish State,* 1896).[21] He also proposed
to influence the European press in favor of the Sultan on the
"Armenian question." In his diary, he gives this version of his
offer: "Let the Sultan give us that piece of land, and in return we
shall set his house in order, straighten out his finances, and
influence public opinion all over the world in his favor" (June 9,
1896). The Sultan told Herzl to go to hell, and, four years later,
Herzl concluded (June 4, 1900): "At present I can see only one
more plan: See to it that Turkey's difficulties increase; wage a
personal campaign against the Sultan, possibly seek contact with
the exiled princes and the Young Turks; and, at the same time, by
intensifying Jewish Socialist activities stir up the desire among the
European governments to exert pressure on Turkey to take in the
Jews."[22]

Turkey's difficulties did increase, with a revolution coming
from the Salonika crypto-Jews, followed by the First World War,
which dismantled the empire altogether.

Lord Balfour's letter to Lord Rothschild

From the Zionist perspective, the purpose of the war was to
shift the control of Palestine from the Ottoman Empire to the
British Empire, before forcing the latter to cede it to the Jews. The
trick required a short letter addressed by the British Foreign
Minister Lord Arthur Balfour to Lord Lionel Walter Rothschild,
president of the Zionist Federation. Prime Minister Lloyd George
later explained the deal in those terms: "Zionist leaders gave us a
definite promise that, if the Allies committed themselves to giving
facilities for the establishment of a national home for the Jews in
Palestine, they would do their best to rally Jewish sentiment and
support throughout the world to the Allied cause. They kept their
word."[23]

It is little known that similar declarations were simultaneously
obtained from other European powers. "Britain could not have
acted alone, because it belonged to an alliance," explains Martin
Kramer. "It would have been unthinkable for Britain to have issued

---

21. Theodor Herzl, *The Jewish State,* on www.jewishvirtuallibrary.org

22. *The Complete Diaries of Theodor Herzl,* Herzl Press & Thomas Yoseloff, 1960,
vol. 1, pp. 362-379, and vol. 3, p. 960.

23. According to a 1937 report of the Palestine Royal Commission, quoted by Alfred
Lilienthal, *What Price Israel?* (1953), Infinity Publishing, 2003, pp. 18-21.

a public pledge regarding the future of territory yet to be taken in war without the prior assent of its wartime allies—especially those that also had an interest in Palestine."[24]

Nahum Sokolow who had become the head of the World Zionist Organization in 1906, obtained from Jules Cambon, one of the great French diplomats of the day, a letter dated June 4, 1917, which not only anticipated the Balfour Declaration but cleared the way for it. It states that the French government "feels sympathy for your cause," namely "the renaissance of the Jewish nationality in that land from which the people of Israel were exiled so many centuries ago." Back in London, Sokolow deposited the Cambon letter at the Foreign Office, where it stimulated a spirit of competition. In January and February 1918, he returned to Paris, this time with the aim of securing a public French declaration in support of the Balfour Declaration.

In his *History of Zionism,* Sokolow praises, among the architects of the secret diplomacy leading to the Balfour Declaration, "the beneficent personal influence of the Honorable Louis D. Brandeis, Judge of the Supreme Court."[25] It was Sokolow who converted Brandeis to Zionism. Brandeis was, with Samuel Untermeyer, one of the most powerful Zionist schemers, exercising an unparalleled influence on the White House. He established a formidable tandem with his protégé Felix Frankfurter, who would succeed him under Roosevelt. "Working together over a period of 25 years, they placed a network of disciples in positions of influence, and labored diligently for the enactment of their desired programs," writes Bruce Allen Murphy in *The Brandeis/Frankfurter Connection.*[26] Brandeis and Frankfurter helped found the American Jewish Congress in 1918, with the aim of presenting a unified American Jewish position at the Paris Peace Conference in 1919.

Thanks to the conspiracy of these modern-day Ezra and Nehemiah, the Treaty of Versailles placed Palestine under the provisional authority of the British, whose "mandate" included the terms of the Balfour Declaration. The Declaration was integrated

24. Martin Kramer, "The Forgotten Truth about the Balfour Declaration," June 5, 2017, on mosaicmagazine.com
25. Nahum Sokolow, *History of Zionism (1600–1918),* vol. 2, 1919, pp. 79–80, quoted in Alison Weir, *Against Our Better Judgment,* 2014.
26. Bruce Allen Murphy, *The Brandeis/Frankfurter Connection,* Oxford UP, 1982, p. 10.

in the preamble of the League of Nations mandate, acquiring then full legal standing in international law.

The story of the Balfour Declaration demonstrates the capacity of Jewish networks to capitalize on a single written statement in a way that its author—in this case Lord Balfour—probably never anticipated. Balfour probably thought that, after the war, his letter, prudently worded and typed on non-official paper, would be of little consequence and easy to dismiss. The key to the Zionists' success in using this piece of paper as a cornerstone to their project is transgenerational persistency. They never let go, and, when they suffer a setback, they persistently look for the next potential Cyrus and push him into power. When the British government proved reluctant to deliver after the Versailles Treaty, the Zionists found their perfect instrument in the ambitious, unscrupulous, and bankrupt Winston Churchill (1874-1965).

"An Old Zionist like me" (Winston Churchill)

Martin Gilbert, author of *Churchill and the Jews: A Lifelong Friendship,* documents Churchill's intimate family ties with the Rothschilds and other Jewish bankers. On the fourth anniversary of the independence of Israel, Churchill declared publicly that he had been "a Zionist from the days of the Balfour Declaration," and he would write to U.S. President Eisenhower in 1956: "I am, of course, a Zionist, and have been ever since the Balfour Declaration." Churchill maintained close ties with Chaim Weizmann from 1919 on, often consulting him in private meetings. Their thoughts, Churchill said, were "99 per cent identical". In 1951, Churchill would refer to himself, in a letter to Weizmann, as "an old Zionist like me."[27]

If Balfour was Cyrus, then Churchill was Artaxerxes. In his 1920 article "Zionism versus Bolshevism: A Struggle for the Soul of the Jewish People," Churchill had already affirmed the British Government's responsibility "of securing for the Jewish race all over the world a home and a centre of national life";

> "if, as may well happen, there should be created in our own lifetime by the banks of the Jordan a Jewish State under the protection of the British Crown, which might comprise three or four millions of Jews, an event would have occurred in the history of the world which would, from every point of view, be beneficial,

---

27. This section is based on Gilbert's book, Henry Holt & Company, 2007.

and would be especially in harmony with the truest interests of the British Empire."[28]

In 1922, as Under Secretary of State for the Colonies, Churchill issued a White Paper aimed at reassuring the Arabs, but giving in fact carte blanche to the Zionists by imposing no limitation either to Jewish immigration in Palestine or to the purchase of lands by Jews, which were the two great concerns of the Arabs. It simply stated: "it is necessary that the Jewish community in Palestine should be able to increase its numbers by immigration. This immigration cannot be so great in volume as to exceed whatever may be the economic capacity of the country at the time to absorb new arrivals."

In 1939, when a new Labour majority undermined Churchill's influence in Parliament and voted a new White Paper limiting Jewish immigration to 75,000 for the next five years, Churchill systematically "refused to allow the 1939 White Paper, despite its passage into law by an overwhelming majority of Members of Parliament, to come into effect. This was certainly unconstitutional," comments Martin Gilbert. In a memorandum that he wrote for the War Cabinet on Christmas Day 1939, Churchill reminded his Cabinet colleagues that the Jews had fulfill their part of the deal for the Balfour Declaration in WW1, and that for winning WW2, "it was more necessary, even than in November 1917, to conciliate American Jewry and enlist their aid in combating isolationist and indeed anti-British tendencies in the United States."

In 1945, Churchill was defeated by a Labour majority. The new Prime Minister Clement Attlee appointed Ernest Bevin, a man ill-disposed toward Zionism, as Foreign Secretary. Churchill understood that the new British government would stick by the 1939 White Paper, and that the hopes of Zionism now rested on the USA. He argued for the U.K. to give up on "a responsibility which we are failing to discharge and which in the process is covering us with blood and shame," and to return the Mandate to the United Nations. As soon as the British handed the Mandate back to the U.N., the Zionists declared the founding of the State of Israel, which the U.S. and the Soviet Union immediately recognized.

---

28. Published on *Illustrated Sunday Herald*, January 8, 1920, on en.wikisource.org

"I am Cyrus" (Harry Truman)

Franklin Roosevelt was opposed to the creation of Israel, and more so after meeting King Ibn Saud of Arabia on the cruiser USS Quincy after the Yalta Conference in February 1945. Roosevelt gave him his word, confirmed by a letter dated April 5, that he "would take no action, in my capacity as Chief of the Executive Branch of this Government, which might prove hostile to the Arab people." In describing his meeting with Ibn Saud, Roosevelt told Congress: "On the problem of Arabia," he said, "I learned more about that whole problem—the Moslem problem, the Jewish problem—by talking with Ibn Saud for five minutes than I could have learned in the exchange of two or three dozen letters."[29]

Roosevelt died on April 12. "If Roosevelt had not died, there might not have been a Jewish state," said Nahum Goldmann, one of the most influential Zionists of the time. "Our great luck was that Roosevelt was replaced by Harry Truman, who was a simple and upright man. He said, 'My friends are Jews; the Jews want the partition, so I am giving it to them.'"[30] David Niles, the *éminence grise* of Zionism in the White House under both Roosevelt and Truman, expressed the same feeling to Stephen Isaacs: "Had Roosevelt lived, Israel would probably not have become a state."[31]

There are suspicions that FDR was actually poisoned. The case was first presented in 1948 by Emanuel Josephson in *The Strange Death of Franklin D. Roosevelt*. Less than four hours after his death, officially of a cerebral hemorrhage, FDR's body had turned black, a typical reaction from arsenic poisoning. Although Georgia law demanded an autopsy, Roosevelt's body was whisked out of the state and no autopsy was done.[32] Emanuel Josephson, a Zionist Jew, blames Stalin, but others who have looked into the case smell a Zionist coup.

According to an anecdote recounted by Craig von Buseck in his hagiography of Truman, *I am Cyrus: Harry S. Truman and the Rebirth of Israel (The Epic Story of Prophecy Fulfilled)*, in November 1953, a few months after leaving the presidency, Harry Truman met a group of Jewish dignitaries at the Jewish Theological Seminary in New York. He was accompanied by his

---

29. Martin Gilbert, *Churchill and the Jews, op. cit.*
30. Nahum Goldmann, *Le Paradoxe juif*, Stock, 1976 (archive.org), pp. 17-18.
31. Stephen Isaacs, *Jews and American Politics,* Doubleday, 1974, p. 244.
32. Emanuel Josephson, *The Strange Death of Franklin D. Roosevelt,* 1948 (archive.org).

good friend and former business partner Eddie Jacobson, who introduced him to the assembled theologians: "'This is the man who helped create the State of Israel.' Truman retorted, 'What do you mean, 'helped to create'? I am Cyrus. I am Cyrus.'"[33]

Like most Cyrus figures, Truman became a Zionist partly by personal necessity. According to the *Jewish World Review*, based on documents revealed by the Truman Library in 2003, including Abraham Feinberg's recorded testimony, "Truman did it to save his own skin." In December 1945, a few months after Roosevelt's death, Truman was still opposed to the idea of a "Jewish state", stating: "The Palestine Government [...] should be the Government of the people of Palestine, irrespective of race, creed or color."[34] But on May 15, 1948, he recognized the State of Israel ten minutes after its unilateral proclamation. This decision went against the recommendations of his Secretary of State George Marshall and his Defense Secretary James Forrestal, whom he would soon discharge. Moreover, it betrayed the Quincy Pact.

In his *Memoirs* published in 1956, Truman commented—in eloquent but somewhat hypocritical terms—on the circumstances of the vote for the 1947 Partition Plan at the General Assembly of the United Nations:

> "The facts were that not only were there pressure movements around the United Nations unlike anything that had been seen there before but that the White House, too, was subjected to a constant barrage. I do not think I ever had as much pressure and propaganda aimed at the White House as I had in this instance. The persistence of a few of the extreme Zionist leaders—actuated by political motives and engaging in political threats—disturbed and annoyed me. Some were even suggesting that we pressure sovereign nations into favorable votes in the General Assembly."[35]

The fact is that Truman, besides being financially dependent on his Jewish donors, was very vulnerable to blackmail, especially because of his past affiliation to the Ku Klux Klan. According to John Loftus and Mark Aarons, authors of *The Secret War Against the Jews: How Western Espionage Betrayed The Jewish People* (sic), the Zionists also blackmailed Nelson Rockefeller, Assistant Secretary of State in charge of Latin America, with information

---

33. Craig von Buseck, *I am Cyrus,* Straight Street Books, 2019.
34. Quoted in Alfred Lilienthal, *What Price Israel?, op. cit.,* pp. xix–xx.
35. Harry Truman, *Years of Trial and Hope,* vol. 2, Doubleday, 1956 (archive.org), p. 158.

about his business dealing with the Nazis, to have him pressure Latin American dictators to vote for the Partition Plan.[36]

In a most interesting report written in 1975, Edwin Wright, member of the Near East-Africa Division (NEA) of the State Department from 1946 to 1966, doesn't mince his words about the way the Zionists manipulated Truman: "they threatened him, they put him under the most intense pressure he ever experienced and eventually he wilted and granted to the Zionists what they wanted." Wright documents how the advice of the NEA was prevented to even reach Truman. In one report dated November 24, 1947, Loy Henderson, Director of NEA, wrote:

> "It seems to me and all the members of my office acquainted with the Middle East, that the policy we are following in New York [at the United Nations, where the U.S. Delegation was favoring the establishment of a Zionist Jewish State on territory overwhelmingly Arab] is contrary to the interests of the United States and will eventually involve us in international difficulties of so grave a nature that the reaction throughout the world, as well as in this country will be very strong. We are incurring long-term Arab hostility, the Arabs are losing confidence in the friendship and integrity of the USA. [It will encourage] Soviet penetration into important areas as yet free from Soviet domination and as vast quantities of petroleum were being discovered in Arab lands, it was essential that normal and mutually advantageous relations with the Arab world should be preserved."

"Before these memoranda could get to the Oval Office in the White House," Wright explains, "they had to pass through the screening of Sam Rosenman, Political Advisor to the President, and David (Nyhus) Niles, Appointments Secretary, both crypto-Zionists. One of these memoranda was returned unopened with a notation, 'President Truman already knows your views and doesn't need this.' That President Truman's attitude toward the NEA had been poisoned is evident from his remarks in his Memoirs that he could not trust his advisors in the State Department because they were 'anti-Semitic.'" These loyal servants of the country were insulted, muzzled or ousted for their loyalty, while Truman was held captive of advisors whose only loyalty was to the Jewish State.[37] According to David Martin, Niles is the most likely

---

36. John Loftus and Mark Aarons, *The Secret War against the Jews,* St. Martin's Griffin, 2017, pp. 212-213.
37. Edwin Wright, *The Great Zionist Cover-Up,* 1975, on newsfollowup.com

mastermind of James Forrestal's assassination in the Navy Bethesda Hospital on May 22, 1949.[38]

Zion and the New World Order

One important thing that Ben-Gurion learned from the Bible is that Israel's destiny is not to be a nation like others, but the center of the world and the ruler of all nations. When asked in 1962 his prediction for the next 25 years, he declared that Jerusalem "will be the seat of the Supreme Court of Mankind, to settle all controversies among the federated continents, as prophesied by Isaiah."[39] Indeed, Isaiah prophesied: "For the Law will issue from Zion and the word of Yahweh from Jerusalem. Then he will judge between the nations and arbitrate between many peoples" (2:3-4).

It should be evident, and it surely is to Netanyahu as it was to Ben-Gurion, that for Jerusalem to become the headquarter of a "Supreme Court of Mankind" that will replace the United Nations, another world war would be necessary. The fall of the American Empire, or at least its total transformation into Zionist occupied territory, is also part of the plan.

Ben-Gurion's prophetic vision has been shared more or less by all subsequent Israeli leaders up to Benjamin Netanyahu. It may be called *Universal Zionism*, which is the actual title of a book by the director of a Jerusalem Summit whose joint declaration recognizes Jerusalem's "special authority to become a center of world's unity," and professes: "We believe that one of the objectives of Israel's divinely-inspired rebirth is to make it the center of the new unity of the nations, which will lead to an era of peace and prosperity, foretold by the Prophets."[40]

Christians will complain that Zionists don't read their Bible correctly. In Isaiah, for example, Christians find hope that one day, people "will hammer their swords into plowshares and their spears into sickles" (Isaiah 2:4). But Zionists correctly start with the previous verses, which describe these messianic times as a *Pax Judaica*, when "the Law will issue from Zion" and Israel "will judge between the nations and arbitrate between many peoples."

---

38. David Martin, *The Assassination of James Forrestal,* McCabe, 2019.
39. David Ben-Gurion and Amram Ducovny, *David Ben-Gurion, In His Own Words*, Fleet Press Corp., 1969, p. 116.
40. Official website: www.jerusalemsummit.org

This is what Ben-Gurion obviously had in mind. Further down in the same book, Zionists read:

> "The riches of the sea will flow to you, the wealth of the nations come to you" (60:5); "For the nation and kingdom that will not serve you will perish, and the nations will be utterly destroyed" (60:12); "You will suck the milk of nations, you will suck the wealth of kings" (60:16); "You will feed on the wealth of nations, you will supplant them in their glory" (61:5-6);

Zionism cannot be a nationalist movement like others, because it resonates with the destiny of Israel as outlined in the Bible: "Yahweh your god will raise you higher than every other nation in the world" (Deuteronomy 28:1). Only by taking into account the biblical roots of Zionism can one understand that Zionism has always carried within it a hidden imperialist agenda.

The Solomon hoax

The history of Israel and Judea that we have today was written as justification for Ezra and Nehemiah's proto-Zionist enterprise, which implied the usurpation of the name and heritage of the ancient kingdom of Israel by a Judean sacerdotal caste. Of course, not everything in the historical books is pure invention: ancient materials were used. But the main narrative into which they have been aggregated is a post-exilic ideological construct.

The central piece of that narrative is the glorious kingdom of Solomon, reaching from the Euphrates to the Nile (1Kings 5:1), with its magnificent temple and its lavish royal palace in Jerusalem (described in detail in 1Kings 5-8). Believe it or not, Solomon had "seven hundred wives of royal rank and three hundred concubines" (11:3) and "received gifts from all the kings in the world, who had heard of his wisdom" (5:14).

We know today that Solomon's kingdom is a complete fabrication, a mythical past projected as the mirror image of a desired future, a fictitious justification for the prophecy of its "restoration". Even the idea that Jerusalem, located in Judea, was once the capital of Israel is blatantly false: before the Judeo-Babylonian colonization, Israel never had any other capital than Samaria. Twentieth-century archeology has definitively exposed the fallacy: there is no trace whatsoever of Solomon and his "united kingdom".[41]

---

41. Israel Finkelstein and Neil Silberman, *David and Solomon,* S&S International, 2007.

The scam is quite evident from the way the authors of the Books of Kings, surely aware of the baselessness of their story, backed it with the testimony of a spurious Queen of Sheba:

> "The report I heard in my own country about your wisdom in handling your affairs was true then! Until I came and saw for myself, I did not believe the reports, but clearly I was told less than half: for wisdom and prosperity, you surpass what was reported to me. How fortunate your wives are! How fortunate these courtiers of yours, continually in attendance on you and listening to your wisdom! Blessed be Yahweh your God who has shown you his favour by setting you on the throne of Israel! Because of Yahweh's everlasting love for Israel, he has made you king to administer law and justice." (1Kings 10:6-9)

When Ben-Gurion declared before the Knesset three days after invading the Sinai in 1956, that what was at stake was "the restoration of the kingdom of David and Solomon,"[42] and when Israeli leaders continue to dream of a "Greater Israel" of biblical proportions, they are simply perpetuating a two-thousand-year-old deception—self-deception perhaps, but deception all the same.

---

42. Israel Shahak, *Jewish History, Jewish Religion: The Weight of Three Thousand Years,* Pluto Press, 1994, p. 10.

2 - CRYPTIC JEWISHNESS
Zionism, Marranism, and the Biblical Hoax

What's a neocon, Dad?

"What's a neocon?" clueless George W. Bush once asked his father in 2003. "Do you want names, or a description?" answered Bush 41. "Description." "Well," said 41, "I'll give it to you in one word: Israel." True or not, that exchange quoted by Andrew Cockburn[1] sums it up: the neoconservatives are crypto-Israelis. Their true loyalty goes to Israel—Israel as defined by their mentor Leo Strauss in his 1962 lecture "Why We Remain Jews," that is, including an indispensable Diaspora.[2]

In his volume *Cultural Insurrections,* Kevin MacDonald has accurately described neoconservatism as "a complex interlocking professional and family network centered around Jewish publicists and organizers flexibly deployed to recruit the sympathies of both Jews and non-Jews in harnessing the wealth and power of the United States in the service of Israel."[3] The proof of the neocons' crypto-Israelism is their U.S. foreign policy: it has always coincided with the best interest of Israel as they see it.

Before 1967, Israel's interest rested on Jewish immigration from Eastern Europe. From 1967, when Moscow closed Jewish emigration to protest Israel's annexation of Arab territories, Israel's interest included the U.S. winning the Cold War. That is when the editorial board of *Commentary,* the monthly magazine of the American Jewish Committee, experienced their conversion to "neoconservatism," and *Commentary* became, in the words of Benjamin Balint, "the contentious magazine that transformed the Jewish left into the neoconservative right."[4] Irving Kristol explained to the American Jewish Congress in 1973 why anti-war activism was no longer good for Israel: "it is now an interest of the Jews to have a large and powerful military establishment in the United States. [...] American Jews who care about the survival of

---

1. Andrew Cockburn, *Rumsfeld,* Scribner, 2011, p. 219.
2. Leo Strauss, "Why we Remain Jews", quoted in Shadia Drury, *Leo Strauss and the American Right,* St. Martin's Press, 1999 (archive.org), pp. 31-43.
3. Kevin MacDonald, *Cultural Insurrections,* Occidental Press, 2007, p. 122.
4. Benjamin Balint, *Running Commentary,* Public Affairs, 2010.

the state of Israel have to say, no, we don't want to cut the military budget, it is important to keep that military budget big, so that we can defend Israel."[5] This tells us what "reality" Kristol was referring to, when he famously defined a neoconservative as "a liberal who has been mugged by reality" (*Neoconservatism: the Autobiography of an Idea,* 1995).

With the end of the Cold War, the national interest of Israel changed once again. The primary objective became the destruction of Israel's enemies in the Middle East by dragging the U.S. into a third world war. The neoconservatives underwent their second conversion, from anti-communist Cold Warriors to crusaders of the "War on Terror" and the "Clash of Civilizations."

In September 2001, they got the "New Pearl Harbor" that they had been calling for in a PNAC report a year before.[6] Two dozens neoconservatives had by then been introduced by Vice President Dick Cheney into key positions, including Richard Perle, Paul Wolfowitz and Douglas Feith at the Pentagon, David Wurmser at the State Department, and Philip Zelikow and Elliott Abrams at the National Security Council. To understand what kind of American patriot is Elliott Abrams, for example, we only need to know that he had written three years earlier that Diaspora Jews "are to stand apart from the nation in which they live. It is the very nature of being Jewish to be apart—except in Israel—from the rest of the population."[7] Perle, Feith and Wurmser had co-signed in 1996 a secret Israeli report titled *A Clean Break: A New Strategy for Securing the Realm,* urging Prime Minister Benjamin Netanyahu to break with the Oslo Accords of 1993 and reaffirm Israel's right of preemption on Arab territories. They also argued for the overthrow of Saddam Hussein as "an important Israeli strategic objective in its own right." As Patrick Buchanan famously remarked, the 2003 Iraq war proves that the plan "has now been imposed by Perle, Feith, Wurmser & Co. on the United States."[8]

How these neocon artists managed to bully Secretary of State Colin Powell into submission is unclear, but, according to his

---

5. *Congress Bi-Weekly,* quoted by Philip Weiss, "30 years ago, neocons were more candid about their Israel-centered views," May 23, 2007, on mondoweiss.net

6. PNAC, "Rebuilding America's Defenses," 2000, on archive.org

7. Elliott Abrams, *Faith or Fear: How Jews Can Survive in a Christian America,* Simon & Schuster, 1997, p. 181.

8. Patrick J. Buchanan, "Whose War? A neoconservative clique seeks to ensnare our country in a series of wars that are not in America's interest," *The American Conservative,* March 24, 2003, on www.theamericanconservative.com

biographer Karen DeYoung, Powell privately rallied against this "separate little government" composed of "Wolfowitz, Libby, Feith, and Feith's 'Gestapo Office'."[9] His chief of staff, Colonel Lawrence Wilkerson, declared in 2006 on PBS that he had "participated in a hoax on the American people, the international community and the United Nations Security Council,"[10] and in 2011, he openly denounced the duplicity of neoconservatives such as Wurmser and Feith, whom he considered "card-carrying members of the Likud party." "I often wondered," he said, "if their primary allegiance was to their own country or to Israel."[11] Something doesn't quite ring true when neocons say "we Americans," as Paul Wolfowitz declaring: "Since September 11, *we Americans* have one thing more in common with Israelis."[12]

The neocons' capacity to deceive the American public by posturing as American rather than Israeli patriots required that mentioning their Jewishness was taboo, and Carl Bernstein, though a Jew himself, provoked a scandal by citing on national television the responsibility of "Jewish neocons" for the Iraq war.[13] But the fact that the destruction of Iraq was carried out on behalf of Israel is now widely accepted, thanks in particular to John Mearsheimer and Stephen Walt's book, *The Israel Lobby and U.S. Foreign Policy,* published in 2007. And even the best liars betray themselves sometimes. Philip Zelikow briefly dropped the mask during a conference at the University of Virginia on September 10, 2002:

> "Why would Iraq attack America or use nuclear weapons against us? I'll tell you what I think the real threat is and actually has been since 1990: it's the threat against Israel. And this is the threat that dare not speak its name, because the Europeans don't care deeply about that threat, I will tell you frankly. And the American government doesn't want to lean too hard on it rhetorically, because it is not a popular sell."[14]

9. Stephen Sniegoski, *The Transparent Cabal: The Neoconservative Agenda, War in the Middle East, and the National Interest of Israel,* Enigma Edition, 2008, p. 156.

10. His interview is on www.pbs.org/now/politics/wilkerson.html

11. Stephen Sniegoski, *The Transparent Cabal, op. cit.,* p. 120.

12. April 11, 2002, quoted in Justin Raimondo, *The Terror Enigma: 9/11 and the Israeli Connection,* iUniverse, 2003, p. 19.

13. April 26, 2013, on MSNBC, "Jewish-American Journalist Carl Bernstein reveals the role 'Jewish Neocons' in Launching Iraq War" on YouTube.

14. Noted by *Inter-Press Service* on March 29, 2004, under the title "U.S.: Iraq war is to protect Israel, says 9/11 panel chief," and repeated by *United Press International.*

Target seven nations

Although the Jewishness of most neocons is not a secret, some have kept it hidden from the public. One example is General Wesley Clark, former Supreme Commander for NATO in Europe (he led the aggression against Serbia in 1999). Only in 1999 did he reveal being the son of Benjamin Jacob Kanne.[15] He has postured as a whistleblower and successfully duped a large segment of the anti-war resistance, by writing in *Winning Modern Wars* (2003) and repeating on Jewish controlled opposition webzines such as Amy Goodman's *Democracy Now*, that one month after September 11, 2001, a Pentagon general showed him a memo "that describes how we're gonna take out seven countries in five years, starting with Iraq, and then Syria, Lebanon, Libya, Somalia and Sudan and finishing off with Iran."[16] As the proud descendant of a lineage of Kohen rabbis, it is hard to believe that Clark/Kanne has never heard about the archetypal "seven nations" marked for destruction by Yahweh for their opposition to Israel. These "seven nations greater and mightier than you," Yahweh told his people, "you must utterly destroy," and "show no mercy to them." As for their kings, "you shall make their name perish from under heaven" (Deuteronomy 7:1-2, 24). The destruction of the "seven nations," also mentioned in Joshua 24:11, is considered a *mitzvah* in rabbinic Judaism, and by the great Maimonides in his *Book of Commandments*,[17] and it has remained a popular motif in Jewish culture.

Is Clark a crypto-Zionist trying to write history in biblical terms, while blaming these wars on WASP Pentagon warmongers instead of his neocon friends? Interestingly, in his September 20, 2001 speech, President Bush also cited seven "rogue states" for their support of global terrorism, but in his list, Cuba and North Korea replaced Lebanon and Somalia. Was it because part of Bush's entourage refused to include Lebanon and Somalia, while his neocon handlers insisted on keeping the number seven for its symbolic value? Whatever the explanation, I suspect that the importance of targeting exactly "seven nations" after 9/11 stems from the same biblical obsession as the need to have ten Nazi officers hanged on Purim day to match the ten sons of Haman

---

15. jewishweek.timesofisrael.com/the-generals-jewish-war-story/
16. Wesley Clark, *Winning Modern Wars*, Public Affairs, 2003, p. 130.
17. "Destroying the Seven Canaanite Nations," on www.chabad.org

hanged in the Book of Esther. Fulfilling prophecy is a symbolic demonstration of supernatural power, meant to impress on Gentiles a sense of helplessness. Just like Rabbi Bernhard Rosenberg can now marvel at how prophetic the Book of Esther is,[18] a few decades from now, Jewish and Christian Zionists will praise their bloodthirsty god for the fulfillment of Deuteronomy 7. Such was the plan, at least. But fulfilling prophecies does not always come easy: Isaiah 17:1, "Behold, Damascus will soon cease to be a city, it will become a heap of ruins," has resisted. Yahweh is not as almighty as he claims.

From crypto-Judaism to crypto-Zionism

Norman Podhoretz, editor-in-chief of *Commentary* (and father-in-law of Elliott Abrams), said that after June 1967, Israel became "the religion of the American Jews."[19] That is, at least, what he started working at. But, naturally, such religion had better remain discreet outside the Jewish community, if possible even secret, and disguised as American patriotism. The neocons have perfected this fake American patriotism wholly profitable to Israel, and ultimately disastrous for Americans—a pseudo-Americanism that is really a crypto-Israelism or crypto-Zionism.

This crypto-Zionism is comparable to the crypto-Judaism that has played a determining role in Christendom in the late Middle Ages. From the end of the fourteenth century, sermons, threats of expulsion, and opportunism made over a hundred thousand Jewish converts to Catholicism in Spain and Portugal, many of whom continued to "Judaize" secretly. Freed from the restrictions imposed on Jews, these "New Christians," called *Conversos* or *Marranos*, experienced a spectacular socio-economic ascension. In the words of historian of Marranism Yirmiyahu Yovel: "*Conversos* rushed into Christian society and infiltrated most of its interstices. After one or two generations, they were in the councils of Castile and Aragon, exercising the functions of royal counselors and administrators, commanding the army and navy, and occupying all ecclesiastical offices from parish priest to bishop and cardinal. [...] The *Conversos* were priests and soldiers, politicians and professors, judges and theologians, writers, poets and legal

---

18. Rabbi Bernhard Rosenberg, "Did Purim heroine Esther prophesy about the Nazis?" March 4, 2015 on eu.mycentraljersey.com
19. Norman Podhoretz, *Breaking Ranks,* Harper & Row, 1979, p. 335.

advisors—and of course, as in the past, doctors, accountants and high-flying merchants. Some allied themselves by marriage to the greatest families of Spanish nobility [...] Their ascent and penetration in society were of astonishing magnitude and speed."[20]

Not all these *Conversos* were crypto-Jews, that is, insincere Christians, but most remained proudly ethnic Jews, and continued to marry among themselves. Solomon Halevi, chief rabbi of Burgos, converted in 1390, took the name of Pablo de Santa Maria, became Bishop of Burgos in 1416, and was succeeded by his son Alonso Cartagena. Both father and son saw no contradiction between the Torah and the Gospel, and believed that Jews made better Christians, as being from the chosen people and of the race of the Messiah.[21]

A new situation was created after the Alhambra Decree (1492) that forced Spanish Jews to choose between conversion and expulsion. Four years later, those who had stayed loyal to their faith and migrated to Portugal were given the choice between conversion and death, with no possibility of leaving the country. Portugal now had a population of about 12 percent so-called New Christians, deeply resentful of Catholicism. They learned and perfected the art of leading a double life. When they were eventually allowed to leave the country and engage in international trade in 1507, they "soon began to rise to the forefront of international trade, virtually monopolizing the market for certain commodities, such as sugar, to participate to a lesser degree in trading spices, rare woods, tea, coffee, and the transportation of slaves."[22] When in 1540, the new Portuguese king introduced the Inquisition following the Spanish model, tracking down Portuguese Judaizers all over Europe and even in the New World, Marranos became more intensely resentful of the Catholic faith they had to fake, and more secretive. They played an important role in the Calvinist or Puritan movement which, after undermining Spanish domination on the Netherlands, conquered England and ultimately formed the religious bedrock of the United States.

Catholic monarchs are to blame for having drafted by force into Christendom an army of enemies that would largely contribute to the ruin of the Catholic empire. By and large, the Roman

---

20. Yirmiyahu Yovel, *L'Aventure marrane,* Seuil, 2011, pp. 119-120.
21. Nathan Wachtel, *Entre Moïse et Jésus,* CNRS éditions, 2013, pp. 54-65.
22. Yirmiyahu Yovel, *L'Aventure marrane, op. cit.,* p. 347.

Church has done much to foster the Jewish culture of crypsis. However, segregation and forced conversions were not the only factor. Crypto-Jews could find justification in their Hebrew Bible, in which they read: "Rebekah took her elder son Esau's best clothes, which she had at home, and dressed her younger son Jacob in them. [...] Jacob said to his father, 'I am Esau your first-born'" (Genesis 27:15-19).

If Jacob cheated his brother Esau of his birthright by impersonating him, why would they not do the same? (Jacob being, of course, Israel, and Esau or Edom being codenames for the Catholic Church.) Crypto-Jews also found comfort and justification in the biblical figure of Esther, the clandestine Jewess who inclined the Persian king favorably toward her people. For generations, Spanish and Portuguese Marranos prayed to "saint Esther."[23] This is significant because the legend of Esther is a cornerstone of Jewish culture: every year the Jews celebrate this fiction by the feast of Purim.[24] Another factor to consider is the ritual prayer of Kol Nidre recited before Yom Kippur at least since the twelfth century, by which Jews absolved themselves in advance of "all vows, obligations, oaths or anathemas, pledges of all names," including, of course, baptism.

Marranos and their descendants had a deep and lasting influence in economic, cultural and political world history, and their culture of crypsis survived the Inquisition. A case in point is the family of Benjamin Disraeli, who defined himself as "Anglican of Jewish race."[25] His grandfather was born from Portuguese Marranos converted back to Judaism in Venice, and had moved to London in 1748. Benjamin's father, Isaac D'Israeli was the author of a book on *The Genius of Judaism,* but had his whole family baptized when Benjamin was thirteen, because administrative careers were then closed to the Jews in England.

What was Disraeli's motivation behind his British imperial foreign policy as Queen Victoria's prime minister? Did he believe in Britain's destiny to control the Middle East? Or did he see the British Empire as the tool for the fulfillment of Israel's own destiny? In mooring the Suez Canal to British interests, did he just

---

23. Yirmiyahu Yovel, *L'Aventure marrane, op. cit.,* pp. 149-151.
24. Elliott Horowitz, *Reckless Rites: Purim and the Legacy of Jewish Violence,* Princeton UP, 2006.
25. Hannah Arendt calls him a "race fanatic" in *The Origins of Totalitarianism,* vol. 1, Meridian Books, 1958, pp. 309-310.

seek to outdo the French, or was he laying the foundation for the future alliance between Israel and the Anglo-American Empire? No one can answer these questions with certainty. But Disraeli's contemporaries pondered them. William Gladstone, his longtime competitor for the prime ministry, accused him of "holding British foreign policy hostage to his Jewish sympathies."[26] So we see that the neoconservatives' loyalty to Israel, and their control of the Empire's foreign policy, is not a new issue. The case of Disraeli highlights the continuity between pre-modern crypto-Judaism and modern crypto-Zionism.

The mask of religion

From his Darwinian perspective, Kevin MacDonald sees crypto-Judaism as "an authentic case of crypsis quite analogous to cases of mimetic camouflage in the natural world."[27] Judaism itself, in its modern form, falls into the same category, according to MacDonald. In the eighteenth century, by claiming to be adepts of a religious confession, Jews gained full citizenship in European nations, while remaining ethnically endogamic and suspiciously uninterested in converting anyone. Referring to the Hebrew school of his childhood, which he attended after regular school hours like all American Jewish schoolchildren of his time, Samuel Roth explained:

> "The preservation of Jewish religion and culture are merely excuses for something else, a smoke-screen. What the Jew really wants and expects to achieve through the instrumentality of the Hebrew school is to cultivate in his son the sharp awareness that he is a Jew and that as a racial Jew—apart from all the other races—he is waging an old war against his neighbors. The young Jew must learn to remember that before anything else he is a Jew, that, before any other allegiance, comes his allegiance to the Jewish People."[28]

Gilad Atzmon points out that the Haskalah motto, "Be a Jew at home and a man in the street" is fundamentally dishonest: "The Haskalah Jew is deceiving his or her God when at home, and misleading the goy once in the street. In fact, it is this duality of

---

26. Stanley Weintraub, *Disraeli: A Biography,* Hamish Hamilton, 1993, p. 579.

27. Kevin MacDonald, *Separation and Its Discontents: Toward an Evolutionary Theory of Anti-Semitism,* Praeger, 1998.

28. Samuel Roth, *Jews Must Live: An Account of the Persecution of the World by Israel on All the Frontiers of Civilization,* 1934 (archive.org).

tribalism and universalism that is at the very heart of the collective secular Jewish identity. This duality has never been properly resolved."[29]

Zionism was an attempt at resolving this duality. Moses Hess wrote in his influential book *Rome and Jerusalem: A Study in Jewish Nationalism* (1862): "Those of our brethren who, for purposes of obtaining emancipation, endeavor to persuade themselves, as well as others, that modern Jews possess no trace of a national feeling, have really lost their heads." For Hess, a Jew is a Jew "by virtue of his racial origin, even though his ancestors may have become apostates." Addressing his fellow Jews, Hess defended the national character of Judaism and denounced the assimilationist Jew's "beautiful phrases about humanity and enlightenment which he employs as a cloak to hide his treason."[30]

In return, Reformed Judaism opposed the nationalist version of Jewishness. On the occasion of their 1885 Pittsburgh Conference, American reformed rabbis issued the following statement: "We consider ourselves no longer a nation, but a religious community, and therefore expect neither a return to Palestine, nor the restoration of a sacrificial worship under the Sons of Aaron, or of any of the laws concerning the Jewish State."[31]

Yet Reformed Judaism promoted a messianic theory that continued to ascribe an exalted role to Israel as chosen people. German-American rabbi Kaufmann Kohler, a star of the Pittsburgh Conference, argued in his *Jewish Theology* (1918) for the recycling of the messianic hope into "the belief that Israel, the suffering Messiah of the centuries, shall at the end of days become the triumphant Messiah of the nations."

> "Israel is the champion of the Lord, chosen to battle and suffer for the supreme values of mankind, for freedom and justice, truth and humanity; the man of woe and grief, whose blood is to fertilize the soil with the seeds of righteousness and love for mankind. [...] Accordingly, modern Judaism proclaims more insistently than ever that the Jewish people is the Servant of the Lord, the suffering Messiah of the nations, who offered his life as an atoning sacrifice for humanity and furnished his blood as the

29. Gilad Atzmon, *The Wandering Who? A Study of Jewish Identity Politics,* Zero Books, 2011, pp. 55-56.

30. Moses Hess, *Rome and Jerusalem*, 1918 (archive.org), pp. 27, 74.

31. Quoted in Alfred Lilienthal, *What Price Israel?* (1953), Infinity Pub., 2003, p. 14.

cement with which to build the divine kingdom of truth and justice."[32]

It is easy to recognize here an imitation of Christianity: the crucifixion of Christ ("by the Jews," Christians used to say) is turned into a symbol of the martyrdom of the Jews (by Christians). Interestingly, the theme of the "crucifixion of the Jews" was also widely used by secular Zionist Jews as a diplomatic argument.[33]

But what is more important to understand is that Reformed Judaism rejected traditional nationalism (the quest for statehood) only to profess a sort of meta-nationalism: Israel as "Messiah of the nations." While affirming their mutual incompatibility and competing for the hearts of Jews, Reformed Judaism and Zionism, dovetailed perfectly: Zionism played the rhetoric of European nationalist movements to claim "a nation like others" (for *Israelis*), while Reformed Judaism aimed at empowering a nation like no other and without borders (for *Israelites*). That explains why in 1976, American Reformed rabbis crafted a new resolution affirming: "The State of Israel and the Diaspora, in fruitful dialogue, can show how a People transcends nationalism while affirming it, thus establishing an example for humanity."[34] In a marvelous example of Hegelian dialectical synthesis, both the religious and the national faces of Jewishness contributed to the end result: a nation with both a national territory and an international citizenry, exactly what Leo Strauss had in mind. Except for a few orthodox Jews, most Jews today see no contradiction between Judaism as a religion and Zionism as a nationalist project.

The question of whether such dialectical machinery was engineered by Yahweh or by B'nai B'rith is open to debate. But it can be seen as an inherent dynamic of Jewishness: the Jewish cognitive elites may find themselves divided on many issues, but since their choices are ultimately subordinated to the great metaphysical question, "Is it good for Jews?" there always comes a point when their oppositions are resolved in a way that reinforces their global position.

---

32. Kaufmann Kohler, *Jewish Theology,* Macmillan, 1918 (www.gutenberg.org).
33. Read for instance Martin H. Glynn, "The Crucifixion of Jews Must Stop!" *The American Hebrew,* October 31, 1919, on www.jrbooksonline.com
34. Quoted in Kevin MacDonald, *Separation and Its Discontents, op. cit.*

Fake universalism

With "what is good for the Jews" in mind, contradictions are easily resolved. All it takes is a bit of Talmudic pilpul. Jewish intellectuals, for example, can be ethnic nationalists in Israel, and pro-immigration multiculturalists everywhere else. A paragon of this contradiction was Israel Zangwill, the successful author of the play *The Melting Pot* (1908), whose Jewish protagonist praises assimilation by mixed marriages: "America is God's Crucible, the great Melting-Pot where all the races of Europe are melting and reforming." The paradox is that when he was writing this, Zangwill was a leading figure of Zionism, that is, a movement affirming the impossibility for Jews to live among Gentiles, and demanding that they be ethnically separated. Zangwill is the author of another famous formula: "Palestine is a land without people for a people without land," and is quoted saying, regarding the Palestinians, "Let them get out! [...]. After all, they have all Arabia with its million square miles, and Israel has not a square inch. There is no particular reason for the Arabs to cling to those few kilometers."[35]

Although it appears to be contradictory for non-Jews, this dual standard is not necessarily so from the point of view of Jewish intellectuals. They may really believe in their universalistic message addressed to the Goyim, while simultaneously believing that Jews should remain a separate people. The implicit logic is that it is good that Jews remain Jews in order to teach the rest of mankind to be universal, tolerant, anti-racists, immigrationists, and caring for minorities (especially Jews). This logic falls under the "mission theory", the secular version of the "messianic nation" theory: Jews, who have invented monotheism, the Ten Commandments and so on, have a moral obligation to keep educating the rest of humankind. For this, they must remain separate. What the "mission" entails is open to reversible interpretations. Rabbi Daniel Gordis, in *Does the World Need Jews?* claims that "Jews need to be different in order that they might play a quasi-subversive role in society [...] the goal is to be a contributing and respectful 'thorn in the side' of society."[36] That naturally tends to upset the Goyim, but it is for their good. It is to free them from their "false gods" that Jews are "a corrosive force", also insists

---

35. Quoted in Henry Ford, *The International Jew* (archive.org), May 28, 1921.
36. Daniel Gordis, *Does the World Need Jews?* Scribner, 1997, p. 177.

Douglas Rushkoff, author of *Nothing Sacred: The Truth About Judaism.*[37]

Preaching universalism to the Goyim in the street while emphasizing ethnic nationalism at home is the great deception. It is the essence of crypto-Judaism and of its modern form, crypto-Zionism. It is so deeply ingrained that it has become a kind of collective instinct among many Jews. It can be observed in many contexts. The following remark by historian Daniel Lindenberg illustrates that Jewish internationalists' relation to Israel in the twentieth century strongly resembled the Marranos' relation to Judaism in pre-modern times:

> "Anyone who has known Communist Jews, ex-Kominternists, or even some prominent representatives of the 1968 generation will know what frustrated crypto-Jewishness means: Here are men and women who, in principle, according to the 'internationalist' dogma, have stifled in themselves all traces of 'particularism' and 'petty-bourgeois Jewish chauvinism,' who are nauseated by Zionism, support Arab nationalism and the great Soviet Union— yet who secretly rejoice in Israel's military victories, tell anti-Soviet jokes, and weep while listening to a Yiddish song. This goes on until the day when, like a Leopold Trepper, they can bring out their repressed Jewishness, sometimes becoming, like the Marranos of the past, the most intransigent of neophytes."[38]

Israel and the Diaspora

If Jews can be alternatively or even simultaneously nationalists (Zionists) and internationalists (communists, globalists, etc.), it is, in the final analysis, because this duality is inherent to the paradoxical nature of Israel.

Until the foundation of the "Jewish state", "Israel" was a common designation for the international Jewish community, for example when on March 24, 1933, the British *Daily Express* printed on its front-page: "*The whole of Israel throughout the world* is united in declaring an economic and financial war on Germany."[39] Until 1947, most American and European Jews were satisfied of being "Israelites", members of a worldwide Israel. They saw the advantage of being a nation dispersed among nations. International Jewish organizations such as B'nai B'rith

---

37. "Corrosive force" on YouTube.
38. Daniel Lindenberg, *Figures d'Israël*, Fayard, 2014, p. 10.
39. Alison Weir, *Against Our Better Judgment*, 2014.

(Hebrew for "Children of the Covenant") founded in New York in 1843, or the Alliance Israélite Universelle, founded in Paris in 1860, had no claim on Palestine.

Even after 1947, most American Jews remained ambivalent about the new State of Israel, knowing that to support it publicly would make them liable to the accusation of dual loyalty. It was only after the Six-Day War that American Jews began to support Israel more actively and openly. There were two reasons for this. First, Zionist control of the press had become such that American public opinion was easily persuaded that Israel had been the victim and not the aggressor in the war that allowed Israel to triple its territory. Secondly, after 1967, the crushing deployment of Israeli power against Egypt, a nation supported diplomatically by the USSR, enabled the Johnson administration to elevate Israel to a strategic asset in the Cold War. Norman Finkelstein explains:

> "For American Jewish elites, Israel's subordination to US power was a windfall. Jews now stood on the front lines defending America—indeed, 'Western civilization'—against the retrograde Arab hordes. Whereas before 1967 Israel conjured the bogey of dual loyalty, it now connoted super-loyalty. [...] After the 1967 war, Israel's military élan could be celebrated because its guns pointed in the right direction—against America's enemies. Its martial prowess might even facilitate entry into the inner sanctums of American power."[40]

Israeli leaders, for their part, stopped blaming American Jews for not settling in Israel, and recognized the legitimacy of serving Israel while residing in the United States. In very revealing terms, Benjamin Ginsberg writes that already in the 1950s, "an accommodation was reached between the Jewish state in Israel and the Jewish state in America"; but it was after 1967 that the compromise became a consensus, as anti-Zionist Jews were marginalized and silenced.[41] Thus was born a new Israel, headquartered in Tel Aviv but with satellites in New York, Paris, and other cities around the world; a nation without borders, delocalized.

Thanks to the powerful diaspora of virtual Israelis now entrenched in all levels of power in the US, France and other nations, Israel is a very special nation indeed. And everyone can now see that it has no intention of being a banal nation. Israel is

---

40. Norman Finkelstein, *The Holocaust Industry,* Verso, 2014, p. 6.
41. Benjamin Ginsberg, *Jews in American Politics,* Rowman & Littlefield, 2004, p. 22.

destined to be an Empire. If Zionism is defined as the movement
for the foundation of a Jewish State in Palestine, then what we see
at work today may be called meta-Zionism, or super-Zionism. It is
the fulfillment of the biblical project.

The national god who claimed to be God

Deeper than the historical deception, at the very core of the
Bible, lies a more essential metaphysical deception that goes a long
way toward explaining the ambivalence of tribalism and
universalism so typical of Jewishness. Once we understand the
historical process of Yahweh's outrageous impersonation of the
universal Great God, we can start seeing Jewish universalism for
what it is: an extreme and pathological form of ethnocentrism. And
we can read through such nonsense of Emmanuel Levinas' claim
that Judaism constitutes a "particularism that conditions univer-
sality" so that "there is an obvious equation between Israel and the
Universal," because "Israel equals humanity."[42]

In the pre-exilic strata of the Bible, Yahweh is a national god
among others: "For all peoples go forward, each in the name of its
god, while we go forward in the name of Yahweh our god for ever
and ever," says pre-exilic prophet Micah (4:5). What sets Yahweh
apart from other national gods is his jealousy, which presupposes
the existence of other gods: "You shall have no other gods to rival
me" (Exodus 20:3). Only in the Persian period does Yahweh really
become the only existing god, and, by logical consequence, God,
the creator of the Universe—the first chapter of Genesis being
demonstrably borrowed from Mesopotamian myths.

That transformation of national Yahweh into the "God of
Heaven and Earth" is a case of crypsis, an imitation of Persian
religion, for the purpose of political and cultural ascendency. The
Persians were predominantly monotheistic under the Achaemenids,
worshipers of the Supreme God Ahura Mazda, whose representations and invocations can be seen on royal inscriptions. Herodotus
wrote about the Persians' customs in the fifth century BC: "they
have no images of the gods, no temples nor altars, and consider the
use of them a sign of folly," preferring to "ascend the summits of
the loftiest mountains, and there to offer sacrifice to Zeus, which is
the name they give to the whole circuit of the firmament"
(*Histories*, I.131).

---

42. Emmanuel Levinas, *Difficult Freedom,* John Hopkins UP, 1990, pp. 22 and 223.

Persian monotheism was remarkably tolerant of other cults. In contrast, Judean monotheism is exclusivist because, although Yahweh now claims to be the universal God, he remains the ethnocentric, xenophobic, jealous god of Israel. And so Persian influence was not the only factor in the development of biblical monotheism, that is, the claim that "the god of Israel" is the One and Only God: Yahweh's sociopathic jealousy, his murderous hatred of all other gods and goddesses, was an important ingredient from pre-exilic times. Being the only god worthy of worship is tantamount to being the only god, and therefore God.

In 1Kings 18, we see Yahweh compete with the great Canaanite god Baal. In ancient Syria, Baal (a name meaning simply "Lord", as the Hebrew *Adonai*), also known as Baal Shamem ("the Lord of Heaven"), was understood as the Supreme God, encompassing all the manifestations of the divine.[43] And so it is ironic that Yahweh, a tribal god, should compete with the great Baal. The cult of Baal received royal support in the powerful kingdom of Israel under the Omrid dynasty (9th century BC). We learn in the Cycle of Elijah (from 1Kings 17 to 2Kings 13) that the Yahwist prophet Elijah challenged 450 prophets of Baal to conjure lightning upon a sacrificial bull: "You must call on the name of your god, and I shall call on the name of Yahweh; the god who answers with fire, is God indeed"—an implausible situation since Baal, being the God of an agrarian society, never required holocausts. Elijah wins the contest, and people then fall on their faces and scream "Yahweh is God! Yahweh is God!" Then they seize all the prophets of Baal, and Elijah slaughters them (1Kings 18).

Later on we read of the Judean general Jehu who, having overthrown and slaughtered Israel's dynasty of King Omri, summoned all the priests of Baal for "a great sacrifice to Baal," and, as sacrifice, massacred them all. "Thus Jehu rid Israel of Baal" (2Kings 10,18-28). This is the perfect illustration of how Yahweh became Supreme God instead of Baal: by the physical elimination of all the priests of Baal, that is, exactly the same way that Jehu became king of Israel by exterminating the family of the legitimate king, as well as "all his leading men, his close friends, his priests; he did not leave a single one alive" (2Kings 10:11).

---

43. Norman Habel, *Yahweh Versus Baal,* Bookman Associates, 1964, p. 41.

These legendary stories have come to us in a post-exilic redaction, and although they may reflect an earlier war between Yahwism and Baalism, the metaphysical claim that Yahweh is the supreme God, the Creator of Heaven and Earth, only became an explicit creed and a cornerstone of Judaism from the Babylonian period. It was a means of assimilation-dissimulation into the Persian commonwealth, comparable to the way Reformed Judaism mimicked Christianity in the nineteenth century.

The Book of Ezra and the prostitute of Jericho

The process of how Yahweh was transformed from national to universal god, while remaining intensely chauvinistic, can actually be documented from the Book of Ezra. It contains extracts from several edicts attributed to succeeding Persian kings. They are certainly not genuine documents, but their content is indicative of the politico-religious strategy deployed by the Judean exiles for their proto-Zionist lobbying. In the first edict, Cyrus the Great declares that "*Yahweh, the God of Heaven*, has given me all the kingdoms of the earth and has appointed me to build him a Temple in Jerusalem*," then goes on to allow Yahweh's people to "go up to Jerusalem, in Judah, and build the Temple of *Yahweh, the god of Israel, who is the god in Jerusalem*" (Ezra 1:2–3). We understand that both phrases refer to the same entity, but the duality is significant.

We find the same paradoxical designation of Yahweh as both "God of Heaven" and "god of Israel in Jerusalem" in the Persian edict authorizing the second wave of return. It is now King Artaxerxes who asks "the priest Ezra, Secretary of the Law of *the God of Heaven*," to offer a gigantic holocaust to "*the god of Israel who resides in Jerusalem*" (7:12-15). We later find twice the same expression "God of Heaven" (*Elah Shemaiya*) interspersed with seven references to "your god," that is, "the god of Israel" (keep in mind that capitalization is irrelevant here, being a convention of modern translators). "God of Heaven" appears once more in the book of Ezra, and it is, again, in an edict signed by the Persian king: Darius confirms Cyrus' edict and recommends that the Israelites "offer sacrifices acceptable to the *God of Heaven* and pray for the life of the king and his sons" (6:10). Everywhere else the Book of Ezra only refers to the "god of Israel" (four times), "Yahweh, the god of your fathers" (once), and "our god" (ten times).

In other words, according to the biblical author, only the kings of Persia imagine that Yahweh is "the God of Heaven"—a common designation of the universal Ahura Mazda—while for the Jews, Yahweh is merely their god, the "god of Israel," the god of their fathers, in short, a national god. Indeed, Persian officials are told that the Jerusalem Temple is dedicated to the God of Heaven, although the idea seems irrelevant to the Judeans themselves: when the Judeans are challenged the right to (re)build their temple by the local Persian governor, they tell him: "We are the servants of the God of Heaven and Earth" (5:11) and refer to Cyrus' edict. And when Nehemiah wants to convince the Persian king let him go to Judea to oversee the rebuilding of Jerusalem, he offers a prayer "to the God of Heaven" (Nehemiah 2:4); but once in Jerusalem, he asks his fellow Jews to swear allegiance to "Yahweh our god" (10:30).

This unmistakable pattern in the books of Ezra and Nehemiah may be taken as a clue of the deepest secret of Judaism, and a key to understanding the real nature of "Jewish universalism": for the Jews, Yahweh is the god of the Jews, whereas Gentiles must be told that he is the supreme and only God. "In the heart of any pious Jew, God is a Jew," writes Maurice Samuel in *You Gentiles* (1924), while to Gentiles, Yahweh must be presented as the universal God—who happens to prefer Jews.[44] The pattern is repeated in the Book of Daniel when Nebuchadnezzar, impressed by Daniel's oracle, prostrates himself and exclaims: "Your god is indeed the God of gods, the Master of kings" (Daniel 2:47).

The hypothesis that the dual nature of Yahweh (god of Israel for the Jews, God of the Universe for Gentiles) was intentionally encrypted into the Hebrew Bible becomes more plausible when we find the same pattern in the Book of Joshua. Its author never refers to Yahweh simply as "God," and never implies that he is anything but "the god of Israel" (9:18, 13:14, 13:33, 14:14, 22:16). Even Yahweh calls himself "the god of Israel" (7:13). When Joshua speaks to the Israelites, he speaks of "Yahweh your god" (1:11, 1:12, 1:15, 3:3, 3:9, 4:5, 4:23-24, 8:7, 22:3-4, 22:5, 23:3,5,8,11, 24:2). The Israelites collectively refer to "Yahweh our god" (22:19), or individually to "Yahweh my god" (14:8). Israel's enemies speak to Joshua about "Yahweh your god" (9:9), and he tells them about "Yahweh my god" (9:23). Yahweh is once called

---

44. Maurice Samuel, *You Gentiles,* New York, 1924 (archive.org), pp. 74-75.

"lord of the whole earth" by Joshua (3:13), and once "the god of gods" by enthusiastic Israelites (22:22), but none of this can be considered to contain any explicit theological claim that Yahweh is the Creator: it is more like the Persian king calling himself king of kings and ruler of the world. Neither can the mention of an altar built by the Israelites as "a witness between us that Yahweh is god" (22:34) be taken to mean anything more than "Yahweh is god between us." If the Yahwist scribe of the Book of Joshua had believed Yahweh to be the universal God, he would have written of whole cities being converted rather than exterminated for the glory of Yahweh.

The only explicit profession of faith that Yahweh is the supreme God, in the whole Book of Joshua, is coming from a foreigner, just like in the books of Ezra and Nehemiah. Not a king, this time, but a prostitute. Rahab is a prostitute in Jericho who is visited by two Israeli spies who spend the night with her, and whom she hides in exchange for being spared, together with her family, when the Israelites will take over the city and slaughter everyone, "men and women, young and old" (6:21). She infiltrates the invading Israelites into the city. As justification for betraying her own people, she tells the Israelites that "Yahweh your god is God both in Heaven above and on Earth beneath" (2:11), something that neither the narrator, nor Yahweh, nor any Israelite in the book ever claims.

Rahab's "profession of faith" may be a post-exilic insertion,[45] because it doesn't fit well with her explicit motivation of saving her life: "we are afraid of you and everyone living in this country has been seized with terror at your approach" (2:9). On the other hand, fear, not faith, is what Yahweh demands, so there is no real contradiction from the biblical point of view.

Whatever the case may be, in the final redaction, the pattern is the same as in the Book of Ezra, and reveals the secret of post-exilic Judaism: to the Jews, Yahweh is their national god, but it is good for the Jews that Gentiles (whether kings or prostitutes) regard Yahweh as the "God of Heaven". It has worked wonderfully: Christians today believe that the God of humankind decided to manifest himself as the jealous "god of Israel" from the time of Moses, whereas the real historical process is the reverse: it is the

---

45. So is Jethro's confession of faith in Exodus 18:10-11, according to Thomas Römer, *The Invention of God,* Harvard UP, 2016, p. 66.

tribal "god of Israel" who impersonated the God of humankind at the time of Ezra.

Worshipping a national god with imperialistic ambitions, while pretending to the Gentiles that they are worshipping the One True God, is manufacturing a catastrophic misunderstanding. A public scandal emerged in 167 AD, when the Hellenistic emperor Antiochos IV dedicated the temple in Jerusalem to Zeus Olympios, the Greek name of the supreme God. He had been led to understand that Yahweh and Zeus were two names for the same cosmic God, the Heavenly Father of all mankind. But the Jewish Maccabees who led the rebellion knew better: Yahweh may be the Supreme God, but only Jews are intimate with Him, and any way the Pagans worship Him is an abomination. Moreover, although the Israelites claimed that their Temple was dedicated to the God of all mankind, they also firmly believed that any non-Jew entering it should be put to death. This fact alone betrays the true nature of Hebrew monotheism: it was a deception from the beginning, the ultimate metaphysical crypsis.

3 - ISRAEL AS ONE MAN
Blood Covenant and Jewish Power

"One outstanding characteristic of the Jewish race is its persistence. What it cannot attain this generation, it will attain next. Defeat it today, it does not remain defeated; its conquerors die, but Jewry goes on, never forgetting, never deviating from its ancient aim of world control in one form or another."[1]

So wrote Henry Ford in *The International Jew.* Indeed, no other people has been capable of such perseverance toward an unwavering goal, pursued step by step over many generations—a hundred generations if we trace the Zionist project back to the period of Ezra. Jews often find themselves divided on crucial issues and involved in radically opposed movements; yet in the end, even their antagonisms seem to synergically advance their collective higher purpose. Many illustrations can be found of the extraordinary capacity of the Jewish elites to separate like a school of fish and then reunite.

Is the Hebrew Bible materialistic?

The American rabbi Harry Waton had a theory to explain the organic unity, persistence and progress of the Jews. He wrote in his *Program for the Jews,* published in 1939: "Hebrew religion, in fact, was intensely materialistic and it is precisely this that gave it persistent and effective reality."

> "Jehovah differs from all other gods. All other gods dwell in heaven. For this reason, all other religions are concerned about heaven, and they promise all reward in heaven after death. For this reason, all other religions negate the earth and the material world and are indifferent to the well-being and progress of mankind on this earth. But Jehovah comes down from heaven to dwell on this earth and to embody himself in mankind. For this reason, Judaism concerns itself only about this earth and promises all reward right here on this earth."

> "While most Jews believe in the general idea of immortality, the Jews that have a deeper understanding of Judaism know that the

---

1. Henry Ford, *The International Jew* (archive.org), November 13, 1920.

only immortality there is for the Jew is the immortality in the
Jewish people. Each Jew continues to live in the Jewish people,
and he will continue to live so long as the Jewish people will
live."

"The [Hebrew] Bible speaks of an immortality right here on earth.
In what consists this immortality? It consists in this: the soul
continues to live and function through the children and grand-
children and the people descending from them. Hence, when a
man dies, his soul is gathered to his people. Abraham, Isaac,
Jacob, Moses, and all the rest continue to live in the Jewish
people, and in due time they will live in the whole human race.
This was the immortality of the Jewish people, and it was known
to the Jews all the time."[2]

This comes close to saying that Jews have only one collective
immortal soul. Significantly, Israel is the only nation bearing the
name of one person: Jacob is given the name Israel in Genesis
32:29.

Waton's understanding of biblical anthropology was informed
by the best scholarship of his days, which has not been contra-
dicted since. It was and still is widely shared among educated
Jews. In his last book, *Moses and Monotheism,* also published in
1939, Sigmund Freud correctly stressed that, on the question of
individual immortality, the Egyptians and the Israelites were on the
opposite end of the spectrum: "No other people of antiquity [than
the Egyptians] has done so much to deny death, has made such
careful provision for an after-life [...]. The early Jewish religion,
on the other hand, had entirely relinquished immortality; the
possibility of an existence after death was never mentioned in any
place."[3]

There is no expectation of an afterlife in the Torah. Instead,
there is an explicit denial of it: "By the sweat of your face will you
earn your food, until you return to the ground, as you were taken
from it. For dust you are and to dust you shall return," says
Yahweh to Adam (Genesis 3:19). That is a logical consequence of
the way "Yahweh God shaped man [*adam*] from the soil of the
ground [*adamah*] and blew the breath of life [*ruah*] into his
nostrils, and man became a living being [*nephesh*]" (2:7). The

---

2. Harry Waton, *A Program for the Jews and an Answer to All Anti-Semites,* 1939
(archive.org), pp. 52, 125, 132.
3. Sigmund Freud, *Moses and Monotheism,* Hogarth Press, 1939 (archive.org), pp. 33-34.

proximity of *adam,* "man", and *adamah,* "earth" or "ground", reinforces the idea.

It has been said, by Cabbalists in particular, that *nephesh* and *ruah* are two terms to designate an immortal spirit. This is a misunderstanding originating from the Greek Septuagint translation: the Hebrew word *nephesh* is translated as *psyche.* But in reality it designates a "living being," animal or human; it sometimes means simply "life" and is associated to blood in the ritual prescriptions of Leviticus 17. The Hebrew word *ruah,* translated as *pneuma,* means "breath," and also designates life. Nowhere in the Hebrew Scriptures do these terms imply any form of individual afterlife.

This biblical anti-spiritualism cannot be explained as a "primitive" trait due to the Hebrew Bible's great antiquity, as if the belief in an Otherworld of the dead was a late development in the history of religious ideas. On the contrary, the Hebrew denial of the afterlife was linked to the rejection of foreign cults, which universally included a concern for the afterlife. The Book of Genesis, whose anthropological materialism is the most explicit, betrays Mesopotamian and Persian influences that cannot be anterior to the Babylonian Exile. Significantly, we find in Genesis an inversion of the Paradise of Indo-European myths ("Paradise" derives from the Persian word for "royal gardens"): instead of making it the future happy world where the righteous dead become immortal by eating from the tree of life, Genesis shifts the Garden and its tree back into a past lost forever for all mankind. It is also the stage of the drama that brought into the world the double scourge of death and labor. For death bears no promise, and work no spiritual reward, for the Hebrew scribes.

Here is one illustration among others: when, in Isaiah 38, the good King Hezekiah "fell ill and was at the point of death," he expressed no hope of meeting his Creator or starting a new life in some Otherworld. Rather, he despaired at the prospect of not seeing Yahweh anymore. For, he told his god, "Sheol cannot praise you, nor the dead celebrate you; those who go down to the pit can hope no longer in your constancy." Sheol is simply "the pit", and it is another common misunderstanding, stemming for its translation as *Hades* in the Septuagint, to think of it as a world where the dead live. There is no life in Sheol, it is a purely negative concept of death, as close as possible to the non-concept of nothingness. The term appears only five times anyway in the Pentateuch: four times in Genesis as a conventional name for death,[4] and once in Numbers 16, in a story about rebellious Jews who, by divine punishment, are suddenly swallowed alive by the earth with all their belongings.

In response to his prayer, Hezekiah only receives an extra fifteen years of earthly life. For Yahweh holds no other reward for the faithful than a long, fertile and wealthy life on earth. Like Hezekiah, the protagonist of the Book of Job expects no afterlife consolation for his enduring faith, but instead gets a 140-year extension on earth, numerous offspring, as well as "fourteen thousand sheep, six thousand camels, a thousand yoke of oxen and a thousand she-donkeys" (Job 42:12). In any other culture, his loyalty to his god would be rewarded by a happy afterlife. But Yahweh does reign over the dead, whom he "remembers no more" (Psalms 88:6).

In fact, Yahweh can hardly be regarded as "a god" if we define a god as a being residing in some world beyond this one. Yahweh claims to rule over this world alone, because he is, literally, a king (*melech*, a title applied to him more than fifty times in the Hebrew Bible). Yahweh is a very special king indeed: invisible, omniscient and eternal—very practical for the hereditary clans of priests and prophets who speak in his name.

Jewishness as racial soul

A "materialistic religion" may sound like a contradiction in terms. Indeed, it is questionable if the concept of "religion", as most people understand it today, applies to biblical Judaism. The evolution of Judaism for the last two thousand years is another story. In the Hellenistic period, Greco-Egyptian dualism infiltrated Jewish thought. The Wisdom of Solomon, written in Greek in Alexandria in the first century BC, asserts that, "God created human beings to be immortal," and criticizes those who "do not believe in a reward for blameless souls" (2:22-23). But such books never made it into the Jewish canon, as rabbinical Judaism vigorously rejected anything Greek. Moreover, even within Hellenistic Judaism, the materialist viewpoint prevailed. According to Ecclesiastes, for example,

> "the fate of humans and the fate of animals is the same: as the one dies, so the other dies; [...] everything comes from the dust, everything returns to the dust." (3:19–20)

---

4. Genesis 37:35; 42:38; 44:29; 44:31.

"The living are at least aware that they are going to die, but the dead know nothing whatever. [...] There is neither achievement, nor planning, nor science, nor wisdom in Sheol where you are going." (9:5-10)

Significantly, the most enduring legacy of Hellenistic Judaism is the metaphor of life after death as *anastasis* ("rising up," generally translated as "resurrection"), but the Jewish version is a materialistic distortion. In the controversy on *anastasis* in Matthew 22:23-33, Jesus defines it as a transformation of mortals into "angels in Heaven," against the Sadducees who, being faithful to the Torah and therefore anti-spiritualists, are unable to conceive of *anastasis* in any other way than physical resuscitation, for which no immortal soul is needed. Hence their reference to the obligation for a man to marry the wife of his dead brother, if she hasn't given him a son—for a male descendant is the only form of immortality conceivable within ancient Judaism. So even the biblical notion of physical resurrection—later adopted by Christian dogma in contradiction to Jesus' teaching—demonstrates that materialism is woven into the fabric of Judaism.

In more recent times, under circumstances comparable to the Hellenistic context, Reformed Judaism has again injected the immortal soul into Judaic anthropology. But it is significant that, when Moses Mendelssohn (1729-1786), the father of the eighteenth-century Haskalah, decided to convince his fellow Jews to accept the creed of the immortality of the individual soul—a necessary condition for the elevation of humanity according to him—he did not rely on the Jewish tradition, but instead produced a Platonic dialogue titled *Phaedo or the Immortality of the Soul*.

Some Jewish intellectuals such as Moses Hess would later protest against the introduction of that foreign body into Jewish thought, and their reaction would contribute to the temporary schism between Reformed Judaism and Zionism. For Zionists, blood, not soul, makes us immortal. In his essay "Zionism, Race, and Eugenics" (1911), Martin Buber makes blood "the deepest, most potent stratum of our being." When he envisions the line of ancestors that led to him, the Jew perceives "what confluence of blood has produced him. [...] He senses in this immortality of the generations a community of blood." [5] According to Zionist historian Benzion Netanyahu, former secretary of Zeev Jabotinsky

---

5. Raphael Falk, "Zionism, Race, and Eugenics," in *Jewish Tradition and the Challenge of Darwinism*, University of Chicago Press, 2006, p. 162.

and father of the current Israeli Prime Minister, defining Jewishness as religion rather than nationality "was the fruit of self-deception." He defends a racial conception that amounts to considering that Jews are only immortal as a nation:

> "Only by intermarriage can a person uproot himself from a nation, and then only in so far as his descendants are concerned. His individuality, which is an extract and an example of the qualities of his nation, may then be lost in future generations, dominated by qualities of other nations. Quitting a nation is, therefore, even from a biological point of view, an act of suicide."[6]

Jewish influential journalist Lucien Wolf tried to have it both ways by claiming that, "in Judaism the religion and the race are almost interchangeable terms," which of course makes no sense within the commonly accepted notion of religion.[7] A religion welcomes converts, but not the "religion" of Israel. There are exceptions: mass forced conversions, on the one hand, and individual sons-in-law who bring added value to the gene pool or the financial pool, on the other, but no case is recorded in the Bible.

What about circumcision, you may ask. Is it not a rite of admission into the Jewish community? Not in the Bible. As the "sign of the covenant" imposed by Yahweh on Abraham, for "you and your descendants after you, generation after generation" (Genesis 17:9), circumcision actually reinforces the strictly genetic, even genital, nature of Jewishness. As a "mark in the flesh" passed on from father to son, it perfectly symbolizes the unspiritual nature of Yahwism.

There is in Genesis 34 a story that illustrates this point in a paradoxical manner. Hamor, the king of the Canaanite city of Shechem, once made the following proposal to Jacob: "My son Shechem's heart is set on your daughter. Please allow her to marry him. Intermarry with us; give us your daughters and take our daughters for yourselves. We can live together, and the country will be open to you, for you to live in, and move about in, and acquire holdings.'" Jacob's sons feigned to agree on the condition that "you become like us by circumcising all your males. Then we will give you our daughters, taking yours for ourselves; and we will stay with you to make one nation." Hamor consented and convinced all his male subjects to be circumcised. Three days later,

---

6. Benzion Netanyahu, *The Founding Fathers of Zionism* (1938), Balfour Books, 2012.
7. Lucien Wolf, "What Is Judaism? A Question of Today," *The Fortnightly Review* 36 (1884), pp. 237-256, on www.manchesterjewishstudies.org/wolf/

"when the men were still in pain," Jacob's sons attacked the town. They "slaughtered all the males," Hamor and Shechem included, and "took all their children and wives captive and looted everything to be found in the houses". This passage records the ambiguity of the relationship between endogamy and circumcision. In theory, people can be integrated into Israelite nationality by circumcision. It may have happened in history, but not in the Bible.

For the anecdote, there is another story of mass circumcision in the Bible, but in this case, those circumcised were slaughtered *before* being circumcised: this is when David killed two hundred Philistines in order to present Saul with their foreskins as bride token for his daughter (1Samuel 18). The Bible doesn't say what Saul did with his prestigious trophy.

In the version compiled and ideologically framed in the post-exilic period, the Hebrew Bible insists on the strict equality between monotheism and racial purity. Yahweh forbids Jews to marry their children to non-Jews *because* "your son would be seduced from following me into serving other gods" (Deuteronomy 7:3-4). When some Israelites took wives among the Moabites (an Abrahamic people), what bothers Yahweh is that these women "invited them to the sacrifices of their gods, and the people ate and bowed down before their gods" (Numbers 25:1-2). From the evolutionary point of view of Kevin MacDonald, the exclusive cult of the jealous god is just a religious pretext for a eugenic project based on strict endogamy, and Judaism is fundamentally a "group evolutionary strategy among peoples."[8]

Endogamy is so highly valued in the Bible that it trumps the prohibition of incest as understood by most cultures. Abraham marries his half-sister Sarah. His son Isaac marries Rebecca, the daughter of his cousin Bethuel (whose mother, Milcah, had married his uncle Nahor). And Isaac's son Jacob marries the two daughters of his maternal uncle Laban. Not to mention Judah, founder of the Judahites (later Jews), who conceives with his daughter-in-law Tamar.

By depriving the Jews of an individual soul, and deifying instead their racial identity, the Torah programs Israel as the most holistic nation. The immortality that is denied the individual is reinvested entirely on the people as a whole ("I instituted an

---

8. Kevin MacDonald, *A People That Shall Dwell Alone,* Praeger, 1994.

eternal people" Isaiah 44:7), as if the Jews were united by a single, national, genetic soul, personified by Yahweh. In an "Essay on the Jewish Soul" (1929), Isaac Kadmi-Cohen actually describes Judaism as "the spiritualization that deifies the race," so that "divinity in Judaism is contained in the exaltation of the entity represented by the race."[9] Israel is possessed by a unique destiny, and each Jew contributes to that destiny. Jewish apologist Maurice Samuel writes in *You Gentiles* (1924): "The feeling in the Jew, even in the free-thinking Jew like myself, is that to be one with his people is to be thereby admitted to the power of enjoying the infinite."[10] And German Zionist Alfred Nossig wrote in 1922: "The Jewish community is more than a people in the modern political sense of the word. [...] It forms an unconscious nucleus of our being, the common substance of our soul."[11]

From a religious point of view, individual immortality appears to be missing in biblical anthropology. But the notion of collective immortality that replaces it is the source of the greatest strength of the Jewish people. An individual has only a few decades to accomplish his destiny, while a nation has centuries, even millennia. Jeremiah can reassure the exiles of Babylon that in seven generations they will return to Jerusalem ("Letter of Jeremiah," in Baruch 6:2). Seven generations in the history of a people is not unlike seven years in the life of a man. While the Goy awaits for his personal final hour on the scale of a century, the chosen people sees much further. The national orientation of the Jewish soul injects into any collective project a spiritual force and endurance with which no other national community can compete.

Israel operates with a totally different time scale from other nations. It defines itself by a panoramic vision that scans millennia into the past and into the future. It keeps a vivid memory of its beginnings 3000 years ago, and it looks with anticipation to the fulfillment of its destiny at the end of times. It makes no difference if its memory is not accurate history. As Yosef Hayim Yerushalmi points out in *Zakhor: Jewish History and Jewish Memory*, "Only in Israel and nowhere else is the injunction to remember felt as a

---

9. Isaac Kadmi-Cohen, *Nomades: Essai sur l'âme juive,* Felix Alcan, 1929 (archive.org), pp. 98, 143.

10. Maurice Samuel, *You Gentiles,* New York, 1924 (archive.org), pp. 74-75.

11. Alfred Nossig, *Integrales Judentum,* 1922, pp. 1-5, on www.deutsche-digitale-bibliothek.de/

religious imperative to an entire people."[12] This characteristic is probably inherited from its nomadic past, for nomadic peoples are more intensely committed to collective memory and genealogy than sedentary peoples, who are also rooted in the land (and the land keeps their memory). Memory defines individuality, and Israel's extraordinary memory makes it an individuality of extraordinary character.

The "national soul" paradigm, rooted in the biblical denial of individual immortality, combines with the "chosen people" paradigm, to make the Jewish soul somehow identifiable to Yahweh. This combination of biblical materialism and biblical ethnocentrism (or pseudo-universalism) is the simple equation, the $E=mC^2$ that explains the "Jewish mind".

The parasitic nation

The holistic principle is not a sufficient explanation for the Jews' persistent effort toward world domination. To some degree, every nation was, until recently, organic. The word "nation" comes from the Latin for "birth" or "race": a nation exists when people living in the same "Fatherland" (*la Patrie*) feel "familiar" with each other, that is, recognize themselves as brothers with common ancestors. To understand how special is the Jewish nation, we need to define more precisely its organic character. Henry Ford has a suggestion:

"The Jewish problem in the United States is essentially a city problem. It is characteristic of the Jew to gather in numbers, not where land is open nor where raw materials are found, but where the greatest number of people abide. This is a noteworthy fact when considered alongside the Jews' claim that the Gentiles have ostracized them; the Jews congregate in their greatest numbers in those places and among those people where they complain they are least wanted. The explanation most frequently given is this; the genius of the Jew is to live off people; not off land, nor off the production of commodities from raw material, but off people. Let other people till the soil; the Jew, if he can, will live off the tiller. Let other people toil at trades and manufacture; the Jew will exploit the fruits of their work. That is his peculiar genius. If this

12. Yosef Hayim Yerushalmi, *Zakhor: Jewish History and Jewish Memory* (1982), University of Washington Press, 2011.

genius be described as parasitic, the term would seem to be justified by a certain fitness."[13]

This national genius is reinforced by the Bible. Yahweh has destined Israel to be, not just an organism like other nations, but a parasitic one. From the time of Moses, Yahweh has sworn to give his people a country "with great and prosperous cities you have not built, with houses full of good things you have not provided, with wells you have not dug, with vineyards and olive trees you have not planted" (Deuteronomy 6:10-11). The prophets encourage the parasitic nature of Israel: "You will suck the milk of nations, you will suck the wealth of kings" (Isaiah 60:16); "Strangers will come forward to feed your flocks, foreigners will be your ploughmen and vinedressers; but you will be called 'priests of Yahweh' and be addressed as 'ministers of our God'. You will feed on the wealth of nations, you will supplant them in their glory" (Isaiah 61:5-6); "the wealth of all the surrounding nations will be heaped together: gold, silver, clothing, in vast quantity" (Zechariah 14:14). "I shall shake all the nations, and the treasures of all the nations will flow in, and I shall fill this Temple with glory, says Yahweh Sabaoth. Mine is the silver, mine the gold! Yahweh Sabaoth declares" (Haggai 2:7-8).

Usury is the quintessential parasitizing, and as far as we know, the Yahwist priests were the first to conceive of enslaving entire nations through debt: "If Yahweh your God blesses you as he has promised, you will be creditors to many nations but debtors to none; you will rule over many nations, and be ruled by none" (Deuteronomy 15:6).

The archetypal parasitic hero is Joseph, son of Jacob. Having risen from the status of a slave to that of chancellor of Pharaoh, he favors his kinsmen and obtains for them "land holdings in Egypt, in the best part of the country." Charged with managing the national grain reserves, he stores large amounts during the years of plenty; then, when famine strikes, he negotiates a high price for the monopolized grain and thus "accumulated all the money to be found in Egypt and Canaan." The following year, having created a monetary shortage, he forces the peasants to relinquish their herds in exchange for grain: "Hand over your livestock and I shall issue you food in exchange for your livestock, if your money has come to an end." One year later, the peasants have nothing left "except our bodies and our land," and so are reduced to begging, then have

---

13. Henry Ford, *The International Jew* (archive.org), November 13, 1920.

to sell themselves in order to survive: "Take us and our land in exchange for food, and we with our land will become Pharaoh's serfs; only give us seed, so that we can survive and not die and the land not revert to desert!" And so the Hebrews, after settling in Egypt, "acquired property there; they were fruitful and grew very numerous" (Genesis 47:11-27), a sure sign of God's blessing. Lawrence Wills, who has compiled several Jewish legends of the Joseph type, writes: "As difficult as it may be for the modern reader to accept, we actually have before us hero legends concerning tax farmers, as if we were reading the Robin Hood legend told from the Sheriff of Nottingham's perspective."[14] A people armed with such a holy book has a huge advantage in the competition for the control of wealth.

Conspiratorial networking

The success of the Jewish elites in advancing their national goals cannot be explained merely by some spontaneous national instinct or group soul that unconsciously binds them together despite their superficial divisions. It is true that the strength of modern Zionism rests on an organic rather than hierarchical bond between Jews, as Gilad Atzmon stresses: "While the organism functions as a whole, the particular organ fulfills an elementary function without being aware of its specific role within the entire system."[15] Nevertheless, as Atzmon also stresses, this organic unity is created, cultivated and used by cognitive elites who are very much aware of the power they can draw from it.

In other words, Israel is not just about blood, it is also about covenant. Religious Jews believe Jewishness goes back to a Mosaic covenant between God and the only people He really cares about. But most of the Jewish intellectual, cultural, financial, political or criminal elite—members of the B'nai B'rith ("Sons of the Covenant"), for example—assume it is a covenant of Jews between themselves.

In practice, the mysterious capacity of Jewish movements to drive history is based on a practice of networking perfected through 2500 years. Ethnic networking means that, unbeknownst to the Gentile public, Jewish elites coordinate their effort on a particular issue so as to apply an irresistible pressure until a desired

---

14. Lawrence Wills, *Jew in the Court of the Foreign King*, Cornell UP, 1995, p. 189.
15. Gilad Atzmon, *The Wandering Who?* Zero Books, 2011, p. 21.

effect is obtained. It is performed in every field and for a great variety of purposes, including in the academic sphere, to create artificial consensus. Brenton Sanderson and Andrew Joyce,[16] both writing on Kevin MacDonald's *Occidental Observer*, have brilliantly demonstrated how concerted efforts from the part of Jewish scholars over a few decades can transform any minor figure, such as Gustav Mahler or Baruch Spinoza, into personifications of the "Jewish genius": "Firstly, inflate the significance of a Jewish figure's intellectual or artistic achievement to the point where it is held to be of 'world changing' magnitude. Secondly, accentuate the Jewish origins and affiliations of the figure so that his 'world-changing' achievement is held to be the natural expression of his Jewish origins and identity."[17] The process illustrates perfectly the connection between the "national soul" aspect of Jewishness and its practical application in networking: for committed Jews, every Jew's achievement is a Jewish achievement, and a particular manifestation of the Jewish soul.

In the inner spheres of deep political power, elite Jews unite in conspiratorial circles to steer history in their desired direction. One such circle was the Order of the Parushim, to which belonged Louis Brandeis (1856–1941), Felix Frankfurter (1882-1965), and probably Samuel Untermeyer (1858-1940). It is described by Sarah Schmidt, professor of Jewish history at the Hebrew University of Jerusalem, as "a secret underground guerilla force determined to influence the course of events in a quiet, anonymous way." At the initiation ceremony, each new member received for instructions:

> "Until our purpose shall be accomplished, you will be fellow of a brotherhood whose bond you will regard as greater than any other in your life—dearer than that of family, of school, of nation. By entering this brotherhood, you become a self-dedicated soldier in the army of Zion."

The initiate responded by vowing:

> "Before this council, in the name of all that I hold dear and holy, I hereby vow myself, my life, my fortune, and my honor to the restoration of the Jewish nation. [...] I pledge myself utterly to

16. Andrew Joyce, "Pariah to Messiah: The Engineered Apotheosis of Baruch Spinoza," parts 1 to 3, May 5, 2019, on www.theoccidentalobserver.net
17. Brendon Sanderson, "Why Mahler? Norman Lebrecht and the Construction of Jewish Genius," April 13, 2011, on www.theoccidentalobserver.net

guard and to obey and to keep secret the laws and the labor of the fellowship, its existence and its aims. Amen."[18]

The group of Leo Strauss' intimate disciples, recipients of the master's "esoteric" teaching, forms another of those conspiratorial circles. Nothing is more revealing of their philosophy than Strauss' understanding of Machiavelli. In his *Thoughts on Machiavelli,* Strauss defines Niccolo Machiavelli as the patriot of the highest degree because he understood that only nations can be immortal, and that the best leaders are those who have no fear of damning their individual soul, since they have none. The true patriot sets no moral limit to what he can do for his country.[19] In an article in the *Jewish World Review* of June 7, 1999, Strauss' disciple Michael Ledeen, founding member of the *Jewish Institute for National Security Affairs* (JINSA), assumes that Machiavelli must have been a "secret Jew," on the ground that, "if you listen to his political philosophy you will hear Jewish music."[20]

The Straussians formed the original core of the Neoconservatives. In two generations, this network of less than a hundred people have parasitized the nerve centers of the American state with the aim of seizing the levers of its foreign and military policies (Greg Felton applies to them the metaphor of the parasite in *The Host and the Parasite*).[21] The Neoconservatives' transgenerational sustainability illustrates the organic background of Jewish networking: Irving Kristol was succeeded by his son William, Donald Kagan by his son Robert, Richard Pipes by his son Daniel, and Norman Podhoretz by his son John and his son-in-law Elliott Abrams.

Such networks of smart, tribal, Machiavellian, conspiratorial Jews are the key to the extraordinary cohesion of worldwide Jewry. We can compare the structure of the Jewish community to concentric orbital spheres in a gravitational field, with Yahweh's ideology and prophecies at the core: in the inner spheres is the elite minority for whom Jewishness and Israel are permanent concerns; in the outer spheres are the "soft" Jews, who are only maintained

---

18. Sarah Schmidt, "The 'Parushim': A Secret Episode in American Zionist History," *American Jewish Historical Quarterly* 65, no. 2, December 1975, pp. 121-139, on ifamericanknew.org/history/parushim.html.

19. Leo Strauss, *Thoughts on Machiavelli,* University of Chicago Press, 1978, p. 42.

20. Michael Ledeen, "What Machiavelli (A Secret Jew?) Learned from Moses," June 7, 1999, on www.jewishworldreview.com/0699/machiavelli1.asp

21. Greg Felton, *The Host and the Parasite: How Israel's Fifth Column Consumed America,* Bad Bear Press, 2012.

in orbit by low gravity, and likely to break away. As fully assimilated Jews, they play an important role in public relations, and most of them can still be rallied when needed under the banner of the fight against anti-Semitism.[22]

The cohesion of the Jewish community is always maintained by the most committed Jews organized in tight networks, who control the Jewish masses through a paranoid terror of extermination combined with a megalomaniac complex of superiority. At critical times in history, such networks are capable of forcing world Jewry to act "as one man" (Judges 20:1). A good example is the campaign launched against Germany in March 1933, by a front-page article in the British *Daily Express* entitled "Judea Declares War on Germany. Jews of All the World Unite," and proclaiming: "The Israeli people around the world declare economic and financial war against Germany. Fourteen million Jews dispersed throughout the world have *banded together as one man* to declare war on the German persecutors of their co-religionists." Samuel Untermeyer, who led the attack, called "traitors to their race" all Jews who refused to join in the German boycott.[23]

Jewishness is a system of mind control of the Jewish masses by the Jewish elites. Whereas in European societies, the extremes tend to be marginalized, in the Jewish community, the opposite is true, notes Kevin MacDonald: "At all the turning points, it is the more ethnocentric elements—one might term them the radicals—who have determined the direction of the Jewish community and eventually won the day. [...] The radical movement begins among the more committed segments of the Jewish community, then spreads and eventually becomes mainstream within the Jewish community. [...] Jews who fail to go along with what is now a mainstream position are pushed out of the community, labeled "self-hating Jews" or worse, and relegated to impotence."[24]

This process can be documented at every turning point in the history of Israel. After the great crisis provoked by the Babylonian Exile, Ezekiel's obsession with purity of blood and purity of cult prevailed over Jeremiah's more internal reform program. As biblical scholar Karl Budde wrote: "the tendency toward the

---

22. Daniel Elazar, *Community and Polity: Organizational Dynamics of American Jewry*, 1976, quoted in Kevin MacDonald, *Separation and Its Discontents*, Praeger, 1998.
23. Detail in my book, *From Yahweh to Zion*, Sifting&Winnowing, 2018, pp. 260-261.
24. Kevin MacDonald, *Cultural Insurrections*, Occidental Press, 2007, pp. 90-91.

complete isolation of Israel from the heathen and the avoidance of every pollution, passed over from Ezekiel's visions into the practical law-books," making Ezekiel the true "father of Judaism."[25] Ezekiel counted himself among the "sons of Zadok" (the Zadokites, called Sadducees in the Gospels) whom he regarded as the only ones allowed to officiate in the Temple sanctuary (44:15).

Ezra also claimed to be of Zadok's lineage and was the spiritual heir of Ezekiel. On learning that the Judeo-Babylonians already returned to Palestine had resorted to mixed marriages, and that "the holy race has been contaminated by the people of the country," Ezra made them swear to "send away all the foreign wives and their children" (Ezra 9:2; 10:3).

In the second century BC, a strong movement toward Helle-nization threatened the integrity of the Jewish nation. As we read in 1Maccabees 1-2, some Israelites said, "let us ally ourselves with the gentiles surrounding us, for since we separated ourselves from them many misfortunes have overtaken us." The extremist Macca-bees then "organized themselves into an armed force, striking down the sinners in their anger, and the renegades in their fury," and established their Hasmonean theocracy.

The problem of Christian individualism

The message of the Gospel is the antithesis of Jewish materialism. Jesus' teaching to "store up treasures for yourselves in heaven" (Matthew 6:20-21) contrasts with Yahweh's greed for "the treasures of all the nations" (Haggai 2:7-8). Jesus' emphasis on personal salvation also comes with a strong hostility to blood ties,[26] and Paul teaches that being reborn through Christ cancels ethnic solidarities, social hierarchies, and even gender identities:

> "There can be neither Jew nor Greek, there can be neither slave nor freeman, there can be neither male nor female—for you are all one in Christ Jesus. And simply by being Christ's, you are that progeny of Abraham, the heirs named in the promise." (Galatians 3:28-29)

---

25. Karl Budde, *Religion of Israel to the Exile,* Putnam's Sons, 1899 (archive.org), pp. 206-207.
26. Matthew 19:10-12, Matthew 19:29, Matthew 22:30, Matthew 24:19, Mark 13:17, Luke 14:26, Luke 21:23, Luke 23:29, 1Corinthians 7:1-8.

Israel's religion is a system of ethnic solidarity. By contrast, Christianity is unfriendly to the concept of race. Catholic doctrine in particular has developed an atomistic, non-genetic and egalitarian conception of the human soul that cannot account for the multi-layered complexity of the human psyche, or the "invisible loyalties" that bind each one to his ancestors.[27] Augustine, the major reference of medieval Catholicism, built a wall between the living and the dead, denouncing any give-and-take between them as the work of the devil. And so by eroding the ties of solidarity between the dead and the living, which are a major part of private and public cults in traditional societies, Catholicism has gradually transformed "solidary death" into "solitary death", in the words of Philippe Ariès.[28]

For these reasons, it has been argued that Christianity laid the foundation for modern Western individualism. Anthropologist Louis Dumont explains in his *Essays on Individualism* that traditional societies are holistic and hierarchical: they subordinate the individual to the community and assign to the individual a value that depends on his/her social role. Such societies admit that some individuals forsake their social existence to seek individual enlightenment, as long as these individuals do not challenge the social order and its holistic dynamic, but remain the exceptions that confirm the rule. Christianity, according to Dumont, has upset that civilizational balance by emphasizing that salvation *from* this world is everybody's business. Every Christian is defined as a "self-in-relationship-to-God", even if he doesn't renounce the world as an hermit or a monk, and so he becomes an "individual-in-the-world." By stages, "holism will have vanished from ideology," and "the outworldly individual will have become the modern, inworldly individual."[29]

The Church did provide a new holistic framework to replace old ones, by emphasizing that the community of Christians forms the "body of Christ." But when this organic body started to disintegrate, all that was left was individualism and egalitarianism. That is when strange political theories arose, holding that man is not a social animal by nature but a selfish individual who engages

---

27. Ivan Boszormenyi-Nagy, *Invisible Loyalties: Reciprocity in Intergenerational Family Therapy,* Harper & Row, 1973, p. 56.

28. Philippe Ariès, *L'Homme devant la mort,* tome 1: *Le Temps des gisants,* Seuil, 1977.

29. Louis Dumont, *Essays on Individualism: Modern Ideology in Anthropological Perspective,* University of Chicago Press, 1992, pp. 23-59.

in social contracts only by self-interest. Thomas Hobbes (1588-1679), the first "social contract" theorist, taught that, in the state of nature, "man is a wolf for man" and only agrees to give up part of his individual freedom for fear of violent death. After Hobbes came Adam Smith (1723-1790), who likewise postulated that each human being is motivated exclusively by his own profit, yet wagered that in a society of free competition, the sum of everybody's selfishness would create a just society. We know the result: the rule of money has thoroughly desocialized Western man, with the smallest organic unit, the nuclear family, barely surviving.

There may be some exaggeration in blaming Western individualism entirely on Christianity, as does Dumont. It is even doubtful if "social contract" theories are of Christian inspiration. They emerged in the deeply Judaized England of Oliver Cromwell, and can be seen as Jewish attacks on the organic substance of Christian nations. Hobbes was a Puritan, but his religious ideas are so Jewish ("the Kingdom of God was first instituted by the ministry of Moses over the Jews," he claims) that some have speculated about his possible Marrano origin.[30]

It is impossible, I think, to come to any simple conclusion about the merits and failures of Christianity, because we cannot objectively distinguish what belongs to Christianity and what doesn't in any of Christendom's achievements. Whether another religion could have done better for Christendom than Christianity is a futile question. What part Christianity played in the decline and fall of Christendom is equally meaningless. Yet the challenges faced by our civilization today require serious anthropological inquiries into Christianity's legacy and deficiencies, and a quest for remedies.

We can learn from some of the Zionist thinkers I have quoted in this essay, who recognize the importance of blood as the link between nature and culture. Another interesting Jewish thinker is Moses Hess, a precursor of Zionism with his book *Rome and Jerusalem: The Last National Question* (1862). According to him, "Nothing is more foreign to the spirit of Judaism than the idea of the salvation of the individual which, according to the modern conception, is the cornerstone of religion." For Hess, the essence

---

30. Robert Kraynak, "The Idea of the Messiah in the Theology of Thomas Hobbes," *Jewish Political Studies Review,* Fall 1992, on jcpa.org.

of Judaism is "the vivid belief in the continuity of the spirit in human history."[31] Hess actually started as a Communist who influenced both Engels and Marx. In his essay on "The Essence of Money" (1845), anticipating Marx's concept of economic alienation, he wrote a relevant indictment of Christian individualism. A realistic conception of the world, he claims "sees life itself in the species and the means to life in the individual." But for Christians,

> "the individual is the end, the life of the species being rather the means to life. They have created for themselves a world apart. The classic theoretical form of this inverted world is the Christian heaven. In the real world the individual dies; in the Christian heaven he lives for ever. In the real world the species acts in and through the individual; in heaven the essence of the species, God, lives outside the individuals."[32]

Some socialist thinkers of more spiritualist orientation, such as the Frenchmen Pierre-Joseph Proudhon or Jean Jaurès, have also reflected on the shortcoming of the Christian concept of individual soul. The socialist predicament is well encapsulated by Jim Casy in John Steinbeck's masterpiece *The Grapes of Wrath*. Casy, a disillusioned preacher, finds a new faith in humanity through social activism. He takes comfort in the idea that, "Maybe all men got one big soul ever'body's a part of."[33] What is lacking, though, in such spiritual universalism, is the recognition of the ethnic principle, the affirmation that man's soul is, to a great extent, national. This insight has been at the heart of German romanticism, which came as a reaction to the dissolving power of English mercantilism and the French Enlightenment.

German holistic reaction

The birth of German romanticism is attached to the name of Johann Gottfried von Herder (1744-1803), a disciple of Kant and a mentor to Hegel, Nietzsche, Goethe, and many others. In his essay, *Ideas on the Philosophy of the History of Mankind* (1784-91), Herder criticizes contractualist political theories, and replaces the individualistic anthropology of the Enlightenment, which postulates an invariable human nature, by a typology of nations. Nations are seen as collective beings having each a particular "genius"

---

31. Moses Hess, *Rome and Jerusalem*, 1918 (archive.org), p. 65.

32. Moses Hess, "The Essence of Money," 1845, on www.marxists.org

33. John Steinbeck, *The Grapes of Wrath* (1939), Penguin Classics, 2000, p. 26.

forged by race, geography and history. Against the French school, which held that a person's nationality is accidental, Herder insisted that the essential qualities of an individual are determined by his nationality. He is the initiator of what is called the ethnic theory of nationalities. His notion of *Volk* influenced Hegel (1770-1831), whose philosophy of history represents the culmination of German nationalism, with his concept of the State as resulting from "the march of God on earth", and his concept of the "world-historical man" unfolding history.

Hitler was a product of this movement. *"Ein Reich, ein Volk, ein Führer"* is an expression of a thoroughgoing organic doctrine, and so is the Nazi catchword *Volksgemeinschaft* ("community of the people"). In *Mein Kampf,* Hitler praises the Aryan's willingness to "put all his abilities at the service of the community."[34] Interestingly, in 1939, Rabbi Harry Waton wrote the following about Hitler and Nazism:

> "Nazism is an imitation of Judaism; Nazism adopted the principles and ideas of Judaism with which to destroy Judaism and the Jews."

> "The Nazi philosophy starts out with the postulate: The blood of a race determines the nature, course of evolution and the destiny of that race. [...] whether consciously or not, the Nazis took this theory from the Bible itself."

> "Hitler's declaration that the Jewish consciousness is poison to the Aryan races is the deepest insight that the Western world has yet achieved in its own nature; and his capacity to realize this is the proof of his genius as well as the secret of his power and of the curious fascination which his personality exerts. [...] it is not the practical power or wealth of the Jews that he fears, but the character of the Jewish mind. [...] It is the hidden penetration of the Jewish spirit into the Gentile mind that is the danger; and it is a danger because the 'Aryan' mind cannot resist it, but must succumb."[35]

Waton was wrong about the source of Hitler's views: they didn't originate from the Hebrew Bible. Neither did they owe anything to the Gospel. They drew from the same cultural current as Herder, which had its main source in a pre-Christian heroic mentality. Beyond that, Hitler's anthropological notions were

---

34. Adolf Hitler, *Mein Kampf,* Raynal & Hitchcock, 1941 (archive.org), pp. 408-409.
35. Harry Waton, *A Program for the Jews,* 1939 (archive.org), pp. 64, 200.

based on universal principles that most Jewish intellectuals of the same period knew very well but preferred Gentiles not to know.

Interestingly, two of the most important founders of modern sociology and anthropology—the scientific study of societies as holistic systems that determine the behaviors and thought patterns of individuals—happen to be German Jews (though neither of them expressed sympathies for the Jews): Emile Durkheim (1858–1917) and Ludwig Gumplowicz (1838-1909). Gumplowicz, professor of political science in Graz, has now fallen in disrepute because his theories show too much proximity with Hitler's. In his major book, *The Struggle of Races* (1883), Gumplowicz formulates the natural law of "syngenism" (from the Greek *syngenea*, meaning kinship). Syngenism refers to a set of factors uniting members of the same race ("race" having then a rather lose meaning, not much different from "people" or "nation"). At the origin of the formation of the syngenic feeling, there is above all consanguinity, but also education, language, religion, custom, law, and way of life (down to cooking habits). In other words, syngenic feelings are based on both physical resemblance and intellectual resemblance.

Western nations are currently suffering from a pathological weakening of syngenic cohesion, resulting mainly—but not exclusively—from mass immigration. Kevin MacDonald refers to several independent studies showing that racial heterogeneity weakens the social fabric and reinforces individualism. Sociologist Robert Putnam, for example, shows that: "immigration and ethnic diversity tend to reduce social solidarity and social capital. New evidence from the US suggests that in ethnically diverse neighbourhoods residents of all races tend to 'hunker down'. Trust (even of one's own race) is lower, altruism and community cooperation rarer, friends fewer."[36] The Europeans' willingness to welcome Third World migrants by the millions, in the name of universalistic moral principles inherited from Christianity, together with the criminalization of any expression of white pride, is therefore a form of "pathological altruism".[37]

Christianity is not solely responsible for this state of affair. It did erode traditional ethnic syngenism, and in the long run, it has

---

36. Robert D. Putnam, "*E Pluribus Unum*: Diversity and Community in the Twenty-first Century," June 15, 2007, on onlinelibrary.wiley.com

37. The standard work on pathological altruism is: B. Oakley, A. Knafo, G. Madhavan and D. S. Wilson (Eds.), *Pathological Altruism*, Oxford UP, 2012.

weakened our collective immune system by its cocktail of individualism and universalism. But the pathological agent itself is not endogenous to Christianity: as MacDonald has also documented,[38] Jewish elites have been the foremost promoters of mass immigration, and the manufacturers of public consent to these policies. By doing so, they have debilitated the national organisms they seek to vampirize, while reinforcing the syngenic vitality of their own national parasitic organism.

A quote from William James' *The Will to Believe* (1896) may serve as a concluding metaphor for the vulnerability of Christian societies to Jewish parasitizing:

> "A social organism of any sort whatever, large or small, is what it is because each member proceeds to his own duty with a trust that the other members will simultaneously do theirs. Wherever a desired result is achieved by the co-operation of many independent persons, its existence as a fact is a pure consequence of the precursive faith in one another of those immediately concerned. [...] A whole train of passengers (individually brave enough) will be looted by a few highwaymen, simply because the latter can count on one another, while each passenger fears that if he makes a movement of resistance, he will be shot before any one else backs him up. If we believed that the whole car-full would rise at once with us, we should each severally rise, and train-robbing would never even be attempted."[39]

38. Kevin MacDonald, *The Culture of Critique: Toward an Evolutionary Theory of Jewish Involvement in Twentieth-Century Intellectual and Political Movements,* Praeger, 2013, chapter 7, "Jewish Involvement in Shaping U.S. Immigration Policy."
39. William James, *The Will to Believe,* Longmans, Green and Co. (gutenberg.org), p. 24.

4 - THE HOLY HOOK
Yahweh's Trojan Horse in the Gentile City

Is the Church the whore of Yahweh?

I concluded my essay on "Cryptic Jewishness" by what I regard as the most important "revelation" of modern biblical scholarship, one that has the potential to free the Western world from a two-thousand-year-old psychopathic bond: the jealous Yahweh was originally just the national god of Israel, repackaged into "the God of Heaven and Earth" during the Babylonian Exile, as part of a public relation campaign aimed at Persians, then Greeks and ultimately Romans. The resulting biblical notion that the universal Creator became Israel's national god at the time of Moses, is thus exposed as a fictitious inversion of the historical process: in reality, it is the national god of Israel who, so to speak, impersonated the universal Creator at the time of Ezra—while remaining intensely ethnocentric.

The Book of Joshua is a good eye-opener to the biblical hoax, because its pre-exilic author never implies that Yahweh is anything but "the god of Israel," that is, "our god" for the Israelites, and "your god" for their enemies (25 times). Joshua shows no interest in converting Canaanite peoples to the cult of Yahweh. However, we find in the Book of Joshua one converted Canaanite woman, a prostitute from Jericho, who acknowledges that, "Yahweh your god is God both in Heaven above and on Earth beneath" (2:11).

The French Catholic *Bible de Jérusalem* adds a footnote to Rahab's "profession of faith to the God of Israel", which, it says, "made Rahab, in the eyes of more than one Church Father, a figure of the Gentile Church, saved by her faith." I find this footnote emblematic of the role of Christianity in propagating among Gentiles the Israelites' outrageous metaphysical claim, that great deception that has remained, to this day, a source of tremendous symbolic power for the Jews. By recognizing her own image in the prostitute of Jericho, the Church claims for herself the role that is exactly hers in history, while radically misleading Christians about the historical significance of that role. It is indeed the Church who, having acknowledged the god of Israel as the universal God, introduced the Jews into the heart of the Gentile city and, over the centuries, allowed them to seize power over Christendom.

This thesis, which I am going to develop here, may seem fanciful, because we have been taught that Christianity was strongly Judeophobic from the start. And that's true. For example, John Chrysostom, perhaps the most influential Greek theologian of the crucial fourth century, wrote several homilies "Against the Jews". But what he is concerned about, precisely, is the tendency of Christians to be influenced by Jews. Many Christians, he complains, "join the Jews in keeping their feasts and observing their fasts" (*First Homily* I.5).

> "Is it not strange that those who worship the Crucified keep common festival with those who crucified him? Is it not a sign of folly and the worst madness? [...] For when they see that you, who worship the Christ whom they crucified, are reverently following their rituals, how can they fail to think that the rites they have performed are the best and that our ceremonies are worthless?" (*First Homily* V.1-7).

To John's horror, some Christians even get circumcised. "Do not tell me," he warns them, "that circumcision is just a single command; it is that very command which imposes on you the entire yoke of the Law" (*Second Homily* II.4). And so, with all its Judeophobia, John Chrysostom's homilies are a testimony to the seduction that Jews have exerted on Gentile Christians in the early days of the triumphant, imperial Church. And no matter how much the Greek and Latin Fathers have tried to protect their flock from the influence of Jews, this influence has persisted as the Church expanded. It can even be argued that the history of Christianity is the history of its Judaization, from Constantinople to Rome, then from Rome to Amsterdam and to the New World.

We commonly admit that the Church has always oppressed the Jews and prevented their integration unless they convert. Were they not expelled from one Christian kingdom after another in the Middle Ages? Again, this is true, but we must distinguish between the cause and the effect. Each of these expulsions was a reaction to a situation unknown in pre-Christian Antiquity: Jewish communities gaining inordinate economic power, under the protection of a royal administration (Jews served as the kings' tax collectors and moneylenders, and made themselves indispensable for war), until this economic power, yielding political power, reaches a point of saturation, causes pogroms and forces the king to take measures.

Let us consider for example the influence of the Jews in Western Europe under the Carolingians. It reached a climax under Charlemagne's son, Louis the Pious. The bishop of Lyon Agobard (c. 769-840) left us five letters written to protest against the power granted to the Jews at the detriment of Christians. In *On the insolence of the Jews*, addressed to Louis the Pious in 826, Agobard complains that the Jews produce "signed ordinances of your name with golden seals" guaranteeing them outrageous advantages, and that the envoys of the Emperor are "terrible toward Christians and gentle towards Jews." Agobard even complains of an imperial edict imposing Sunday rather than Saturday as market day in order to please the Jews. In another letter, he complains of an edict forbidding anyone to baptize the slaves of the Jews without the permission of their masters.[1]

Louis the Pious was said to be under the influence of his wife Judith—a name that simply means "Jewess". She was so friendly to Jews that the Jewish historian Heinrich Graetz hypothesizes that she was a secret Jewess, in the manner of the biblical Esther. Graetz describes the reign of Louis and Judith (and "the treasurer Bernhard, the real ruler of the kingdom" according to him) as a golden age for the Jews, and points out that in the emperor's court, many regarded Judaism as the true religion. This is illustrated by the resounding conversion of Louis' confessor, Bishop Bodo, who took the name of Eleazar, had himself circumcised, and married a Jewess. "Cultured Christians," writes Graetz, "refreshed themselves with the writings of the Jewish historian Josephus and the Jewish philosopher Philo, and read their works in preference to those of the apostles."[2] The Judaization of the Roman Church at this time is appropriately symbolized by the adoption of unleavened bread for communion, with no justification in the Gospel. I say "the Roman Church", but perhaps it should be called the Frankish Church because, from the time of Charlemagne, it was taken over by ethnic Franks with geopolitical designs on Byzantium, as Orthodox theologian John Romanides has convincingly argued.[3]

---

1. Adrien Bressolles, "La question juive au temps de Louis le Pieux," 1942, on www.persee.fr

2. Heinrich Graetz, *History of the Jews,* Jewish Publication Society of America, 1891 (archive.org), vol. III, ch. VI, p. 162.

3. John Romanides, *Franks, Romans, Feudalism, and Doctrine: An Interplay Between Theology and Society,* Holy Cross Orthodox Press, 1981, on www.romanity.org

The Old Testament was especially influential in the Frankish spheres of power. Popular piety was focused on the Gospel narratives (canonical or apocryphal), the worship of Mary, and the ubiquitous cults of the saints, but kings and popes relied on a political theology drawn from the Tanakh. The Hebrew Bible had been a major part of Frankish propaganda from the late sixth century. Gregory of Tours' *History of the Franks*, the primary—and mostly legendary—source for Merovingian history, is framed on the providential ideology of the Books of Kings: the good kings are those who support the Catholic Church, and the bad kings those who resist the growth of its power. Under Louis the Pious, the rite of anointment of the Frankish kings was designed after the model of the prophet Samuel's anointment of King David in 1Samuel 16. And it not without rationale that French Jewish author Éric Zemmour can title one chapter of his book *Destin français,* "Saint Louis, le roi juif."[4]

The Old Testament as Israel's Trojan Horse

In pre-Christian times, pagan scholars had shown little interest in the Hebrew Bible. Some Jewish writers (Aristobulus of Paneas, Artapan of Alexandria) had tried to bluff the Greeks on the antiquity of the Torah, claiming that Homer, Hesiod, Pythagoras, Socrates and Plato had been inspired by Moses, but no one before the Church Fathers seems to have taken them seriously. Jews had even produced fake Greek prophecies of their success under the title *Sibylline Oracles,* and written under a Greek pseudonym a *Letter of Aristea to Philocrates* praising Judaism, but again, it was not until the triumph of Christianity that these texts were met with Gentile gullibility.

Thanks to Christianity, the Jewish Tanakh was elevated to the status of authoritative history, and Jewish authors such as Josephus and Philo gained undeserved reputation—while being ignored by rabbinic Judaism. Christian academia uncritically tuned to the rigged history of the Jews. While Herodotus had crossed Syria-Palestine around 450 BC without hearing about Judeans or Israelites, Christian historians decided that Jerusalem was then the center of the world, and accepted as fact the totally fictitious empire of Solomon. Until the nineteenth century, world history

---

4. Éric Zemmour, *Destin français,* Albin Michel, 2018.

was calibrated on a fanciful biblical chronology (Egyptology is currently trying to recover from it).[5]

The sanctification of the Tanakh combined its effect with the obsession of converting the Jews. The Church advertised itself to the Jews as the gateway out of the prison of the Law, into the freedom of Christ. But Jewish converts were not asked to leave their Torah on the doorstep. The Jews who entered the Church entered with their Bible, that is to say, with a big part of their Jewishness, while being freed from all the civil restrictions imposed on their non-converted brethren.

When Jews were judged too slow to convert willingly, they were sometimes forced into baptism under threats of expulsion or death. The first documented case goes back to Clovis' grandson, according to Bishop Gregory of Tours:

"King Chilperic commanded that a large number of Jews be baptized, and he himself held several on the fonts. But many were baptized only in body and not in heart; they soon returned to their deceitful habits, for they really kept the Sabbath, and pretended to honor the Sunday." (*History of the Franks,* chapter V)

Such collective forced conversions, producing only insincere and resentful Christians, were conducted throughout the Middle Ages. Hundreds of thousands of Spanish and Portuguese Jews were forced to convert at the end of the fifteenth century, before emigrating throughout Europe. Many of these "New Christians" not only continued to "Judaize" among themselves, but could now have greater influence on the "Old Christians". The penetration of the Jewish spirit into the Roman Church, under the influence of these reluctantly converted Jews and their descendants, is a much more massive phenomenon than is generally admitted.

One case in point is the Jesuit Order, whose foundation coincided with the peak of the Spanish repression against Marranos. Of the seven founding members, four at least were of Jewish ancestry. The case of Loyola himself is unclear, but he was noted for his strong philo-Semitism. Robert Markys has demonstrated, in a groundbreaking scholarly work titled *The Jesuit Order as a Synagogue of Jews*, how crypto-Jews infiltrated key positions in the Jesuit Order from its very beginning, resorting to nepotism in order to eventually establish a monopoly on top positions that

---

5 . Read Gunnar Heinsohn, "The Restauration of Ancient History," on www.mikamar.biz/symposium/heinsohn.txt and John Crowe, "The Revision of Ancient History – A Perspective," on www.sis-group.org.uk/ancient.htm

extended to the Vatican. King Phillip II of Spain called the Order a "Synagogue of Hebrews."[6]

Marranos established in the Spanish Netherlands played an important role in the Calvinist movement. According to Jewish historian Lucien Wolf, "the Marranos in Antwerp had taken an active part in the Reformation movement, and had given up their mask of Catholicism for a not less hollow pretense of Calvinism. [...] The simulation of Calvinism brought them new friends, who, like them, were enemies of Rome, Spain and the Inquisition. [...] Moreover, it was a form of Christianity which came nearer to their own simple Judaism."[7]

Calvin himself had learned Hebrew from rabbis and heaped praise on the Jewish people. He wrote in his commentary on Psalm 119: "Where did Our Lord Jesus Christ and his apostles draw their doctrine, if not Moses? And when we peel off all the layers, we find that the Gospel is simply an exhibition of what Moses had already said." The Covenant of God with the Jewish people is irrevocable because "no promise of God can be undone." That Covenant, "in its substance and truth, is so similar to ours, that we can call them one. The only difference is the order in which they were given."[8]

Within one century, Calvinism, or Puritanism, became a dominant cultural and political force in England. Jewish historian Cecil Roth explains: "The religious developments of the seventeenth century brought to its climax an unmistakable philo-Semitic tendency in certain English circles. Puritanism represented above all a return to the Bible, and this automatically fostered a more favourable frame of mind towards the people of the Old Testament."[9] Some British Puritans went as far as to consider the Leviticus as still in force; they circumcised their children and scrupulously respected the Sabbath. Under Charles I (1625–1649), wrote Isaac d'Israeli (father of Benjamin Disraeli), "it seemed that religion chiefly consisted of Sabbatarian rigours; and that a British

---

6. Robert A. Markys, *The Jesuit Order as a Synagogue of Jews,* Brill, 2009, on www.oapen.org/search?identifier=627427. Read Andrew Joyce's review on theoccidentalobserver.net

7. Lucien Wolf, *Report on the "Marranos" or Crypto-Jews of Portugal,* Anglo-Jewish Association, 1926.

8. Vincent Schmid, "Calvin et les Juifs," 2008, on www.racinesetsources.ch.

9. Cecil Roth, *A History of the Jews in England* (1941), Clarendon Press, 1964, p. 148.

senate had been transformed into a company of Hebrew Rabbis."[10] Wealthy Jews started to marry their daughters into the British aristocracy, to the extent that, according to Hilaire Belloc's estimate, "with the opening of the twentieth century those of the great territorial English families in which there was no Jewish blood were the exception."[11]

The influence of Puritanism on British society naturally extended to the United States. The national mythology of the "Pilgrim Fathers" fleeing "Egypt" (Anglican England) and settling into the Promised Land as the new chosen people, set the tone. The Judaization of American Christianity led to its Zionization in the early twentieth century, with a little help from outside. Again, the Old Testament was used as the Trojan Horse of Zionism within the Christian city. The best example is the Scofield Reference Bible, published in 1909 by Oxford University Press, under the sponsorship of Samuel Untermeyer, a Wall Street lawyer, Federal Reserve co-founder and devoted Zionist. The Scofield Bible is loaded with highly tendentious footnotes. For example, Yahweh's promise to Abraham in Genesis 12:1-3 gets a two-thirds-page footnote explaining that "God made an unconditional promise of blessings through Abram's seed to the nation of Israel to inherit a specific territory forever," although Jacob, who first received the name Israel, was not yet born. The same note explains that, "Both O.T. and N.T. are full of post-Sinaitic promises concerning Israel and the land which is to be Israel's everlasting possession," accompanied by "a curse laid upon those who persecute the Jews," or "commit the sin of anti-Semitism."[12]

As a result of this kind of gross propaganda, most American Evangelicals regard the creation of Israel in 1948 and its military victory in 1967 as miracles fulfilling biblical prophecies and heralding the second coming of Christ. Jerry Falwell declared, "Right at the very top of our priorities must be an unswerving commitment and devotion to the state of Israel," while Pat Robertson said, "The future of this Nation [America] may be at stake, because God will bless those that bless Israel." As for John Hagee, chairman of Christians United for Israel, he once declared:

10. Isaac Disraeli, *Commentaries on the Life and Reign of Charles the First,* 1851, quoted in Archibald Maule Ramsay, *The Nameless War*, 1952 (archive.org).
11. Hilaire Belloc, *The Jews,* Constable & Co., 1922 (archive.org), p. 223.
12. Joseph Canfield, *The Incredible Scofield and His Book*, Ross House Books, 2004, pp. 219-220.

"The United States must join Israel in a pre-emptive military strike against Iran to fulfill God's plan for both Israel and the West."[13]

Gullible Christians not only see God's hand whenever Israel advances in its self-prophesized destiny of world domination, but are ready to see Israeli leaders themselves as prophets when they announce their own false-flag crimes: Evangelical author Michael Evans believes that Isser Harel, founder of Israeli secret services, had a prophetic inspiration when, in 1980, he predicted that Islamic terrorists would hit the Twin Towers. [14] Benjamin Netanyahu also boasted on CNN in 2006 to have prophesized 9/11 in 1995.[15] To the less naive, this tells a lot about the Jewish gift of prophecy, which is really predictive programming.

Christians' learned helplessness

By recognizing the Jews' special status as the people of the Old Testament, once chosen by God among all nations, Christians have granted them an extraordinary symbolic power that no other ethnic community can compete with.

For two thousand years, Christianity has taught Gentiles to consent to the delusional claim of the Jews to divine election: are they not the first and only ethnic group whom the God of the universe has addressed personally, the people whom He has loved to the point of exterminating its enemies? It matters not that Christians tell the Jews that they have lost the election because they rejected Christ: the main price is theirs. To accept the biblical notion of "chosen people", whatever the reservations, is to accept the metaphysical superiority of the Jews. If Christ is Israel's Messiah, then truly, "salvation is from the Jews" (John 4:22).

We are experiencing today the final consequences of this submission, which the peoples of Antiquity could never have imagined in their worst nightmares. The exalted status of the Jews and of their "holy history" is the deeper reason for their influence on the affairs of the world. By accepting the triple biblical paradigm—Jealous God, Chosen People, Promised Land—, Christian Churches, Catholic and Protestant in particular, have become complicit with the imperialistic project of the Hebrew

---

13. Jill Duchess of Hamilton, *God, Guns and Israel,* The History Press, 2009.
14. Michael Evans, *The American Prophecies,* 2005, quoted in Christopher Bollyn, *Solving 9-11: The Deception That Changed the World,* C. Bollyn, 2012, p. 71.
15. "Netanyahu Predicted 9/11 in 1995" on YouTube.

Bible. Therefore, there will be no definitive emancipation from Zion without mental and moral emancipation from the biblical matrix.

When reading the Book of Joshua, a Christian is supposed to approve, as a matter of principle, the extermination of the inhabitants of the cities of Canaan and the stealing of their land, since it was ordained by God. The editors of my *Bible de Jérusalem* explain in a footnote to chapter 3: "Joshua was considered by the Fathers as a figure of his namesake Jesus [their names are identical in Hebrew], and the Jordanian passage as a figure of Christian baptism." How can Joshua be a figure of Jesus? What has Jesus' Sermon on the Mount to do with Joshua's bloodthirsty fanaticism? How can the xenophobic god of Joshua be the Father of Christ? A crippling cognitive dissonance has seized Christian peoples, causing a chronic inability to see and resist the inherent violence of Israel, which is only a reflection of the violence of the psychopathic god Yahweh.

As a matter of principle, the Christian is supposed to approve Yahweh's sentence on those who ate with the Moabites and took wives among them: "Yahweh said to Moses, 'Take all the leaders of the people. Impale them facing the sun, for Yahweh, to deflect his burning anger from Israel'" (Numbers 25:4). But then, why blame the Jerusalem priestly caste for sending Jesus to the torture? Explain to me in which way they were unfaithful to the Torah! Not to mention, of course, the inherent contradiction in blaming them for the Cross, since, according to the Gospel, "the Son of man was destined to suffer grievously, and to be rejected by the elders and the chief priests and the scribes, and to be put to death, and after three days to rise again" (Mark 8:31).

The sanctification of Yahweh's bloody leadership during the Exodus and the conquest of Canaan has made Gentiles incapable of understanding the ideological foundation of Jewishness, and helpless in the face of its intrinsic violence today. It has created a blind spot in Christians' mind: they may see the effects of Zion's evil power, but not its cause, falsely assuming that the moral corruption they see in Jews comes from the Talmud or the Kabbalah.

Christians cannot even see the Jewish plan for world domination that is written in plain language, right under their nose. If the Jewish Tanakh had not become the Christians' Holy Book, it would have been exposed as the proof for Israel's racist and

supremacist ambitions long ago. But when it comes to the Old
Testament, Christians are seized by a severe reading disorder:
when their Good Book says "Israel will conquer and enslave the
nations of the world", they think it means "the Church will convert
the world to the love of Christ."

If the "Jewish question" is about the inordinate power of Israeli
elite networks within nations, then the Jewish question is also a
Christian question: it is about the built-in vulnerability of Christian
societies to this power. Deep down, anyone who grew up a
Christian knows that the chosen people will have the last word,
because if Yahweh is God, his promise is eternal, as he himself
declares, in his inimitable megalomaniac style: "By my own self I
swear it; what comes from my mouth is saving justice, it is an
irrevocable word" (Isaiah 45:23). One can even speak of the
"learned helplessness" of Christians, whose Scriptures tell them
again and again of God's merciless humiliation of the Jews'
enemies. Deeper than that, Christians' helplessness comes from
having as ultimate model a man crucified by the Jews: how can the
"imitation of Christ" save us from the high priests' power to lobby
and corrupt Pilatus?

The Judeo-Babylonian metaphysical hoax makes God not just
ridiculously anthropomorphic, but Judeomorphic. To be fooled by
it is to mistake the Creator of the Universe for a topical demon
rumbling and spitting fire from a Midianite volcano (Exodus 19),
adopted as tutelary deity by a confederation of Semitic nomadic
tribes craving for a piece of the Fertile Crescent. It is to internalize
an extremely primitive and unspiritual image of the divine that is
obstructive of sound metaphysical thinking: the divorce between
philosophy (the love of Wisdom) and theology (the science of
God) is one manifestation of the resulting mental split in Western
thought. In the final analysis, the jealous Yahweh, destroyer of all
pantheons, is so unconvincing in the garb of the Great universal
God that he is fated to be discarded in his turn. Atheism is the end
result and the mirror image of biblical monotheism: it is the
rejection of the biblical God, mistaken for the true God. "If
Yahweh is God, no thanks," has been the simple rationale for
atheism in Christendom since the Enlightenment: Voltaire, for
example, scorned Christianity by quoting the Old Testament.
Yahweh has ruined men's natural faith in a divine Creator.

How Christianity reinforced Jewish alienation

Also to consider is the effect that the Christian sanctification of the Jewish Tanakh has had on Jews themselves. It has discouraged Jews from questioning their scriptures and breaking free from their psychopathic bond with Yahweh. Any Jew who questioned the divine inspiration of the Torah was not only banned from his community, but found no shelter among Christians: this happened to Baruch Spinoza and many others. For two thousand years, Christians have prayed that the Jews would open their heart to Christ, but they have done nothing to free them from Yahweh.

Critics of Jews in pagan Antiquity had a simple logic: although Jews were considered an *ethnos,* it was commonly admitted that their misanthropy was due to their religion. It was the fault of Moses, who had taught them to scorn the gods and the traditions of others. Hecataeus of Abdera gives in his *Aegyptiaca* (around 300 BC) an alternative version of the Exodus: to appease their gods during a plague, the Egyptians expelled from their lands the many tribes of migrant foreigners, and some of them settled in Judea under the conduct of their leader Moses who, "because of their expulsion, [...] introduced a kind of misanthropic and inhospitable way of life."[16] The Roman historian Tacitus tells a similar story and also attributes to Moses the introduction of "new religious practices, quite opposed to those of all other religions. The Jews regard as profane all that we hold sacred; on the other hand, they permit all that we abhor" (Tacitus, *Histories* V.3-5). Plutarch reports in his treatise on *Isis and Osiris* that some Egyptians believed the god of the Jews to be Seth, the murderer of Osiris, banned from the council of the gods and exiled in the desert, from where he periodically returns to bring famine and discord. This opinion was so widespread in the Greco-Roman world that many people believed that the Jews worshiped in their Temple the golden head of a donkey, symbol of Seth in the divine bestiary of Egypt. The Roman general Pompey is reported to have been surprised not to find this famous donkey idol when he entered the Holy of Holies in 63 BC.

Judeophobia was simple, then: the Jews were not racially, but religiously degenerate. But the Christian Fathers, who held that only the Jews had worshiped the true God before the coming of

---

16. Peter Schäfer, *Judéophobie: Attitudes à l'égard des Juifs dans le monde antique,* Cerf, 2003, pp. 13-15.

Jesus Christ, had to elaborate a sophisticated explanation for the Jews' asocial behavior, one which is so self-contradicting that its message to the Jews amounts to a "double bind": on the one hand, the Jews are told that their Yahweh is the true God and that their Bible is holy, but on the other hand, they are criticized for behaviors they have learned precisely from Yahweh and the Bible. They are accused of plotting to rule the world, although it is the very promise that Yahweh made to them: "Yahweh your God will raise you higher than every other nation in the world" (Deuteronomy 28:1). They are blamed for their materialism and their greed, but that also they learned from Yahweh, who dreams only of plunder: "I shall shake all the nations, and the treasures of all the nations will flow in" (Haggai 2:7).

Above all, they are rebuked for their separatism, although this is the very essence of Yahweh's message to them: "I shall set you apart from all these peoples, for you to be mine" (Leviticus 20:26). The Church Fathers endorse Yahweh's endless complaint against his people's irrepressible tendency to socialize with other nations, by pacts, shared meals and intermarriage. But are not these "stiff-necked Jews" who rebelled against the tyrannical yoke of the Levites, precisely those who sought to extricate themselves from the Jewish alienation by assimilating into the surrounding civilizations? Were they not doing exactly what we would like Jews to do today? The contradiction is in many Christian writings. John Chrysostom, for example, writes in his *First Homily Against the Jews* (II.3):

> "Nothing is more miserable than those people who never failed to attack their own salvation. When there was need to observe the Law, they trampled it under foot. Now that the Law has ceased to bind, they obstinately strive to observe it. What could be more pitiable that those who provoke God not only by transgressing the Law but also by keeping it?"

This amounts to telling the Jews: "Damned if you do, damned if you don't." Christians accuse them of having rebelled against Yahweh yesterday, and they accuse them of obeying Yahweh today, under the pretext that Yahweh's orders no longer stand. How unconvincing to the Jews!

Anti-Yahwism is the only effective criticism of Israel because it is the only fair criticism. It cuts short the accusation of anti-Semitism, since it aims at liberating the Jews from the sociopathic god who has taken control of their destiny—and who is, of course, only the puppet of the Levites.

Zionist pioneer Leo Pinsker wrote in his booklet *Auto-Emancipation* (1882), that the Jews are "the people chosen for universal hatred." They are indeed, but not because Gentiles are universally affected by a "psychic aberration," a "variety of demonopathy" known as Judeophobia, as Pinsker believes; rather because their covenant with Yahweh has programmed them to be hated wherever they go.[17]

It is time to tell the Jews what Christians have been unable to tell them: You were never chosen by God. You have just been misled by your Levites to take your vindictive tribal god for the universal Father in Heaven. This cognitive short-circuit has caused in your collective psyche a grave narcissistic personality disorder. For our own misfortune, we Gentiles have been fooled by your self-delusion and have fallen, too, under the psychopathic bond of your leaders. But we are now waking up, and as soon as we recover our senses and our dignity, we'll help you out of it too.

Christianity as "controlled opposition"

"Inside every Christian is a Jew," stated Pope Francis.[18] That may not be *the* essential truth of Christianity, but it is an essential truth none the less. Most Christians are not aware of this Jew inside them, yet he commands a large part of their worldview. Meditating on this truth can be a mind-opening experience, radiating in a multiplicity of questions. Should we use Sigmund Freud's concept of "projection" and say that most Christians who hate Jews really hate the Jew inside them? Or is this Jew inside them a self-hating Jew, like every Jew according to Theodor Lessing (*Jewish Self-Hatred,* Berlin, 1930)? Perhaps inside every Christian are two Jews, one hating the other, Moses and Jesus. From whichever side we want to look at it, the fact is that Christians are, by New Testament definition, the spiritual heirs of Yahweh's promise to Israel. They are new branches grafted onto the trunk of Israel, according to Paul's metaphor (Romans 11:16-24).

---

17. Leon Pinsker, *Auto-Emancipation: An Appeal to His People by a Russian Jew* (1882), on www.jewishvirtuallibrary.org/jsource/Zionism/pinsker.html.
18. Josephine Mckenna, "Pope Francis: 'Inside every Christian is a Jew,'" *Washington Post,* June 123, 2014, on www.washingtonpost.com

What still needs to be explained is how Paul and his followers succeeded in convincing tens of thousands of Gentiles to become a new synthetic Israel, at a time when the very name of Israel was hated all around the Mediterranean Sea? How is it that the religion that converted the Roman Empire to the worship of a Jewish Messiah, was born at the time when the biggest wave of Judeophobia was sweeping across the Empire? To answer that question, let's examine the context.

At the turn of the millennium, during the prosperous reign of Augustus, Jews had gained advantageous situations in many parts of the Empire. They enjoyed freedom of cult and judicial autonomy, and were exempted from the civil formality of emperor worship, from all obligations on the Sabbath, and from military service. Moreover, they were allowed to collect funds and send them to the Jerusalem Temple bureaucracy.[19]

As Jews abused of their privileges and conspired to increase them, Gentile resentment grew and anti-Jewish riots followed. In the year 38 AD, the Greeks of Alexandria sent a delegation to Rome, whose leader Isidoros complained that the Jews are "trying to stir up the entire world."[20] The emperor issued an edict declaring that, if the Jews continued to sow dissent and "to agitate for more privileges than they formerly possessed, [...] I will by all means take vengeance on them as fomenters of what is a general plague infecting the whole world." This edict was followed by another addressed to all the Jewish communities of the empire, asking them not to "behave with contempt towards the gods of other peoples."[21]

Tensions were high in Jerusalem, where the pro-Roman Herodian dynasty faltered. It was at this time that Pharisees and Sadducees denounced Jesus to the Romans as a seditious would-be king of the Jews, calculating, according to the Fourth Gospel, that "it is to [the Jews'] advantage that one man should die for the people, rather than that the whole nation should perish" (John 11:50). Flavius Josephus mentions several Jewish revolts in the same period, including one during the Passover of 48 or 49 AD, after a Roman soldier assigned to the entrance of the Temple committed the irreparable: "raising his robe, he stooped in an

---

19. Michael Grant, *Jews in the Roman World,* Weidenfeld & Nicolson, 2011, pp. 58-61.
20. Joseph Mélèze Modrzejewski, *The Jews of Egypt, From Rameses II to Emperor Hadrian,* Princeton UP, 1995, p. 178.
21. Quoted in Michael Grant, *Jews in the Roman World, op. cit.,* pp. 134-135.

indecent attitude, so as to turn his backside to the Jews, and made a noise in keeping with this posture" (*Jewish Wars* II.224).[22] In 66 the Jewish War broke out, when the Sadducees defied Roman power by banning from the Temple the daily sacrifices offered in the name and at the expense of the Emperor. After the destruction of the Temple by the future emperor Titus in 70, the embers of Jewish messianism continued to hatch for 70 more years, and ignited Palestine for the last time with the revolt of Simon Bar Kochba, which provoked in retaliation the complete destruction of Jerusalem, its conversion into a Roman city renamed Aelia Capitolina, and the banning of Jews from it. By then, enmity against the Jews had reached a climax throughout the Empire.

This is precisely the time when Christian missionaries spread the cult of Christ in all the major urban centers of the Empire, starting with those inhabited by large Jewish communities, such as Antioch, Ephesus and Alexandria. A reasonable explanation for their success among Gentiles is that Christianity, in its Pauline version, is a fundamentally Judeophobic religion that surfed on the greatest wave of Judeophobia. As the cult of a demi-god victim of the Jews, it satisfied the general perception of Jews as a "race hated by the gods" (Tacitus, *Histories* V.3). But that explanation fails to account for the fact that the triumphant Judeophobic religion is not a pagan religion, but the fundamentally Jewish cult of a Jewish Messiah allegedly fulfilling Jewish prophecies. What we have here is a bizarre case of Hegelian dialectic, one in which the "antithesis" is controlled by the "thesis" and absorbed into it.

Through Christianity, Roman Judeophobia became Judaized. The Gospel narrative makes the Jews the plotters against the Son of God, but this Son of God is a Jew, and soon the "Mother of God"—as Isis, Ishtar or Artemis were called—would be turned into a Jewess too. Most importantly, Judeophobic Christians will adopt the Tanakh and the bizarre Jewish paradigm of the "jealous god" with his "chosen people". From that point of view, it is as if Christ nailed on the Cross had been used as a bait to pull anti-Jewish Gentiles, by the fishing line of the Old Testament, into worshipping Jewishness.

This process fits the concept of "Jewish controlled opposition" conceptualized by Gilad Atzmon in his book *Being in Time*. Whenever Jewish power becomes threatened by the Gentiles'

---

22. Quoted in Michael Grant, *Jews in the Roman World, op. cit.,* p. 148.

resentment against it, it produces "a satellite Jewish dissent" designed to control and stir Gentile opposition. This Jewish dissent monopolizes the protest and keeps non-Jewish dissenters in line. According to a parable proposed by Atzmon, the purpose is to make sure that any Jewish problem suffered by the Gentiles is treated by Jewish doctors, whose fundamental interest is that the problem is not solved. By claiming to have the solution to the problem, dissident Jews deceive Gentiles on the nature of the problem, and ultimately aggravate the problem.

As Atzmon sees it, the process does not necessarily result from a secret agreement between Jewish power and Jewish dissent. The Jewish opposition intellectuals "are not necessarily consciously deceiving us; indeed, they may well be doing their best, within the context of a limited tribal mindset. The truth is, they cannot think out of the box, they cannot climb over the ghetto walls that enclose their own tribal beings."[23] We can see this tribal mindset as a collective instinct of conservation that is part of the essence of Jewishness. Ideological quarrels between Jews may be intense and sincere, but they remain quarrels between Jews, who tacitly agree to speak louder than Gentiles and exclude from the discussion any radical criticism of Jewishness.

In the light of Atzmon's analysis, it becomes conceivable that Christianity's primary function was to absorb Greco-Roman Judeophobia into a movement that would ultimately reinforce the symbolic status of the Jews, by spreading the "chosen people" propaganda myth fabricated five centuries earlier. Ezra had convinced the Persians that the Jews worshipped the God of Heaven like them; the Church went on convincing the Romans that, before Jesus, the Jews had been the *only* people worshipping the true God and loved by Him. Such creed from the Gentiles is worth a thousand Balfour declarations, in the march toward world domination by way of deception. In the Christian narrative that says, "God chose the Jewish people, but then rejected them," the benefit from the first part is much higher than the cost of the second, which hardly makes sense anyway.

If the Italian rabbi Elijah Benamozegh is right in saying that "The constitution of a universal religion is the ultimate goal of Judaism," then Christianity is a great step toward that glorious future: "In Heaven, one God of all men, and on earth a single

---

23. Gilad Atzmon, *Being in Time: A Post-Political Manifesto*, Skyscraper, 2017, p. 208.

family of peoples, among whom Israel is the eldest, responsible for the priestly function of teaching and the administration of the true religion of humanity."[24] Christianity has prepared the way for the next stage: the cult of the crucified Jew is now being superseded by the cult of the exterminated Jews (the Holocaust world religion).

Christianity without the Old Testament?

In the second century AD, Marcion of Sinope had asserted the incompatibility of the Hebrew Bible and the Gospel: Yahweh cannot be the Father of Christ, he said, because everything opposes them. The covenants of Moses and Christ are so contrary in their terms that they must have been passed with deities totally alien to each other. According to the German specialist Adolf von Harnack, it was Marcion who founded the first hierarchical church, established the first Christian canon, to which he first gave the name of *evangelion*. In the early third century, his doctrine "has invaded the whole earth," complained Tertullian, who was from the Semitic city of Carthage, as was Augustine and other Latin Fathers who emphasized the Jewish roots of Christianity.[25] Had Marcionism prevailed, Christianity would have broken with Judaism, which might have withered in a few centuries.[26] Islam would never have emerged. On the other hand, perhaps Christianity itself would not have prevailed, and would be remembered today as just another transient otherworldly oriental religion, alongside its Manichean cousin.

Can we really separate the New Testament from the Old anyway? We are told that Marcion's canon consisted of Paul's letters and a short version of Luke, but it is hard to imagine how he could have completely sanitized the later from its 68 references and allusions to the Old Testament. Admittedly, the original Gospels contained less Old Testament items than it does today: for example, Mark's only apocalyptic passage (in chapter 13), a condensation of apocalyptic imagery from the books of Daniel, Isaiah, and Ezekiel, was a secondary addition. Many scholars even consider all of Jesus' apocalyptic prophecies in Matthew and Luke

---

24. Élie Benamozegh, *Israël et l'humanité* (1914), Albin Michel, 1980, pp. 28-29.

25. Adolf von Harnack, *Marcion, l'évangile du Dieu étranger* (1924), Cerf, 2005.

26. If we follow the logic of Peter Schäfer, *The Jewish Jesus: How Judaism and Christianity Shaped Each Other*, Princeton UP, 2012.

as foreign to Jesus' original message, and some regard the bulk of the Book of Revelation (from 4:1 to 22:15), which refers neither to Jesus nor to any identifiable Christian theme, as a Jewish book framed between a Christian prologue and epilogue.[27]

Alternate history is fun, but quite pointless. Christianity came to us with the Old Testament and a heavily Judaized New Testament. The fruit came with the worm, whose name is Yahweh. The question is: what can we expect from Christianity today? From the viewpoint I have adopted here, it seems that Christianity cannot be the solution to the problem it has created.

Yes, we can rejoice at the rebirth of the Russian Church, and its role in fostering a healthy public morality and reviving national dignity. Orthodox Christianity is the closest to the original, and by far the least Judaized. Persecuted during seventy years of communism, it is certainly not much infiltrated by crypto-Jews, at the moment. But can it overcome the inherent problem that I have highlighted here? Can it ever challenge the Jews' megalomaniac and narcissistic claim to their metaphysical exceptionality?

A radically critical approach of the Old Testament is, I believe, an indispensable tool for Gentiles to emancipate themselves mentally and recover their natural defense mechanism against the Yahweh-Zion matrix. Theologians should, at the very least, be allowed to say that Yahweh is a grossly distorted Judeomorphic image of God. Islam has an advantage here, since Muslims have always admitted that the Jewish Tanakh is fraudulent. Not that I see Islam as a solution, far from it, but a consensus between Muslims and Orthodox Christians on the problematic nature of the Hebrew Scriptures could be a first step toward emancipation.

It is important also not to overrate the impact of these issues on popular piety, as an argument against addressing them. The average Christian's faith would not be much disturbed if the Old Testament would cease to be read in Church, or even if it would be openly criticized. It is also important not to confuse Christendom with Christianity: Notre-Dame was not built by bishops, priests or saints, but by the people of Paris. The same can be said of every cathedral or village church. Johan Sebastian Bach was not a priest (and certainly never composed under the inspiration of the Old Testament), and neither were any of the great geniuses who built

---

27. See for example James Charlesworth, *Jesus within Judaism,* SPCK, 1989.

our civilization. Exposing the impostor god of the Old Testament will not undermine Christian civilization.

Finally, I have zoomed here on a problematic aspect of Christianity, but other viewpoints are possible. I have developed the antithesis to the common thesis that Christianity is anti-Jewish, but there is truth also in the thesis. Christianity is certainly not entirely Jewish: it is also profoundly pagan. Jesus' legend is a Greek heroic myth. The cults of the Virgin Mary and of the saints are pagan traditions superficially Christianized, with no roots in the Old or New Testament. To acknowledge, accept and celebrate those pagan roots, could be a welcome development within Christianity, as a counterweight to the Old Testament burden.

5 - THE VOLCANO GOD
The Arabian Cradle of Judaism

When Yahweh resided in an Arabian volcano

"Yahweh came from Sinai" (Deuteronomy 33:2; Psalms 68:18). It is in Sinai that Moses first encounters Yahweh; it is back to Sinai that Moses leads Yahweh's people from Egypt; and it is from Sinai that, two years later, on Yahweh's order again, Moses sets off with them to conquer a piece of the Fertile Crescent. But where is Sinai, with its Mount Horeb? The answer is given in Exodus.

Moses' encounter with Yahweh in Sinai resulted from his having murdered an Egyptian official: "Looking this way and that and seeing no one in sight, he killed the Egyptian and hid him in the sand". Upon learning that his deed "has come to light," Moses got "frightened" and fled "into Midianite territory," where he was hosted by "a priest of Midian with seven daughters." He "agreed to stay on there with the man, who gave him his daughter Zipporah in marriage" (Exodus 2:12-21). Moses' father-in-law is named Reuel in Exodus 2:18, but Jethro in Numbers 3:1, "Hobab son of Reuel the Midianite" in Numbers 10:29, and "Hobab the Kenite" in Judges 1:16. We'll call him Jethro, his most popular name. His daughter gave Moses two sons: Gershom (2:22) and Eliezer (18:4). It is while grazing his father-in-law's flocks that Moses finds himself near Mount Horeb, "to the far side of the desert" (3:1), where he hears Yahweh call his name. By implication, Sinai is in Midian.

And where is Midian? Greek authors unanimously place it in northwestern Arabia, on the eastern shore of the Gulf of Aqaba. Even Paul the Apostle, who spent three years in Arabia, knew that "Sinai is a mountain in Arabia" (Galatians 4:25). It was not before the fourth century that the biblical Sinai was misplaced in the Egyptian peninsula, probably for geopolitical reasons (Egypt was within the control of the Roman Empire, unlike Arabia, under Persian influence). But placing the biblical Sinai west of the Gulf of Aqaba didn't make any sense, since that region had always belonged to Egypt (archeology has confirmed it). Why would the

Israelites have settled there when chased by the Egyptian army? The same goes for Moses' earlier flight from Egypt as a wanted murderer. Never mind if these stories are true or not: the point is that their authors could not possibly have placed Sinai and Mount Horeb within Egyptian territory.

Where, then, did the Israelites cross the Red Sea? They probably didn't: the biblical "Red Sea" is a mistranslation originating from the Greek Septuagint. These waters are simply referred to in Hebrew as *Yam Suph* (23 times), which means "Sea of Reeds," and suggests a body of shallow fresh water, which Yahweh simply "dried up" before the Israelites, according to Joshua 2:10. It could be anywhere, in this land of ephemeral wadis.

The precise location of Mount Horeb or Mount Sinai (both names are used interchangeably) can be deduced from the phenomena witnessed by the Israelites there:

> "there were peals of thunder and flashes of lightning, dense cloud on the mountain and a very loud trumpet blast; and, in the camp, all the people trembled. Then Moses led the people out of the camp to meet God; and they took their stand at the bottom of the mountain. Mount Sinai was entirely wrapped in smoke, because Yahweh had descended on it in the form of fire. The smoke rose like smoke from a furnace and the whole mountain shook violently. Louder and louder grew the trumpeting. Moses spoke, and God answered him in the thunder." (Exodus 19:16-19)

If Mount Horeb shakes like a volcano, rumbles like a volcano, smokes like a volcano, and spits fire like a volcano, then it should be a volcano. No matter how much fantasy the final redactors introduced into the story, it still contains very realistic descriptions of a powerful volcanic eruption, such as the vision of Yahweh as a "pillar of cloud" by day, and a "pillar of fire" by night to guide them toward Sinai (Exodus 13:21). When Moses went up the mountain, Yahweh warned him that "no human being can see me and survive," but finds him a spot from where he will be able to get a glance of him safely:

> "Here is a place near me. You will stand on the rock, and when my glory passes by, I shall put you in a cleft of the rock and shield you with my hand until I have gone past. Then I shall take my hand away and you will see my back; but my face will not be seen." (Exodus 33:20-23)

Moses got somewhat irradiated by a long exposure to "Yahweh", for when he came down, "the skin on his face was so radiant that they were afraid to go near him" (34:30).[1]

The region of Midian in northwestern Arabia happens to be a volcanic area, unlike the Egyptian Sinai. Volcanic activity was still reported there in the Middle Ages.[2] Explorer Charles Beke was one of the first modern scholars to point out that Mount Sinai must be a volcano (*Mount Sinai a Volcano*, 1873), and to place it in Arabia (*Sinai in Arabia and of Midian*, 1878). New arguments were added in 1910 by Czech orientalist and explorer Alois Musil, who in turn inspired other investigators and scholars. The theory became widely accepted, and Sigmund Freud adopted it in his *Moses and Monotheism* (1939).[3]

One likely candidate for Sinai-Horeb is Jabal Maqla, which is part of the Jabal al-Lawz mountain range in northwestern Saudi Arabia. Its summit, reaching almost 8500 feet, consists of metamorphic rocks of volcanic origin. The Jabal al-Lawz candidacy has gained the support of a growing number of scholars. What was originally a confidential scholarly debate began to be popularized in the 1990s, in books by adventurers such as Larry Williams,[4] or Howard Blum,[5] and documentary films such as "Searching for the real Mt Sinai," or "Search for Mt. Sinai-Mountain of Fire").

Two new books appeared recently, one by a Christian Evangelical, Joel Richardson (*Mount Sinai in Arabia*), and the

1. Read more arguments and references in ohmyvolcano.blogspot.com
2. Colin Humphreys, *The Miracles of Exodus,* HarperOne, 2003.
3. Sigmund Freud, *Moses and Monotheism*, Hogarth Press, 1939 (archive.org), p. 55.
4. Larry Williams, *The Mountain of Moses,* Wynwood Press, 1990.
5. Howard Blum *The Gold of Exodus,* Simon & Schuster, 1998.

other by a Jewish rabbi, Alexander Hool (*Searching for Sinai*). And in 2018, the Doubting Thomas Research Foundation launched a couple of websites, SinaiInArabia.com and jabalmaqla.com, dedicated to present the complete evidence for the Arabian Sinai. It has produced the best documentary so far, "Finding the Mountain of Moses: The Real Mount Sinai in Saudi Arabia."

NEOM and the Saudi-Israeli secret deal

The Saud royal clan, while well aware of possessing the true Sinai and the archeological remnants surrounding it, have prohibited their access to foreign adventurers and archeologists. But it may soon become an issue in the war of holy places in the Middle East. During their occupation of the Egyptian Sinai between 1967 and 1982, the Israelis had engaged in intense but fruitless archaeological search there; the Arabian alternative for the Mountain of God cannot leave them indifferent. Huge symbolic power is at stake. As everything biblical, the issue has far-reaching geopolitical implications in the eyes of the lords of Zion. Not to mention the financial prospect. Joel Richardson's introduction to his *Mount Sinai in Arabia* sounds like a touristic pamphlet aimed at Yahweh worshippers worldwide:

> "This was the very place where God Himself 'came down'. [...] This is a mountain that is literally drenched with divine history. [...] The time is ripe. Within the sovereignty of God, I fully believe that the season has come in which Jebel al-Lawz will finally be fully opened not only to archeologists but to the whole world."[6]

The growing popularization of the Arabian Sinai cannot be unrelated to the NEOM project announced in October 2017 by Saudi Crown Prince Mohammad bin Salman (MSB): a high-tech, ultra-connected, transnational mega city and economic zone, covering 10,230 square-miles (about the size of Massachusetts), which happens to correspond roughly to ancient Midian. Operating under a specific legal regime geared for a Western lifestyle and insulated from Islamic law, NEOM will also target luxury tourism. Richardson hopes that Jebel al-Lawz will be part of the attraction:

> "If current plans continue, the Saudi Kingdom will soon be opening to tourism for the first time in its history. Is the sovereign hand of God at work? [...] In the current atmosphere of increasing

---

6. Joel Richardson, *Mount Sinai in Arabia,* WinePress Media, 2019.

unbelief, the same God who descended upon the mountain before multitudes has ordained that it now emerge from the relative shadows to be marveled upon by an even greater multitude."[7]

Israel, whose city of Eilat will be just a few miles away with direct access by boat, is a major, although discreet, stakeholder in the mega-project. A *Jerusalem Post* reporter claims to have seen "correspondence between Arab diplomats and Israeli businessmen confirming that talks are ongoing over economic cooperation, and a number of Israeli companies are already selling cybersecurity tools to the Saudi government." This joint venture, comments the Israeli reporter, is "a blow to the decades-long Arab League boycott of the Jewish state."[8] Indeed, the legendary Saudi-Israeli enmity is morphing before our very eyes into an overt alliance for the control of the Middle East at the expense of Iran. MBS may now be reversing 70 years of Saudi boycott of Israel, saying, "Jews has a right to their own land."[9]

What sparked this romance was love potion # 9/11. The sophisticated false flag operation orchestrated by the crypto-Zionist neocons in 2001 had an inbuilt device to blackmail Saudi Arabia into alignment (or, let's say, force the Sauds to purge their anti-Israeli elements): besides Osama bin Laden, 15 of the 19 alleged hijackers were Saudis. That was a message in itself, and David Wurmser hammered it with an article in the *Weekly Standard* of October 29, 2001, entitled: "The Saudi Connection: Osama bin Laden's a Lot Closer to the Saudi Royal Family Than You Think." Many books and articles were written with the same line.[10] Pressure increased when the *New York Times*, July 26, 2003, revealed that a 28-page section detailing possible involvement of specific Saudi officials had been censored from the 9/11 Commission Report. One of the key men in this blackmailing operation was Senator Bob Graham, brother-in-law of *Washington Post* owner Katharine Graham (born Meyer), with his book[11] and interviews, notably on *Democracy Now*. To anyone aware that bin

7. Joel Richardson, *Mount Sinai in Arabia,* WinePress Media, 2019.

8. Max Schindler, "Israeli companies talking to Saudi Arabia about $500b. 'Smart City'," October 25, 2017, on www.jpost.com

9. "Saudi Arabia's Mohammad bin Salman suggests Jews have a right to their own land," on www.thejc.com

10. For instance, Dore Gold, *Hatred's Kingdom: How Saudi Arabia Supports the New Global Terrorism,* Regnery Publishing, 2004.

11. Bob Graham, *Intelligence Matters: The CIA, the FBI, Saudi Arabia, and the Failure of America's War on Terror,* Random House, 2004.

Laden had nothing to do with 9/11, it should be obvious that the 28 "censored" pages of the 9/11 Commission report are a sham like the rest of it, an integral part of the false flag to blackmail Saudi Arabia into a new Israel-friendly policy.

It was effective, judging from the good job the Saudis have done for Israel in the last decade, by directing their jihadists against Libya and Syria. "Israel is said to be working with Saudi Arabia on an Iran strike plan," according to *The Times of Israel,* November 17, 2013. The Saud's war in Yemen, directed against the Houthi Ansarullah movement, mostly Shiite and Israelophobic ("Death to Israel, Curse on the Jews," they are heard chanting), is another proof of their readiness to serve Zion.

Some believe that the Saudi-Israeli secret alliance actually goes back to the very foundation of Saudi Arabia. A strong argument can be made that the simultaneous creation of Saudi Arabia by Great Britain in the early twentieth century fitted the Zionist agenda.[12] The twin States of Israel and Saudi Arabia were made and maintained by the same Anglo-Zionist forces.

The Zionist plan aims at fulfilling Yahweh's promise to Abraham (taken as a promise to the Jews): "To your descendants I give this land, from the river of Egypt to the great river, the Euphrates" (Genesis 15:18-21). It means that northern Arabia must one day fall under Israeli control. Which is what NEOM may really be about. The signs of a "Greater Israel" hidden agenda are everywhere, including in such headlines as *Haaretz*'s "Before Islam: When Saudi Arabia Was a Jewish Kingdom" (a perfect example of Israelis' propensity to use insignificant or fraudulent archeological findings to support their imperial hubris).[13]

There are actually rumors that both Muhammad ibn Saud (1710-1765), founder of the Saud dynasty, and his partner Muhammad ibn Abd-al-Wahhab (1703-1792), founder of Wahhabism, were Jews of ancient stock. The Memoirs of a British spy named Hempher, made known in 1888 by Ottoman admiral Ayyub Sabri Pasha, claims that Abd-al-Wahab was from a family of Dönmeh, and that his reform was covertly supported by the British as part of a strategy to foment division within Islam and destabilize Ottoman rule. This source is taken seriously in an Iraqi Military Intelligence

---

12. Read Nu'man Abd al-Wahid, "How Zionism helped create the Kingdom of Saudi Arabia," January 7, 2016, on mondoweiss.net
13. Ariel David, "Before Islam: When Saudi Arabia Was a Jewish Kingdom," November 29, 2017, on www.haaretz.com

report dated 2002 and entitled "The Birth of Al-Wahhabi Movement and its Historical Roots", translated by the U.S. Department of Defense.[14] The Iraqi report also refers to other Arabian sources claiming that ibn Saud was descended from a Jewish merchant from Basra. These claims receive a lot of echo in the Islamic world. It is common among Iranian Shiites to consider that "Wahhabism has its roots in Judaism," as IRGC general Qassem Soleimani had stated.[15] Indeed, Wahhabis do seem to be driven by the same bloodthirsty demon that spoke to Moses, Joshua and Elijah, a point appropriately illustrated by their fury against Baal, whose ancient temple in Palmyra the Islamic State blew up in 2015.

Although the crypto-Jewish origins of Wahhabism and/or the Saud dynasty seem impossible to authenticate, they are not implausible. There have been powerful Jewish communities in Arabia from very ancient times. At the time of the prophet Muhammad, writes Gordon Newby in *A History of the Jews of Arabia*, "Jews were present in all areas of Arabian society. There were Jewish merchants, Jewish bedouins, Jewish farmers, Jewish poets, and Jewish warriors. Jews lives in castles and in tents. They spoke Arabic as well as Hebrew and Aramaic."[16] They bore Arab names and their tribal organization was no different from that of other Arabs. Many converted to Islam over the centuries but some may have maintained some secret Jewishness. The most powerful Jewish community that Muhammad had to deal with was that of Khaybar, a hundred miles north of Medina. In the twelfth century, there were still 50,000 Jews in that region, according to Jewish traveller Benjamin of Tuleda. They "go forth to pillage and to capture booty from distant lands in conjunction with the Arabs, their neighbors and allies."[17] In 1875, Charles Montagu Doughty found that they had become "Moslems outwardly, but, in secret, cruel Jews that will suffer no stranger to enter among them."[18] Itzhak Ben-Zvi postulates a form of crypto-Judaism to explain the

---

14. fas.org/irp/eprint/iraqi/wahhabi.pdf
15. Seth Frantzman, "IRGC General Soleimani says roots of Wahhabism are Jewish, linked to ISIS," *Jerusalem Post,* February 22, 2019, on jpost.com
16. Gordon Darnell Newby, *A History of the Jews of Arabia, From Ancient Times to Their Ecclipse under Islam,* The University of South Carolina Press, 1988, p. 49.
17. *The Itinerary of Benjamin of Tuleda,* ed. Marcus Nathan Adler, 1907, p. 47-48, on www.teachittome.com
18. *Ibid,* footnote by Marcus Nathan Adler, p. 47.

simultaneity of the decline of north Arabian Jewry and the rise of the Wahhabis.[19]

The Arabian origin of Judaism

The question of the Jewish origins of the Sauds belongs to the larger issue of the threefold ties between Judaism, Islam, and Arabia. In the rest of this essay, I will present the overwhelming evidence for the Arab origin of the Israelites, then the equally overwhelming evidence for the Jewish origin of Islam, which explains the Mosaic pattern in the Islamic conquest of Syria. By connecting the two, we'll get a broader perspective on the deep cultural current that has kept spreading from the Arabian desert since Moses' time.

First, let's get back to Moses' story. As I have said earlier, the scholarly consensus is that the first compilation of the Tanakh dates from the exilic period. But the Exodus story itself is older and, apart from miracles and revelations, it has the ring of historical plausibility. The name "Israelites" must be anachronistic, though, since the kingdom named Israel existed long before being converted to Yahwism by Judeans. The Bible indicates that Moses' people were called "Hebrews" by the Egyptians (14 times in Exodus) and by the Philistines (8 times in 1Samuel), a term also employed with the vulgar meaning of "bandits" or "robbers" in Isaiah 1:23 and Hosea 6:9.[20] That name may be identical to the *habirus* mentioned in the Amarna tablets discovered in Middle Egypt; these tablets were sent from Canaan some time during the second millennium BC to implore the speedy aid of the Pharaoh against the nomadic tribes of *habirus*.[21] Moses and Joshua's throng of migrants was probably not the first wave of such *habirus* to covet Canaan, and certainly not the latest.

Canaan was a prosperous region, unlike the poorer lands of its southern fringe. Its inhabitants, portrayed as detestable idolaters in the Bible, were members of a technologically and culturally advanced civilization, organized in city-states, producing wheat, wine, oil, and other valuable products in large quantities.

19. Itzhak Ben-Zvi, *The Exiled and the Redeemed,* Jewish Publication Society, 1957, p. 193, quoted in Gordon Newby, *A History of the Jews of Arabia, op. cit.,* p. 104.

20. Niels Peter Lemche, *The Israelites in History and Tradition,* John Knox Press, 1998, pp. 58-60.

21. Karl Budde, *Religion of Israel to the Exile,* New York, 1899 (archive.org), pp. 5-11.

According to the report of the tribal chiefs sent by Moses in reconnaissance, "It does indeed flow with milk and honey. […] At the same time, its inhabitants are a powerful people; the towns are fortified and very big" (Numbers 13:27-28).

The classic biblical paradigm for the relationship between Jews and Arabs is the Genesis story of the half-brothers Isaac and Ishmael. But a more informative background is provided by the Exodus story of the Israelites' interaction with the Midianites, a semi-nomadic people known for their advanced skill in domesticating camels, and for their extensive commercial activity.[22]

As in a palimpsest, the narrative presenting Moses as the true discoverer of Yahweh seems to be written over an older story presenting Yahweh as a Midianite god adopted by Moses from his father-in-law, who is said to be a "priest" (*kohen*). Exodus hints that Mount Horeb was already known "holy ground" when Moses approached it (3:5). And the Bible so much emphasizes that marrying a non-Israelite woman leads to adopting her gods that we may apply it to Moses, especially since it is Moses' Midianite wife who, "taking up a flint, […] cut off her son's foreskin" in order to appease Yahweh's anger (Exodus 4:24-26).

In Exodus 18, after leading his people from Egypt and establishing his camp in the Midianite desert, "Moses went out to meet his father-in-law, bowed to him and kissed him." Then Jethro "offered a burnt offering and other sacrifices to God; and Aaron and all the elders of Israel came and ate with Moses' father-in-law in the presence of God" (18:7-12). Here it is Jethro who acts as a priest of Yahweh, while Moses and Aaron are merely guests in the ceremony. Soon afterward, when Moses feels overwhelmed by the task of governing alone a great number of people, it is Jethro who, again with the authority of a priest of Yahweh, advises him to institute the Judges; "Moses took his father-in-law's advice and did just as he said" (18:19-25). Moses then needs his father-in-law to guide him to Canaan, telling him: "You know where we can camp in the desert, and so you will be our eyes. If you come with us, we shall share with you whatever blessings Yahweh gives us" (Numbers 10:31-32). From Judges 1:16, we understand that Moses' father-in-law agreed and "marched up with the sons of Judah."

---

22. Thomas Römer, *The Invention of God,* Harvard UP, 2016, p. 57.

The sum of all these stories suggests that the cult of Yahweh originated with the Midianites. This hypothesis was first formulated in German by Friedrich Wilhelm Ghillany in 1863,[23] then in English by Karl Budde in 1899.[24] The theory has gained wide support, and is today convincingly presented by Swiss scholar Thomas Römer.[25] It doesn't necessarily imply that the Hebrews only adopted Yahweh under Moses' guidance: when Yahweh mandates Moses to tell his people in Egypt, "Yahweh, the god of your ancestors, has appeared to me" (3:16), the implication is rather that he is talking to Midianites who already know Yahweh. The situation is historically plausible, since nomadic tribes are believed to have migrated into the pastureland of the border-districts of Egypt, from where they could be put to forced labor for any great building operations.[26]

Moses' most significant innovation to the Midianite cult, apparently, was to provide Yahweh with mobility, thanks to the Ark and the Tabernacle, a luxurious gold-plated tent (using the gold stolen from the Egyptians), the detailed specifications of which are given in Exodus, chapters 25 to 31. Far from his volcanic abode, Yahweh became invisible. But Moses remedied this by convincing his followers that he could continue to see Yahweh inside the Tabernacle, where he alone was allowed, and talk to him "face to face, as a man talks to his friend" (33:11). The privilege was transferred to Joshua after Moses' death. That delocalization of Yahweh can be regarded as the first stage in the long process of turning Yahweh from a volcano-dwelling deity into the omnipresent "God of Heaven and Earth."

Yet Yahweh long remained attached to the volcanic crater from where he first emerged into this world. On the eve of the migration from Sinai to Canaan, there is a vague notion that he wouldn't really leave his mountain, but will "send an angel" to guide Moses (Exodus 23:20).[27] Centuries after the Exodus, the prophet Elijah walks 40 days on a pilgrimage to "the mount of God, to Horeb," where, after a hurricane, an earthquake and a fire eruption, he received God's word (1Kings 19). Yahweh continues

---

23. Under the pseudonym of Richard von der Alm (Thomas Römer, *The Invention of God, op. cit.*, p. 67).

24. Karl Budde, *Religion of Israel to the Exile, op. cit.*, p. 19.

25. Thomas Römer, *The Invention of God, op. cit.*, 2016.

26. Karl Budde, *Religion of Israel to the Exile, op. cit.*, p. 12.

27. In Judge 4:8, "the Angel of Yahweh" gives victory to the Israelites.

to be called El Shaddai, possibly meaning "the god from the mountain" (Genesis 17:1, Exodus 6:2–3).[28] His taste for the carbonized flesh of holocausts (Genesis 8:21) can be ascribed to his volcanic genes. And he definitely keeps a volcanic character throughout: he is "a consuming fire" (Deuteronomy 4:24), expected in prophetic visions to "glow like a furnace," and "set ablaze" all evil-doers (Malachi 3:19).

That Yahweh was originally the personification of a terrifying volcanic irruption, exploited by Moses to seize control of a few gullible Midianite tribes, goes a long way toward explaining the nature of ancient Judaism. Fear of Yahweh's fire and brimstones is the foundation of Yahwism, and fear is what Yahweh keeps demanding from the Israelites throughout the Tanakh. Even the Jewish notion that Yahweh's name should not be uttered is proof enough that fear has remained the essence of Judaism; for ethnography informs us that, everywhere in the world, it is the names of evil demons that must not be uttered, lest we attract their attention or offend them.

Other Abrahamic peoples

According to Genesis 25:2-4, the Midianites are descendants of Abraham by his second wife Keturah. They are therefore heirs of the Abrahamic covenant, just like the Ishmaelites, descendants of Abraham by his servant Agar. Midianites and Ishmaelites are actually more or less confused in Genesis 37, where it is said that Joseph was sold by Midianites to Ishmaelites who took him to Egypt (37:28), then that "the Midianites had sold him in Egypt" (37:36).

In addition to the Midianites, the Israelites interact with a series of peoples on their way to Canaan, notably the Moabites, the Edomites (or Idumeans), and the Amalekites. Although they practice agriculture around urbanized crossroads, all these peoples are mostly semi-nomadic pastors and merchants. They are all given as descendants of Abraham in Genesis: Moab is Abraham's nephew (19:31-38), Edom or Esau is Abraham's grandson (25:25), and Amaleq is Esau's grandson (36:12). Kinship doesn't necessarily rhyme with friendship. The Israelites are told in Deuteronomy, "You must not regard the Edomite as detestable, for he is your brother" (23:8), but Moabites must be excluded from the commu-

---

28. Thomas Römer, *The Invention of God, op. cit.*, p. 108.

nity to the tenth generation (23:4-5). As for the Amalekites, who "occupy the Negeb area" according to Numbers 13:29, they deserve to be eradicated from the face of the earth according to 1Samuel 15:2.

In Judges 1:16, Moses' father-in-law is called a Kenite rather than a Midianite. It is commonly assumed that the Kenites were a tribe among the larger nation of the Midianites, and that the Israelites had a special alliance with the Kenites, rather than with the Midianites as a whole. The name of the Kenites actually means "blacksmiths" or "iron-workers", and it makes sense for such people to worship a volcano. Tribes of blacksmiths were more or less nomadic because their skills were required over a very wide area. They were the objects of superstitious fears, because the art of metalworking is associated with magic. Strangely, the name of the Kenites (*Qayn* in Hebrew) is identical to the name of Cain, whose descendants are described in Genesis 4 as "restless wanderers" living in tents, inventors of ironwork, makers of metallic musical instruments, and protected from harm by a mysterious mark. The original Cain and Abel story must have originated from a people who claimed Cain as their ancestors,[29] because the third brother Seth appears to be a secondary addition: his children's names in Genesis 5:6-32 are a copy of Cain's children's names in Genesis 4:17-18. Other biblical traditions may be derived from Kenite folklore, according to Hyam Maccoby.[30]

According to 1Chronicles 2:55, the Kenites are "descended from Hammath, father of the House of Rechab." This makes the Kenites identical or kindred to the Rechabites. Jonadab the son of Rechab stands at the side of the Judean Yahwist general Jehu when he exterminates the priests of Baal in the northern kingdom of Israel (2Rois 10). The prophet Jeremiah commends the Rechabites for their fidelity to Yahweh and to their ancestor who ordered them not to "drink wine, build houses, sow seed, plant vineyards or own them, but [to] live in tents all your lives" (Jeremiah 35:6-7). Benjamin of Tuleda mentions Rechabites in Arabia in the twelfth century, and several explorers still find them there in the early nineteenth century.[31]

---

29. Yuri Slezkine cites other ethnic groups of wanderers who conceived their mode of existence "as divine punishment for an original transgression" (*The Jewish Century*, Princeton UP, 2004, pp. 22-23).

30. Hyam Maccoby, *The Sacred Executioner*, Thames & Hudson, 1982, pp. 13-51.

31. Gordon Newby, *A History of the Jews of Arabia, op. cit.*, pp. 100-103.

The Kenites and Rechabites are the only peoples besides the Israelites who are presented systematically in benevolent terms in the Bible. Saul spares the Kenites when he exterminates the Amalekites among whom they dwell, because, he tells them, "you acted with faithful love towards all the Israelites when they were coming up from Egypt" (1Samuel 15:6). When David "sent parts of the booty to the elders of Judah, town by town," some of it goes to "the towns of the Kenites" (1Samuel 30:26-29).[32] In contrast, the rest of the Midianites are presented negatively from the beginning of the conquest of Canaan. In Numbers 31, Midianites dwelling in the land of Moab are blamed for inciting the Israelites to intermarry with the Moabites, bringing on them "the vengeance of Yahweh." Moses formed an army to slaughter all the Midianites. (Yet in Judges 6, the Midianites are still a powerful people, allied with the Amalekites to oppress the Israelites.)

Finally, we need to mention the Benjaminites. Although they are presented as one of the twelve tribes, the last chapters of Judges (19 to 21) show them at war with the other eleven tribes. Benjamin means *Ben Yamin,* or "son of Yemen." Does that mean they came from Yemen, the southwestern part of Arabia? Not necessarily, since *yemen* simply means "south" (or "right," looking at the sunrise). But it is a possibility. There is a very ancient Jewish presence in Yemen, going back at least to the Himyarite Kingdom that controlled Arabia from the beginning of the Christian era or earlier. It is believed that the king of Himyar converted to Judaism in 380 and that in the sixth century, the last Jewish king, Yûsuf Dhû Nuwâs, unleashed a great massacre of Christians, but fell in his turn when the Ethiopian Christian king invaded Yemen. The dates and details of this story are uncertain, and the origin of the Yemenite Jews (most of them relocated in Israel in 1949-50) remains partly mysterious. According to one of their legends, they were descended from the union of King Solomon and the Queen of Sheba. According to another, they had migrated from Israel before the destruction of the First Temple, and had refused to return from exile at the time of Ezra.[33] Genetic studies show that they are

---

32. See also Numbers 24:21 and Judges 5:24.
33. Gordon Newby, *A History of the Jews of Arabia, op. cit.,* pp. 18, 33-34.

closely related to other Jewish groups, and linguistic studies show that Yemenite Hebrew is archaic.[34]

In conclusion, we have found an abundance of biblical evidence that Yahweh was originally a Midianite god, perhaps specially worshipped by the Kenites and the Rechabites, and that those presented as "Israelites" originated from Arabia (whether or not they had spent time in eastern Egypt).

There is also extra-biblical evidence of an ancient connection between Jews and Arabs. The three Jewish tribes residing in Yathrib (Medina) at the time of Muhammad claimed they had been living in the Hijaz since the time of Moses. Orientalist David Samuel Margoliouth believed their presence may well be that ancient. He also argued that many Hebrew names, including that of Yahweh, were Arabic, and that the Book of Job, among other biblical stories, "ostensibly comes from Arabia."[35]

The story of Joseph looks totally Arabian to Kamal Salibi, professor of history and archeology in Beirut. In *The Bible Came from Arabia* (1985), he proposes a radical hypothesis: he relocates in western Arabia all biblical place names and therefore all biblical history, from Abraham to Solomon through Moses. Egyptian researcher Ashraf Ezzat comes to a similar conclusion in his book *Egypt Knew no Pharaohs nor Israelites*. I do not find those theories very strong, but the evidence of the Arabic origin of Yahwism, the matrix of Jewish culture, is overwhelming.

The Judaic cradle of Islam

I mentioned earlier the thesis that Wahhabism is a Jewish creation. But was not Islam itself a Jewish creation from the beginning? The influence of Judaism on Muhammad is beyond question. It is reflected in many Quranic references to Moses (*Musa*), Abraham (*Ibrahim*), Joseph, David, Jonah, Solomon, and other biblical figures. Whole *surahs* are devoted to biblical legends, "often with postbiblical midrashic embellishments presumably gathered from local Jewish oral traditions," writes professor Mark Cohen in the *A History of Jewish-Muslim*

---

34. Gordon Newby, "The Jews of Arabia at the Birth of Islam," in Abdelwahab Meddeb and Benjamin Stora (eds), *A History of Jewish-Muslim Relations – From the Origins to the Present Day*, Princeton UP, 2013, pp. 39-57 (40).

35. David Samuel Margoliouth, *Relations Between Arabs and Israelites Prior to the Rise of Islam*, Oxford UP, 1924 (archive.org).

Relations. "At the outset, most scholars agree, Muhammad assumed the Jews would flock to his preaching and recognize him as their own prophet—indeed, the final, or 'seal' of the prophets."[36] He prayed toward Jerusalem, adopted the Jews' prohibitions, and fasted on the same days. He married a woman from the Banu an-Nadir, one of the two wealthiest Jewish tribes of Yathrib (Medina), considered to be of priestly origin, which puts him in a position strikingly reminiscent of Moses marrying the daughter of a Midianite priest.

The Jewish tribes of Yathrib "were supposed to have derived from a migration of priests to Arabia some time after the destruction of the Second Temple," explains Gordon Newby, author of a respected *History of the Jews of Arabia.* "The presence of a [Jewish] priestly influence in Arabia will help account for the plethora of eschatological traditions ascribed to Jews in Islamic literature or utilized by Muslim exegetes based on Jewish writings".[37] According to Newby, "Islam developed against the background of an Arabia strongly under the influence of Judaism."

"Islam and Judaism in Arabia during Muhammad's lifetime were operating in the same sphere of religious discourse: the same fundamental questions were discussed from similar perspectives; moral and ethical values were similar; both religions shared the same religious characters, stories, and anecdotes. We can see this when we look at the implied context of the Qur'ânic message. There is no expectation that the stories we call biblical are anything but familiar to the Arabian listeners. [...] Muhammad's expectations that he might convert the Jews to his view were not unreasonable. It is clear that Muhammad did not think that he was starting a 'new' religion but, rather, restoring and reforming the Abrahamic heritage among the Jews and Christians of Arabia."[38]

It is also clear that Muhammad had no intent to create a new independent holy book. His surahs rather appear as rambling commentaries on the Jewish Tanakh, as sometimes explicitly said:

"And We [Allah] had certainty settled the Children of Israel in an agreeable settlement and provided them with good things. [...] So if you are in doubt, [O Muhammad], about that which We have

---

36. Mark Cohen, "Islamic Policy toward Jews from the Prophet Muhammad to the Pact of 'Umar," in A. Meddeb and B. Stora (eds), *A History of Jewish-Muslim Relations, op. cit.,* pp. 58-70.

37. Gordon Newby, *A History of the Jews of Arabia, op. cit.,* pp. 17, 47.

38. Gordon Newby, *A History of the Jews of Arabia, op. cit.,* pp. 105, 84-85.

revealed to you, then ask those who have been reading the
Scripture before you." (Surah Yunus 10:93-94)

"And before it was the scripture of Moses to lead and as a mercy.
And this [the Quran] is a confirming Book in an Arabic tongue to
warn those who have wronged and as good tidings to the doers of
good." (Sura Al-Ahqaf 46: 12)[39]

It was under Abu Bakr, Muhammad's successor as first Caliph,
that the Quran became canonized and standardized. According to
the Jewish scholar Joseph Schwarz, Abu Bakr, who gave
Muhammad his six-year-old daughter Aicha when he made
allegiance to him, was a Jewish rabbi, whose influence "induced
Mahomet to give up his terrible intention to destroy the Jews in his
country, and thus did Rabbi Shallum save his people."[40]

Sunnis assert that Abu Bakr's daughter Aisha was
Muhammad's favorite wife and attribute thousands of hadith to
her, but Shiites are very critical of her and do not consider her a
reputable source of hadith. Some Shiite clerics even teach that
Muhammad was murdered by Abu Bakr and Umar, the second
Caliph, through the means of their daughters, Aisha and Hafsa,
feeding him poison.[41]

It was Abu Bakr who led the Arab conquest of Palestine,
although French specialist Alfred-Louis de Prémare argued that it
had been planned and even initiated by Muhammad.[42] Like the
Israelite conquest ten centuries before, the Arab conquest started as
a systematic raid. It "appealed to the greed for booty of ever larger
circles of Arabs," wrote historian Hichem Djait. "Almost all Arabs
who participated in the wars of conquest found themselves
enriched by booty, to the point that we can say that booty became
the incentive for the conquest."[43] Like the Israelites, they had a
strong ethnic consciousness: the Prophet and most of his
companions, as well as all the caliphs up to the thirteenth century,
came from a single Arab tribe, the Quraych, who already
controlled the sanctuary of Mecca in pre-Islamic times. (I cannot
here delve into the issue of the original Mecca (the Bakkah of the

39. Taken from quran.com. See also Surah Al-Israa 17:2 and Sura Al-Jathiyah 45:16
40. Joseph Schwarz, "From the Accession of the Mahomedans to that of the
Europeans," in *Descriptive Geography and Brief Historical Sketch of Palestine*
(1850), on www.jewish-history.com/palestine/period2.html
41. Yasser Al-Habib, "Who Killed Allah's Messenger?" on www.alqatrah.net/en/al28
42. Alfred-Louis de Prémare, *Les Fondations de l'islam,* Seuil, 2002, pp. 131-135.
43. Hichem Djaït, *La Grande Discorde. Religion et politique dans l'islam des
origines,* Gallimard, 1989, pp. 70-71, 96.

Quran), but I strongly recommend the documentary "The Sacred City: Discovering the Real Birthplace of Islam" based on Dan Gibson's research, leading to the conclusion that Islam was born in Petra, north of Midian.)

The context of the Arab conquest was strikingly similar to that of the biblical conquest of Canaan. Moses had taken advantage of the centuries-long struggle between Egypt and Assyria for the control of Syria. Muhammad and his successors took advantage of the war between the Persians and the Byzantines for the control of the very same territory. These Byzantine-Sasanian wars had exhausted both empires' military resources, and revived among Jewish communities the messianic hope of seizing power over the ancient land of Israel. In 614, the Jews helped the Persians conquer part of Palestine. When the Byzantines took back Palestine in 628, and when their emperor Heraclius made a triumphal entry into Jerusalem in 630, many Jews took refuge to Arabia, Persia or Egypt. More fled when, two years later, weary of his Jewish subjects' betrayals, Heraclius published an unprecedented decree compelling all the Jews and Samaritans of his empire to become Christians. Although the decree was not systematically enforced, it increased the Jews' anti-Byzantine messianic fever. Several Jewish apocalyptic and prophetic texts were written in that period, some predicting that "the Empire will soon pass to Israel." The *Sefer Zerubavel* (or *Apocalypse of Zerubbabel*) announced the restoration of Israel and the establishment of the Third Temple, designating Heraclius (under the cryptogram Armilius) as the Antichrist. It is noteworthy that the Islamic conquest of Syria followed within a few years of the proclamation by Heraclius of his "final solution" to the Jewish question.[44]

In their groundbreaking yet controversial book *Hagarism: The Making of the Islamic World,* professors Patricia Crone and Michael Cook find the origin of Islam in a form of Jewish messianism assigning to the Ishmaelites (or Hagarenes, from the name of Ishmael's mother Hagar) a share in God's promise to Abraham, and the mission to take possession of the Promised Land in cooperation with the sons of Israel who have lost it.[45] The non-

---

44. Gilbert Dagron and Vincent Déroche, *Juifs et chrétiens en Orient byzantin,* Centre de recherche d'histoire et civilization de Byzance, 2010, p. 41.
45. Patricia Crone and Michael Cook, *Hagarism: The Making of the Islamic World,* Cambridge UP, 1977 (archive.org), pp. 6-30. Other revisionist historians of Islam include John Wansbrough, with his *Qur'anic Studies* (Oxford UP, 1977), prolonged

Islamic sources of the seventh century used by the authors are not many, but they are very consistent in their accounts of "a wider intimacy in the relations of Arabs and Jews" at the time of Muhammad, and "the warmth of the Jewish reaction to the Arab invasion," as well as "a marked hostility towards Christianity on the part of the invaders."

For example, the *Doctrina Jacobi* is a book written in Palestine in the 630s, in the form of a dialogue between a sincerely converted Jew named Jacob and other Jews, either baptized by force or non-baptized. It mentions Muhammad as a prophet from the Saracens who is proclaiming "the advent of the anointed one who is to come" and the redemption of the Promised Land for all children of Abraham. The *Secrets of Rabbi Simon ben Yohay* is a Jewish apocalypse of the mid-eighth century, asserting that God "brings the kingdom of Ishmael" in order to save the Jews from the wickedness of Byzantium. "He raises up over them a Prophet according to His will and will conquer the land for them and they will come and restore it in greatness, and there will be great terror between them and the sons of Esau." Another important source is an Armenian Chronicle written in the 660s and ascribed to Bishop Sebeos. According to Crone and Cook, it presents the Islamic conquest as "an irredentism directed to the recovery of a divinely conferred birthright to the Promised Land," in a partnership between the Sons of Ishmael and the Sons of Israel exiled in Arabia. It begins with the exodus of Jewish refugees from Edessa following its recovery by Heraclius from the Persians in 628. The Jews who fled to Arabia sought the help of the Ishmaelites, but "could not convince the mass of the people, because their cults were different." Then appeared among them Muhammad, who told them:

> "God has promised this land to Abraham and his posterity after him forever; he acted according to His promise while he loved Israel. Now you, you are the sons of Abraham and God fulfills in you the promise made to Abraham and his posterity. Only love the God of Abraham, go and take possession of your country which God gave to your father Abraham, and none will be able to resist you in the struggle, for God is with you."

The general picture drawn from non-Islamic sources finds confirmation in a few fossilized elements within the Islamic

---

in *The Sectarian Milieu* (Oxford UP, 1978). Twenty years after Crone and Cook, their student Robert Hoyland wrote *Seeing Islam As others saw It,* The Darwin Press, 1998.

tradition, such as the "Constitution of Medina," "a patently anomalous and plausibly archaic element of the Islamic tradition," documenting the alliance between Muhammad and the powerful Jewish tribes of Yathrib.

It was only after the Arab conquest of Jerusalem that Jews and Arabs parted ways, leading to a rewriting of their relationship in Islamic sources. Crone and Cook find evidence of "an overt quarrel between Jews and Arabs over the possession of the site of the Holy of Holies, in which the Arabs frustrate a Jewish design to restore the Temple and build their own oratory there instead." Simultaneously, "as the Hagarenes broke with their erstwhile Jewish protégés and acquired large numbers of Christian subjects, their initial hostility to Christianity was clearly liable to erosion." The messianic significance of the conquest was toned down, and Jesus was recognized as Messiah.

However, Islam never lost contact with its Jewish origin, and even "acquired its classical rabbinic form in the shadow of Babylonian Judaism, probably in the aftermath of the transfer of power from Syria to Iraq in the middle of the eighth century."

Some scholars prefer to see Islam as rooted in Judeo-Christian heresies, rather than in Judaism *stricto sensu*.[46] The arguments include a hadith about Waraka ibn Nawfal, a relative of Muhammad's first wife Khadija, presented as a priest of the "Nazarenes" and the first believer in Muhammad's calling (*Sahih al-Bukhari Hadith*, 1.3). When Muhammad told him about the angel's visit, Waraka told him this was the same angel that God had sent to Moses. Waraqa "knew both the Torah and the Gospel," and "copied in Hebrew all the part of the Gospel that God wanted him to transcribe." Clearly, Waraqa is more Jewish than Christian, as were "Nazarenes" in general, a term referring generally to Jewish believers in the messiahship of Jesus who remained loyal to the Torah and circumcision.

What did the Muslims do for the Jews?

By combining what we have learned about the Arab origin of Mosaic Judaism, on the one hand, and about the Jewish origin of Islam, on the other, we get a very broad historical perspective. The conquest of Canaan launched by Moses and achieved by Joshua,

---

46. Karl-Heinz Ohlig and Gerd-Rudiger Puin (dir.), *The Hidden Origins of Islam,* Prometheus Books, 2010.

which gave birth to Judaism, and the conquest of Syria launched by Muhammad and achieved by Abu Bakr, which gave birth to Islam, appear as two tidal waves of the same irresistible drive of Arabs and other *habirus* to leave their inhospitable deserts and conquer the weakest and closest part of the Fertile Crescent.

Each wave is supported by the previous one and contributes to empower it. In all their conquests, the Arabs were favorably received by the Jews, who helped them overthrow Byzantine power. When Syria fell into Arab hands after the decisive battle of Yarmouk against the Byzantines in 636, the Holy City, from where the Jews had been banned since 135, became open to them again, and they rushed in. Although Islam then took some distance from Judaism, Jews assisted the Arabs in their subsequent conquest of Persia. And nowhere was the cooperation between Jews and Muslims more intimate than in the conquest of Catholic Visigothic Spain in 711. Muslim and Catholic sources agree that the conquering army, composed mostly of Berbers, included also many Jews, and that Iberian Jews provided valuable aid to the invaders. They were so trusted that conquered cities were left under the control of Jews.[47]

In return, the Islamic conquest remained a godsend for Jewish communities everywhere, even though their messianic expectations were not fully realized. Previously, the Jews were divided into two empires at war with each other; the Jews of the Byzantine Empire were cut off from the intellectual center of Babylon, under Persian rule. A century after Muhammad's death, virtually every Jew in the world lived in a unified political space. As *dhimmis,* they were still second-class citizens, but that was preferable to the status of non-citizens they had previously. In a world where, for two centuries, Muslims remained a minority, Jews were now equal to Christians, and enjoyed a very broad social autonomy. Arab conquerors, who needed skilled administrators, opened up for the Jews unexpected prospects for social advancement.

Jews no longer had to fear forced conversions. In fact, they were not even encouraged to convert by their Muslim masters. For in the ideology of the early conquerors, Hichem Djait explains, "converting other peoples was not part of the agenda." The aim was to rule over them and live off their work through heavy tax

---

47. Norman Roth, *Jews, Visigoths and Muslims in Medieval Spain,* Brill, 1994, pp. 79-90.

(the *jizyah*).[48] Unlike the Christians, who for a long time remained attached to their Coptic, Syriac or Greek languages, the Jews quickly adopted Arabic, a Semitic language close to Aramaic and Hebrew, while developing for internal use a Judeo-Arabic language that allowed them to maintain a separation. Hebrew, which had been dead, was revived as a sacred language, on the model of the Arab language. "The revival of Hebrew in our own times would be entirely unthinkable without the services rendered to it by Arabic in various ways a thousand years ago," wrote S. D. Goitein.[49] After the end of the Islamic conquest of Persia in the mid-eighth century, the Talmudic institutions (*Yeshiva*) of Babylonia became the supreme spiritual authorities of the Jewish world, serving as centers of knowledge and organs of world government. Still in the sixteenth century, Jewish communities as far away as Spain sought guidance from Baghdad. "Islamic rule not only transformed Judaism but enabled its consolidation and diffusion," writes historian Marina Rustow.[50]

Considering all this, David Wasserstein states in an article published in the *Jewish Chronicle*, entitled "So, what did the Muslims do for the Jews?":

> "Islam saved Jewry. This is an unpopular, discomforting claim in the modern world. But it is a historical truth. The argument for it is double. First, in 570 CE, when the Prophet Mohammad was born, the Jews and Judaism were on the way to oblivion. And second, the coming of Islam saved them, providing a new context in which they not only survived, but flourished, laying foundations for subsequent Jewish cultural prosperity— also in Christendom— through the medieval period into the modern world. [...] Had Islam not come along, Jewry in the West would have declined to disappearance and Jewry in the east would have become just another oriental cult.[51]

Today, Israel benefits from Islam in different ways. First, it can use Islam to defuse the only real threat it faces in the Middle East: Arab nationalism. Arab secular states, such as those of Nasser, Saddam, Gaddaffi or al-Assad, have been the most dangerous

48. Hichem Djaït, *La Grande Discorde, op. cit.*, p. 70.
49. S. D. Goitein, *Jews and Arabs: Their Contacts through the Ages,* Schocken Books, 1970, pp. 7-8.
50. Marina Rustow, "Jews and Muslims in the Eastern Islamic World," in A. Meddeb and B. Stora (eds), *A History of Jewish–Muslim Relations, op. it.*, pp. 75-96.
51. David J Wasserstein, "So, what did the Muslims do for the Jews?" *Jewish Chronicle,* May 24, 2012, on www.thejc.com

enemies of the State of Israel, while political Islam has been
Israel's *de facto* ally in the weakening or the destruction of these
states. It started with the Muslim Brotherhood in Egypt. More
recently, Israel has been supporting financially, militarily, and
even medically, the jihadists who have plunged Syria into chaos.
In Europe also, "Islam is the broom of Israel," says French rabbi
David Touitou.[52]

---

52. "L'islam est le balai d'Israël" on YouTube.

6 - THE CRUCIFIED GODDESS
The Rise and Fall of Western Romanticism

"Love is civilization's miracle", wrote Stendhal in his insightful essay on *Love*.[1] He was talking about the high ideal of love elaborated in Western Europe, from twelfth-century courtly love to nineteenth-century romanticism. That ideal is pretty much dead, buried under the heaps of obscenities produced industrially every day by our degenerate sub-culture. As the fish stinks by the head, so are the Harvey Weinstein and the Jeffrey Epstein affairs good indicators of the current state of rot of the Western Eros.

They are also emblematic of the role of Israel (in the sense of International Jewry) in the moral corruption of our once Christian civilization. Jews have always excelled as sex trafficking. As documented by Hervé Ryssen in "Israel and the White Slave Trade," it was not a "Russian Mafia" that lured about 500,000 young women from Eastern Europe into worldwide prostitution networks during the 1990s, but ethnic Jews with Israeli citizenship.[2] A 2000 *Amnesty International* report identified Israel as the central hub of this traffic, in which unsuspecting young girls were sequestrated, beaten, raped, enslaved and mentally destroyed.[3]

Pornography, a specialization of prostitution, is almost a Jewish monopoly. Professor Nathan Abrams of the University of Aberdeen broke the taboo in 2004 with an article in the *Jewish Quarterly* (reprinted in a collection of essays titled *Jews and Sex*): "there's no getting away from the fact that secular Jews have played (and still continue to play) a disproportionate role throughout the adult film industry in America. Jewish involvement in pornography has a long history in the United States, as Jews have helped to transform a fringe subculture into what has become a primary constituent of Americana."[4] The expression "secular

---

1. Stendhal, *Love,* Penguin Classics, 2000, p. 83.
2 . herveryssen.files.wordpress.com/2018/09/hervc3a9-ryssen-israel-and-the-white-slave-trade.pdf
3. "Human rights abuses of women trafficked from countries of the former Soviet Union into Israel's sex industry," on www.amnesty.org
4. "Triple exthnics: Nathan Abrams on Jews in the American Porn Industry," *Jewish Quarterly,* vol. 51, n°4 (2004), pp. 27-31, on www.tandfonline.com

Jews" is a convenient euphemism. Porn journalist Luke Ford, author of *A History of X: 100 Years of Sex in Film,* similarly insists that the business is run by "non-Jewish Jews," by which he means "Jews alienated from Judaism." He writes: "They're acting in a manner contrary to everything Jewish—the Torah, Israel, God, synagogue and everything the Jewish tradition considers holy."[5]

We've heard that line before: Jewish Bolsheviks were not Jews either, because they didn't behave Jewishly. In this essay, I will try to show that, just like Jewish Bolsheviks, Jews who abduct, enslave, sell, or even sacrifice ritually Gentile girls are behaving much in accordance with the Torah. I insist: with the Torah, not just with the Talmud.

32,000 shikses *and other biblical stories*

The Torah forbids the Israelites to "have intercourse with an animal," under penalty of death (Exodus 22:18)—although I've heard the Talmud is more lenient—but there is not a trace of a prohibition to exploit sexually young Gentile girls. On the contrary, there is Moses' blessing upon it.

In Numbers 31, Moses ordered his men to slaughter all the Midianites, because they had persuaded the Israelites to intermarry with the Moabites. Moses' soldiers killed all the men but took "the Midianite women and their little ones captive." Moses "was enraged with the officers of the army" and rebuked them: "Why have you spared the life of all the women? They were the very ones who [...] caused the Israelites to be unfaithful to Yahweh." He finally compromised: "So kill all the male children and kill all the women who have ever slept with a man; but spare the lives of the young girls who have never slept with a man, and keep them for yourselves." At the end of the day, the booty amounted to thousands of sheep, goats, cattle, donkeys, "and in persons, women who had never slept with a man, thirty-two thousand in all." Since no age is specified, and since girls were married very young in nomadic societies, we can guess that the 32,000 girls taken as human booty were mostly children. Nothing is said of their fate, but the very criterion of their selection (having never slept with a man) leaves us in no doubt about their utility. They were certainly not taken as legitimate wives, since the whole story is about the prohibition against marrying non-Jews. So we have here, I think,

---

5. "Why are there so many Jews in porn?" on lukeford.net/blog/?p=103821

an unmistakable biblical precedent for the sexual enslavement of Gentile girls on a massive scale.

But it gets worse: the booty, including the 32,000 virgin girls, was divided in two: half for the combatants, half for the rest. From the combatants' half, Yahweh required as his own "portion", "one out of every five hundred persons, oxen, donkeys and sheep." So Yahweh's portion included 32 girls, who were all entrusted to the sacrificial priest Eleazar, for him to offer them to Yahweh. How were they offered to Yahweh? The Good Book doesn't say. But we know that animals were always served to Yahweh as holocausts, and the wording of Numbers 31 makes no distinction between human and animal spoils, but rather insists on putting them in the same bag. So there is no reason to suppose that "Yahweh's portion" of virgin girls were offered to Yahweh in any other way than Yahweh's portion of oxen, donkeys and sheep: they were burnt to produce Yahweh's favorite fragrance.

Incidentally, the fate of the remaining 31,948 Midianite virgins informs us on the logic behind the rule of transmission of Jewishness by the mother. This rule, never explicit in the Torah, has nothing to do with any particular respect for women. It follows directly from the fact that sex with foreign girls is lawful, as long as any bastard thus conceived is kept apart from the community (Deuteronomy 23:3). The opposite situation needed not be considered: by biblical standards, a Jewish woman having sex with a Gentile would be stoned to death before giving birth.

Unless, of course, she is acting for a higher purpose. Wealthy Jews such as the Rothschilds, although highly endogamous, have often married their daughters into politically influential families. The biblical prototype, in this case, is Mordecai's niece Esther, who, by marrying the Persian king, saved the Jews from Haman's evil scheme. The story ends happily with the Jews slaughtering 75,000 Persians, men, women and children, after which "the various peoples were now all afraid of the Jews" (9:2), and "Mordecai the Jew was next in rank to King Ahasuerus" (10:3). Esther is the archetypal Jewish heroin who marries a Goy for the sake of the Jews.

Some rabbinical tradition claims that Esther was not only Mordecai's niece, but also his wife. In that case, Mordecai was following the example of Abraham. Married to his half-sister Sarah (his father's daughter), Abraham introduced her as his sister to Pharaoh who took her as a concubine, then compensated

Abraham with "flocks, oxen, donkeys, men and women slaves, she-donkeys and camels" (Genesis 12:16). Abraham repeated the trick with the Philistine king Abimelech and got again "sheep, cattle, men and women slaves" (Genesis 20:14).

Such stories do not convey much reverence for women, but rather betray a utilitarian and mercantile view of women. The story of how Jacob married the two daughters of his uncle Laban (Genesis 29) is also representative. Jacob wants Rachel as "wages" for seven years of work for Laban. But he is duped by Laban who slips Leah into his bed at night instead of Rachel. Jacob has to work seven more years to get Rachel too.

One story that shows an even more sinister view of women is found in Judges 19. A Levite from the highlands of Ephraim travels to Bethlehem in Judah with his concubine, and stops in the Benjaminite city of Gibeah, where he receives the hospitality of an old native from Ephraim.

> "While they were enjoying themselves, some townsmen, scoundrels, came crowding round the house; they battered on the door and said to the old man, master of the house, 'Send out the man who went into your house, we should like to have intercourse with him!' The master of the house went out to them and said, 'No, brothers, please, do not be so wicked. Since this man is now under my roof, do not commit such an infamy. Here is my daughter; she is a virgin; I shall bring her out to you. Ill-treat her, do what you please with her, but do not commit such an infamy against this man.' But the men would not listen to him. So the Levite took hold of his concubine and brought her out to them. They had intercourse with her and ill-treated her all night till morning; when dawn was breaking they let her go. At daybreak the girl came and fell on the threshold of her husband's host, and she stayed there until it was light. In the morning her husband got up and, opening the door of the house, was going out to continue his journey when he saw the woman, his concubine, lying at the door of the house with her hands on the threshold. 'Get up,' he said, 'we must leave!' There was no answer. He then loaded her on his donkey and began the journey home. Having reached his house, he took his knife, took hold of his concubine and cut her, limb by limb, into twelve pieces." (Judges 19:22-29)

The Levite sent the pieces to different Israelite towns with a call for vengeance against Gibeah. The Israelites slaughtered everyone in Gibeah and set the city on fire, while six hundred Benjaminite warriors had escaped into the desert. Then, as a token of reconciliation, they decided to provide these Benjaminites with new wives. For this, they attacked the town of Jabesh in Gilead, where they killed "all males and all those women who have ever slept with a man," and gathered four hundred virgins to offer to the Benjaminites (21:10-24).

The way the Levite and his host in Gibeah offer their concubine and daughter for gang rape is reminiscent of the story of the two daughters of Lot (Abraham's nephew), who are also proposed by their father (Genesis 19) to the Sodomites who wanted to "have intercourse" with the two "messengers of Yahweh" accommodated by Lot. "Look," said Lot, "I have two daughters who are virgins. I am ready to send them out to you, for you to treat as you please, but do nothing to these men since they are now under the protection of my roof" (Genesis 19:8). Lot's daughters were saved by the "messengers" miraculously blinding the Sodomites so that "they could not find the doorway" (double meaning?). The Hebrew for "messengers" is *malachim* in Hebrew, translated as *angeloi* in Greek, and although these "messengers of Yahweh" are understood as "angels," they might have been Levites in the original story, which would then be a variation on the Judges 19 story.

Later on, Lot's daughters got their father drunk to conceive with him Moab and Ben-Ammi, ancestors of the Moabites and Ammonites (Genesis 19:31–38). That brings us to the main purpose of Israelite women: provide male heirs to their husbands. There are numerous examples in the Bible highlighting this absolute imperative. For instance, when Rachel found herself barren while her elder sister Leah had already given Jacob four sons, Rachel asked Jacob to unite with her servant Bilha, who gave him two sons as Rachel's substitute. Then "Leah, seeing that she had ceased to bear children, took her slave-girl Zilpah and gave her to Jacob as concubine" (Genesis 30:9).

In biblical anthropology, there is no other immortality for a man than through his male offspring. From that derives a man's duty to substitute for a brother who died without a son. In Genesis 38, after the death of his son Er, Judah asked his other son Onan to sleep with his sister-in-law Tamar "to maintain your brother's line" (Genesis 38:8). Onan was reluctant, and gave his name to "onanism". Finally, Tamar dressed as a prostitute and slept with her father-in-law. Without her, there would have been no tribe of Judah. Tamar and Ruth exemplify the second type of Jewish heroin, who commits incest or adultery to save the clan or the tribe from extinction.

All these stories are pretty consistent in their representation of women and sexuality. Women have two functions: sex slaves if they are non-Jewish, and reproductive mates if they are Jewish. It would be hard to find any exception. The only biblical book that strikes a different note is the Song of Songs; but it is probably not of Israelite origin, and was only adopted in the Hebrew corpus in the first century AD, due to an allegorical interpretation of Rabbi Akiva, who sees in it a symbolic declaration of the love between God and his people, although God is never mentioned. At any rate, its poetic eroticism does not rise above the comparison of love with drunkenness.

The Queen of Heaven

Having outlined the "anthropology of Eros" implicit in the Tanakh, we can turn to theology, with the understanding that theology and anthropology mirror each other: the general mentality and attitude to love, sex and women in any given civilization is reflected in—and influenced by—its mythology. India, for example, has a rich erotic mythology: the Kalika Purana tells how Brahma created Dawn, radiant of youth and vitality, and himself succumbed to her charms.

Nothing of that sort can be found in the Bible. Yahweh is a male god who abhors not only every other god, but goddess as well. His feminine nemesis is Asherah. Her name appears forty times in the Tanakh, either to designate and curse the goddess, or to designate her symbol in the form of "sacred poles". The Books of Kings report that Asherah was sometimes worshipped alongside Yahweh in Judea, and there is corroborating archeological evidence: inscriptions asking for the blessing of "Yahweh and his Asherah," from the eighth century BC, were found in the ruins of Kuntillet Ajrud (the Sinai Peninsula).[6] But from the point of view adopted by the scribes, Asherah worship is an unbearable abomination. The Judean king Manasseh is loathed for having "set up altars to Baal and made an *Asherah* [sacred pole] in the two courts of the Temple of Yahweh" (2 Kings 21:2–5), whereas his grandson Josiah is praised for having removed Asherah's symbol

6. Raphael Patai, *The Hebrew Goddess,* 3rd ed., Wayne State UP, 1990, p. 34.

from the temple and "burnt it, reducing it to ashes and throwing its ashes on the common burial-ground" (23:6).

Throughout Antiquity, most civilized peoples worshipped a great goddess, and generally agreed to identify her with the great goddesses worshipped under other names by other peoples. From the third millennium BC, the Sumerians had worshipped the goddess Inanna, whose name probably means "Lady of Heaven." She was associated to the planet Venus, the morning star, whom Greeks would call lightbearer, which was Latinized as Lucifer. She became known to the Assyrians as Ishtar, who was herself known as Astarte in the Phoenician city states of Sidon, Tyre, and Byblos, and identified with the other Syrian goddess Asherah. No cult was more syncretic, and all these goddesses merged under the title of "Queen of Heaven". It can be argued that the worship of the great motherly Goddess fostered the sense of the universal brotherhood of men, in a way that no male divinity could do. Perhaps that is why Yahweh hated Asherah so much.

Under King Josiah, Yahweh complains to his prophet Jeremiah that the Israelites keep worshipping the "Queen of Heaven": "The children collect the wood, the fathers light the fire, the women knead the dough, to make cakes for the Queen of Heaven; and, to spite me, they pour libations to alien gods" (Jeremiah 7,18). We read in Jeremiah 44 that, after the Babylonians took Jerusalem, Judeans who had fled to Egypt persisted in their abominable worship of the Queen of Heaven. Yahweh tells them that the destruction of Jerusalem was their punishment for these "wicked deeds [...] offering incense and serving other gods" (44:2-3). He threatens them with complete extermination if they persist: "Why bring complete disaster on yourselves [...] by provoking my wrath by your actions, [...] as though bent on your own destruction and on becoming a curse and a laughing-stock for all the nations of the earth?" (44:7-8). Unimpressed, the rebellious Jews respond to Jeremiah:

> "We have no intention of listening to the word you have just spoken to us in Yahweh's name, but intend to go on doing all we have vowed to do: offering incense to the Queen of Heaven and pouring libations in her honour, as we used to do, we and our ancestors, our kings and our chief men, in the towns of Judah and the streets of Jerusalem: we had food in plenty then, we lived well, we suffered no disasters. But since we gave up offering incense to the Queen of Heaven and pouring libations in her honour, we have

been destitute and have perished either by sword or by famine"
(44:16-18).

True to the jealous god he is serving, Jeremiah claims that it is
precisely for having sacrificed to the Queen of Heaven that the
Judeans were punished with the Babylonian army. But history
proves him wrong: Manasseh's 55-year reign, when Asherah was
worshipped inside the Jerusalem temple, was an exceptionally long
period of peace and prosperity, while Josiah brought disaster to
Judea.

In the Hellenistic period, most great goddesses were identified
to the Egyptian Isis, whose cult radiated from Alexandria across
the Mediterranean Basin. Isis became known as the "myrionyme"
goddess ("of ten thousand names"). In Apuleius' second-century
novel *The Golden Ass,* she calls herself "Queen of Heaven" and
"the natural mother of all things," and declares: "my divinity is
adored throughout the world, in divers ways, in various customs,
and by many names."

Isis is a nourishing mother, for she taught the cultivation of
wheat and the making of bread to the Egyptians, who introduced it
to the Greeks.[7] Joseph Campbell notes that the Goddess is
especially dear to sedentary agrarian societies, but not so to
pastoral nomads, probably because "life in the desert doesn't leave
you feeling terribly grateful toward the Mother Goddess."[8] As a
matter of fact, Yahweh doesn't like vegetal offerings, and rejected
Cain's offering for that very reason. He also finds the incense
offered to the Queen of Heaven "repellent" (Jeremiah 44:21).
What he liked was the "pleasing smell" of holocausts.

Isis is also the goddess of love. After her husband Osiris was
murdered and dismembered by his jealous younger brother Seth,
she gathered the pieces and, through her lamentations and prayers,
brought Osiris back to life. She then conceived with the revived
Osiris a son, Horus, who would return as an adult to complete the
deliverance of Osiris by taking vengeance on Seth and reign over
Egypt. This is the timeless story of love's triumph over death—the
only love story worth telling. It is akin to the tale type known to
folklorists as "Beauty and the Beast", in which the sacrificial love
of a woman heals the heart of a dead man, or breaks the spell put
upon him. But it also incorporates the redemptive virtue of

7. George Foucart, *Les Mystères d'Éleusis,* Picard, 1914 (archive.org).
8. Joseph Campbell, *Goddesses*, 2013, "Chapter 1: Myth and the Feminine Divine."

vengeance, found for instance in Shakespeare's *Hamlet*, in which the king is murdered by his brother and avenged by his son.

The Virgin Mother Mary

In the early centuries AD, Artemis was the name of the universal goddess in Ephesus (now in Turkey), where her gigantic temple was considered one of the Seven Wonders of the World. She was referred to as "the Mother of the gods", although Christians called her "mother of the demons". We read in the Acts of the Apostles (19:23-28) of a "serious disturbance" in Ephesus, when "a silversmith called Demetrius, who provided work for a large number of craftsmen making silver shrines of Artemis," complained about Paul's preaching:

> "'This threatens not only to discredit our trade, but also to reduce the sanctuary of the great goddess Artemis to unimportance. It could end up by taking away the prestige of a goddess venerated all over Asia, and indeed all over the world.' This speech roused them to fury, and they started to shout, 'Great is Artemis of the Ephesians!'" (Acts 19:23-28)[9]

Although the author of Acts belittles the Ephesians' concern as purely economic, this was a religious conflict. It lasted several centuries, and in 401, the Temple of Artemis was burned down by Christians. Thirty years later, the Eastern Roman emperor Theodosius II convened at Ephesus a council, at which the title *Theotokos* was officially bequeathed to the Virgin Mary. And so Artemis was given back to the Ephesians, only under a new identity. The pilgrims who had converged to Ephesus for centuries to pay homage to Artemis could now pray in front of the same statues and walk the same torchlight processions. Mary naturally became known as the Queen of Heaven, and adorned by a crown of twelve stars, recalling the zodiac that Artemis wore as a necklace. A Christian tradition asserts that Mary retired to Ephesus in her later years, from where she ascended to heaven.

In Egypt, Libya, Italy and Gaul, Mary merged perfectly with Isis, and the figure of Mary shedding tears at the foot of the cross echoed the lamentations of Isis. The crucified and resurrected Jesus made an excellent avatar of Osiris, who was used to absorbing other heroes and gods—for instance Antinous in the

---

9. I have restored here the name of Artemis, arbitrarily replaced in the New Jerusalem Bible by Diana.

second century AD. As for Horus, known to the Greeks as
Harpocrates (from the Egyptian *Har pa khrad*, "Horus the child"),
he was transformed into the figure of the Infant Jesus. In the
Egyptian myth, Horus is conceived at the spring equinox, the time
of harvest, and his birth is celebrated every year at the winter
solstice, like Jesus' birth. Isis hid Horus to protect him from the
evil uncle whom he was destined to overthrow as king of Egypt,
just as Mary hid Jesus—in Egypt precisely—to save him from
King Herod who feared for his throne (Matthew 2). The
representations of Isis with little Horus on her knees are believed
to have influenced Christian art.

In a mostly illiterate society, it may seem fairly simple to
convince a majority of people that the Mother of God and Queen
of Heaven worshipped by their ancestors was in fact the mother of
a Jewish Messiah. Syncretism was, after all, in the very nature of
the Goddess. But Christianization met strong resistance among the
aristocratic and literate elite. The Christian version of the Goddess
was frustratingly reductive: her exclusive human incarnation in
Palestine restricted her universal significance. The Virgin Mary is
hardly a nurturing mother in the agrarian sense. More importantly,
she lacked some aspects of femininity. Although Mary is "full of
grace," there is a limit to Marian mysticism: Eros is out of the
question.

As for Jesus, the idea that he might have had a sexual life is
anathema. Yet sex does not appear among the three satanic
temptations that he overcomes in Matthew 4. This suggests that it
was not such an issue in the earliest days of the Jesus movement.
The gospels show Jesus surrounded by women, and it is to Mary
Magdalene, who had followed him from Galilee, that he first
appeared after his death (Mark 16:9). This evokes the classic folk
motif of the young man's ghost appearing to his loved one. Jesus'
relationship with Mary Magdalene has inspired much speculation.
The heresiologists tell us that the early Gnostics considered Mary
Magdalene as the "concubine" of Christ, although they may have
conceived this relation as platonic. Some Gnostic sects claimed to
be guardians of a tradition secretly transmitted by Mary
Magdalene, and the theme of her opposition to Peter (the first
"Pope") is widespread in Gnostic literature (*Pistis Sophia, Gospel
of Mary, Gospel of Philip, Gospel of Thomas*), and survived among
the Cathars, as Elaine Pagels explains in her book *The Gnostic*

Gospels.[10] Catholicism normalized the cult of Mary Magdalene, when her body was officially "discovered" in Vézelay in 1279.

The cult of Virgin Mary also served to absorb that embarrassing Mary Magdalene, who was actually closer to Isis, the sister-wife of Osiris, than Christ's mother could ever be. It was perhaps not before the twelfth century that the cult of Mary was firmly established in Western Europe. Bernard de Clairvaux (1090–1153) was the main promoter of this cult in France, and the first to call her "Our Lady" ("Notre Dame"). All the Gothic cathedrals from then on were consecrated to her. Yet in the South of France, many "Black Madonnas" produced as late as the thirteenth century are thought to have been made for Isis, rather than Mary. And even after the triumph of the Gregorian Reform in 1215 (Fourth Council of the Lateran), the ancient cult of Isis seems to have continued to irrigate secretly western civilization, as an underground stream. We are now going to follow this stream until its resurgence in the romantic movement of the nineteenth century.

The courtly tradition of fin'amor

We should not imagine Western medieval society as immersed in a homogeneous Catholic faith, with only a few heretical groups at the fringe. We get a more accurate idea of medieval civilization if we consider that it had two distinct and antagonistic cultures: there is on one side the Latin culture of the clerics, with a near monopoly on the written word, and on the other, a rich culture in vernacular languages, mainly oral but leaving us enough written material from the twelfth century. Unlike clerical culture, which is written in prose and concerned with doctrinal orthodoxy, lay culture is mostly narrative and poetic. It is of aristocratic origin, but permeates popular classes. In its highest expressions, such as Chrétien de Troyes' masterpieces, it excels in polysemy and symbolism. Although we may call it "secular", it possesses its own religiosity, which includes ideas about the world of the dead completely at odds with Christian doctrine.[11]

Aristocratic non-clerical culture values love as the source of the greatest spiritual joy, and therefore cannot conceive of Paradise without it. Some poems sarcastically reject the loveless Christian

---

10. Elaine Pagels, *The Gnostic Gospels,* Weidenfeld & Nicolson, 1979.
11. Laurent Guyénot, *La Mort féerique. Anthropologie du merveilleux (XIIe-XVe siècles),* Gallimard, 2011.

Paradise: the male protagonist of the twelfth-century poem *Aucassin et Nicolette*, threatened with Hell by a cleric if he persists in loving Nicolette, answers that he prefers Hell, if that is where those who value love, chivalry and poetry are destined to go. In Guillaume de Lorris' *Roman de la Rose* (1225-1230), the narrator dreams himself in a wonderful garden with a Fountain of Love and the most beautiful woman he has ever seen. According to specialist Jean Dufournet, we find in this work "the elements of a very strong spiritual current that make the protagonist an emulator of the mystics." The god Amor who strikes the narrator's heart may be a poetic hypostasis, but he poses as a competitor of the Catholic God of asceticism and virginity; incidentally, Amor is Roma in reverse.

These notions played a crucial role in the tradition known today as "courtly love", first formalized in the troubadours' poetry in Aquitaine, where the duchess Alienor (1122-1204), grand-daughter of the first troubadour, introduced it to the court of her first husband, the King of France, then to that of her second husband, the King of England, where it combined harmoniously with the Celtic traditions of Wales and Britain, to produce for example the fairy lays of Marie de France or the Arthurian romances of Chrétien de Troyes.

As its name indicates, the *fin'amor* required the refinement or the crude sexual impulse. In the central episode of Chrétien de Troyes' *Erec and Enide,* Erec meets a lovely damsel in a paradisiac garden magically protected, but must fight the terrible red knight who keeps her prisoner. Erec wins the fight, and learns that it is in fact the red knight who was prisoner of his lady, and is now free. Erec also learns that the lady was Enide's cousin, and he can now celebrate with Enide the "Joy of the Court" (*La Joie del Cort*). When we are familiar with the codes of Chrétien de Troyes, such as his taste for puns and his cryptic duplication of characters as brothers or cousins, we understand that, not only the two women are one, but the red knight is also the *alter ego* of Erec himself—his dark, impulsive, side, that Erec must overcome in order to experience the "Joy of the Heart" (*La Joie del Cor* in Old French) with his lady.

In his memorable essay *Love in the Western World* (originally published in French in 1938, revised in 1952, and followed in 1961 by *Essays on the Myths of Love*), French author Denis de Rougemont sought to understand the intricate relationship between the erotic and the religious in the tradition of the troubadours and their romantic heirs. He recognizes that this poetry is fundamentally religious, but foreign and opposed to Christianity. Because it developed at the same time (12th century) and in the same region (Occitania) as Catharism—sometimes even the same castles—De Rougemont tried to link the two, but most historians have rejected his hypothesis of the troubadours' secret Catharism. A simpler explanation for the proximity of the two traditions is the climate of religious tolerance and pluralism that existed in the South of France before the Albigensian Crusades (1209-1229).

De Rougemont has highlighted the fact that the *Dame* of the troubadours often seems an ideal, distant, almost intangible figure. Her name is generally kept secret, and when it is not, it suggests an allegorical fiction rather than a real person. A good example is Geoffrey Rudel (12th century), who, "after long being in love with the image of a woman he has never seen, beholds her at last after a sea passage and dies in the arms of the Countess of Tripoli as soon as she has bestowed upon him a single kiss of peace and a greeting." De Rougemont also notes that the stereotypic form of the troubadours' poetry gives the impression that they all love the same Lady.[12]

De Rougemont finds here an argument for his thesis that the experience of passionate love, that "invention" of the troubadours, is an illusion, a lie: when the lover thinks he is loving a woman, he is, in fact, loving an ideal woman that doesn't exist. But that is an unfair judgment. From a Platonic viewpoint, the Idea is more real than its manifestations on earth, and for the medieval poet as for the medieval philosopher, visible realities are always the symbol and the sign of more essential, invisible realities (Étienne Gilson, *The Spirit of Mediaeval Philosophy,* 1922). The troubadours believed that to love a woman perfectly is to perceive and worship the immaterial Goddess through her. From that perspective, the psychological phenomenon that Stendhal called "crystallization", which makes the beloved appear to the lover glowing with all perfections, takes on a very different meaning. Love does not lie; simply, its truth is not of this world.

Dante and the Fedeli d'Amore

Our fragmentary knowledge of the troubadours' tradition does not permit any certainty about their underlying philosophy. There

---

12. Denis de Rougemont, *Love in the Western World*, Princeton UP, 1983, pp. 84-97.

is no conclusive evidence of a religion of the Goddess encrypted in their art. But the love poetry of their immediate successors, namely Dante Alighiery (1265-1321), Petrarch (1304-1374) and Boccaccio (1313-1375), is easier to decrypt. All are from Florence, a city where many Occitans took refuge after fleeing the Frankish crusaders and the Roman Inquisition.[13] Literary critics have often wondered if the ladies to whom they addressed their most beautiful verses (respectively Beatrix, Laura and Fiametta) were real or archetypal women. Each of them was allegedly encountered during Holy Week, and died shortly after, so that the poet addresses her as a disembodied creature, living in Paradise where she transforms herself into Divine Light. Her lover then takes the title of pilgrim, and undertakes a spiritual journey to reach her.

What we think we know about Dante's Beatrice comes exclusively from Boccaccio, who wrote fifty years later a commentary on the *Divine Comedy*. But Boccaccio had his own reason for claiming that Beatrice was a real woman. There is a strong argument that she was not. Dante's poems are enigmatic, and the poet urges his readers to find the hidden meaning in his verses: "Men of sound intellect and probity, weigh with good understanding what lies hidden behind the veil of my strange allegory" (*Inferno*, IX, 61-63). Luigi Valli published in 1928 a book that made a great impression on thinkers like René Guénon, Julius Evola or Henri Corbin: *Il linguaggio segreto di Dante e dei "Fedeli d'amore"*.[14] The "faithful of love" mentioned by Dante may have been a circle of poets, artists and philosophers, mostly Florentines, sharing highly heterodox religious conceptions, and a hostility to the new world order imposed by the Roman Church. These poets, writes Valli, made their love feelings "a material for expressing mystical and initiatory thoughts [...] in a symbolic love language."

The key to Beatrice's cryptic identity in the *Divine Comedy* is provided by Dante in an earlier book titled *Vita Nuova (The New Life)*. Here Dante first introduces "my mind's glorious lady, [...] she who was called by many Beatrice, by those who did not know what it meant to so name her" (the name Beatrice means "*she who confers blessing*"). Nine times in his life, Beatrice appeared to

---

13. Philippe Guiberteau, "Dante, Guido Cavalcanti et les Épicuriens de Florence," *Bulletin de l'Association Guillaume Budé*, October 1969, on www.persee.fr
14. Valli's research was expanded by Alfonso Ricolfi in *Studi sui "Fedeli d'amore"*. Soc. Anonima Dante Alighieri, 1933-1940.

him, Dante says. The first time, Beatrice "greeted me so virtuously, so much so that I saw then to the very end of grace." For Beatrice's "greeting", Dante uses the Italian word *saluto,* which is close to *salute,* "salvation". Beatrice's *saluto,* says Dante, fills men with repentance, humility, forgiveness, and charity— hardly the qualities of the ordinary lover.

> "In her eyes my lady bears Love,
> by which she makes noble what she gazes on:
> where she passes, all men turn their look on her,
> and she makes the heart tremble in him she greets,
> so that, all pale, he lowers his eyes,
> and sighs, then, over all his failings:
> anger and pride fleeing before her.
> All sweetness, all humble thought
> are born in the heart of him who hears her speak,
> and he who first saw her is blessed."

Beatrice is the essence of feminine grace and virtues, manifested in all women to various degrees: "my lady came into such grace that not only was she honoured and praised, but through her many were also honoured and praised." In several passages, Dante indicates that when he is sensitive to the charm of real women (Beatrice's friends, for example), it is Beatrice that he sees through them: "They have seen perfection of all welcome / who see my lady among the other ladies."

We need not take the cryptic nature of Dante's message as a form of "esotericism", as did René Guénon (*The Esoterism of Dante,* 1925). In those times, crypsis was necessary for any non-suicidal heterodox thinker. A close friend of Dante, Cecco d'Ascoli (1269-1327), was accused by the Inquisition of "speaking badly" of the Catholic faith and burnt at the stake, and Dante himself came under suspicion.

With some exaggeration perhaps, Robert Graves wrote that, "The purpose of poetry is religious invocation of the Muse," whom he also called the White Goddess and the Mother of All Living.[15] Painters and sculptors have also devoted much effort to capturing and communicating the essence of feminine grace. The aesthetic experience, according to Schopenhauer, means getting lost in the contemplation of the Platonic Idea behind the phenomenon, thus escaping the cycle of unfulfilled desires. Surely Yahweh's second

---

15. Robert Graves, *The White Goddess: A Historical Grammar of Poetic Myth* (1948), Farrar Strauss Giroux, 1966, pp. 4, 24.

commandment not to make "any image of anything" (Exodus 20:4) has much to do with the absence in Hebrew culture of reverence for woman as an object of worship.

Two centuries after Dante, another Florentine genius, Leonardo da Vinci (1452-1519), would give us a portrait of the Goddess under the name Mona Lisa. Just like for Dante's Beatrice, scholars say they know her identity. Lady Lisa (Mona is a diminutive of Madonna, or Ma Donna) is said to have been the wife of a rich merchant who commissioned her portrait to the painter, who was then at the height of his glory. But the painting respects none of the codes of the portrait of the time (lack of jewelry, for example). And Leonardo worked on it uninterruptedly for ten years, with extraordinary devotion, religiously superimposing thousands of layers of paints and varnish of extreme thinness. He never parted from it until his death at the court of François 1st. Many have supposed, correctly I believe, that this painting is not the portrait of a lady, but the icon of *the* Lady, Donna l'Isa (Isa being a variant of Isis). The black veil that can be seen rejected on her left shoulder is a reference to the famous veil of Isis that "no mortal ever raised," mentioned by Plutarch.

Romanticism and the Divine Sophia

According to Julius Evola (*Metaphysics of Sex*, 1934), Dante's Beatrice, Petrarch's Laura and Boccaccio's Fiametta all symbolize Wisdom or Gnosis, the divine source of enlightenment. This is consistent with Dante's admiration for Boethius, whom he places in Paradise. In his *Consolation of Philosophy* (524), Boethius told how, while awaiting death in the jails of King Theodoric, he had been visited by *Philosophia* in the form of a majestic woman, and entrusted his soul to her.

Technically, *philosophia* is the love of Sophia, Wisdom. The divinization of Sophia is a very ancient tradition. It survived in Christian Byzantium, as the very name of the basilica Hagia Sophia (Holy Wisdom) bears witness. The tradition has even persisted in the fringe of Russian Orthodoxy. Philosopher and poet Vladimir Solovyov (1853-1900) experienced mystically the divine Sophia in the form of a celestial female being who made him feel that "All was one, a single image of womanly beauty" (*Three meetings*). Unfortunately, Solovyov's attempt to reconcile the

Trinitarian doctrine with the Platonic notion of Divine Wisdom met with opposition in the Orthodox hierarchy.

From a theological viewpoint, if the Supreme Being is seen as masculine, it makes sense that Wisdom, the intermediary principle that brings the world into being, be viewed as feminine. From a psychological, spiritual or mystical viewpoint, it makes even more sense. Sophia is to be understood as Truth, and the love of Sophia is really the love of Truth. This is a masculine impulse. Beauty, on the other hand, is a feminine attribute because it is the sensible manifestation of Truth, the way Truth appears to the Truth-lover (this is also the function of art). That is why Truth, or Sophia, manifests herself mystically as a Goddess to the man who loves her unconditionally.

Danish philosopher Søren Kierkegaard brings a precious insight on the relationship between the masculine desire for Truth, which he calls "Ideality," and the worship of feminine Beauty. He remarks that the seed of Ideality is sown by nascent love in the soul of the adolescent. In other words, it is the Goddess that awakens Ideality. (It follows that to defile the image of woman in the mind of adolescents through mass pornography, is to raise generations of men devoid of ideality.)

Kierkegaard, who renounced marrying the woman he loved in order to cultivate his genius, wrote in *In Vino Veritas* (1845):

> "It is through woman that ideality is born into the world and— what were man without her! There is many a man who has become a genius through a woman, many a one a hero, many a one a poet, many a one even a saint; but he did not become a genius through the woman he married, for through her he only became a privy councilor; he did not become a hero through the woman he married, for through her he only became a general; he did not become a poet through the woman he married, for through her he only became a father; he did not become a saint through the woman he married, for he did not marry, and would have married but one—the one whom he did not marry; just as the others became a genius, became a hero, became a poet through the help of the woman they did not marry."

This dilemma is at the heart of the romantic or heroic conception of love. Love aspires to fusion and permanence, but only survives through separation and instability, and sometimes reaches perfection and immortality through death. This is best illustrated by the German poet Novalis (1772-1801), who first coined the term "romanticism." In his *Hymns to the Night*, Novalis evokes his young fiancée Sophie, whose death triggered his poetic gift, exactly as Beatrice did for Dante. As he was shedding tears on Sophie's tomb, she appeared to him:

> "through the cloud I saw the glorified face of my beloved. In her eyes eternity reposed. I laid hold of her hands, and the tears became a sparkling bond that could not be broken. Into the distance swept by, like a tempest, thousands of years. On her neck I welcomed the new life with ecstatic tears. It was the first, the only dream, and just since then I have held fast an eternal, unchangeable faith in the heaven of the Night, and its Light, the Beloved."

"I have for Sophie religion, not love," commented Novalis. Sophie became for him the Goddess. Gérard de Nerval (1808-1855), the emblematic French romantic poet, gave another beautiful expression of this theme in his last novel *Aurélia* (he was found dead soon after finishing it). As the narrator gets convinced by some sign that his death is near, he falls sick and, in his delirium, sees a woman of supernatural beauty, whose body grows until embracing the whole cosmos. She bears the features of Aurelia, the love of his youth, whom he had lost by some tragic misunderstanding and who, he will learn later, has just died. In another dream, she tells him she has been with him all the time: "I am the same as Mary, the same as your mother, the same as all the forms you have always loved." And so the narrator concludes:

> "I set my thoughts on the eternal Isis, the mother and the sacred wife; all my aspirations, all my prayers were confounded in this magical name, I felt reviving in her, and sometimes she appeared to me under the figure of the ancient Venus, sometimes also in the features of the Virgin of the Christians."

The Jewish assault on love

The romantic ideal of love as a mystical encounter with the eternal feminine, or the Goddess, has had a profound influence on European culture. Naturally, an ideal is never fully attained. Perhaps it is only approached by a blessed few, an aristocracy of love. Yet it glitters in the sky for all to see, and it attracts like a magnet the collective soul. Certainly, the ideal is the source of much disillusion and suffering, as De Rougemont insisted and as the romantic poets knew. But, as Byron said, "sorrow is knowledge."

Conversely, the absence of ideality in relationship to love in the Hebrew tradition has had a profound influence on the Jewish mind. The main reason why romanticism is foreign to Jewish culture is that there can be no truly romantic conception of love without faith in the immortality of the soul, and Jewish anthropology is fundamentally materialistic (as I explained in "Israel as One Man"). It is therefore no surprise that romanticism has been regarded with contempt by most Jewish intellectuals. Moses Hess judged it "decadent," preferring Jewish novels, since "the Jews alone had the good sense to subordinate sexual to maternal love."[16] He admits, however, that Jewish writers are perfectly capable of imitating romanticism, like anything else.

The enthusiasm of the Jewish cultural elites for Freud's theory may be seen in the light of this "clash of cultures". Kevin MacDonald (*A Culture of Critique,* ch. 4) explains it by an inherited Jewish culture where love is seen "as an invention of the alien gentile culture and thus morally suspect."[17] Otto Rank's idea that Jews had a more primitive, and therefore healthier sexuality ("The Essence of Judaism," 1905) was widely shared among Freud's disciples. Which makes John Murray Cuddihy argue, in his insightful essay *The Ordeal of Civility,* that Freud's theory of sublimation resulting from repression came straight from the *shtetl* Jews' inner struggle over integration: "In psychoanalysis, the 'id' is the functional equivalent of the 'Yid' in social intercourse."[18] Sexual liberation became a new version of the messianic ideal of universal redemption by the Jews, the "light of the nations." And as we know, in practice, the Jewish way to save the nations is to defile their most sacred values—their gods, and, above all, the Goddess.

From the 1930s, American Jewish authors found in the theories of Freud and his Jewish disciples the justification for assaulting the romantic ideal and challenging the obscenity laws, as Josh Lambert shows in *Unclean Lips: Obscenity, Jews, and American Culture.* Ludwig Lewisohn, "the most prominent Jewish writer in interwar America," is a case in point. He had been analyzed briefly by Freud, and was a close friend of Otto Rank. Like Rank, Lewisohn liked to "portray traditional, unassimilated Jewish

---

16. Moses Hess, *Rome and Jerusalem,* 1918 (archive.org), pp. 82, 86.

17. Kevin MacDonald, *The Culture of Critique,* Praeger, 1998, p. 125.

18. John Murray Cuddihy, *The Ordeal of Civility: Freud, Marx, Lévi-Strauss, and the Jewish Struggle with Modernity,* Delta Book, 1974 (archive.org), p. 23.

sexuality as uniquely healthy." He also shared Wilhelm Reich's idea (*The Mass Psychology of Fascism*, 1934), that anti-Semitism is a symptom of sexual frustration and can be cured by liberating the Gentiles' libido (a message echoed in Herbert Marcuse's *Eros and Civilization,* 1955, as well as in Theodor Adorno's *The Authoritarian Personality,* 1950). So did Isaac Rosenfeld, who said: "I regard anti-Semitism as a symptom of a serious, underlying psycho-sexual disease of epidemic proportion in our society." According to Josh Lambert,

> "Much of the sexual utopianism and amateur sexology that appeared in the fiction and essays of Norman Mailer, Saul Bellow, Allen Ginsberg, and Isaac Rosenfeld in the 1940s and 1950s elaborated upon Reich's attempt to cure the sexual ills of all of Western civilization, and, in so doing, to relieve Jews of their role as scapegoats."[19]

In their endeavor to elevate obscenity to the status of art, Jewish authors received the active support of Jewish lawyers and judges. "Jews participated in these obscenity trials not only as defendants, but also in key juridical roles," writes Lambert, citing Jewish Supreme Court justices Benjamin Cardozo, Louis Brandeis, Felix Frankfurter, Arthur Goldberg, and Abe Fortas.[20]

In 1969 Philip Roth unleashed his novel, *Portnoy's Complaint,* the confession of a sex-obsessed American Jew, who lusted after the *shikses* as a teenager ("My circumcised little dong is simply shriveled up with veneration. [...] How do they get so gorgeous, so healthy, so blond?"), before securing for himself a blond *shiksa,* whom he nicknamed The Monkey. "Hating Your Goy and Eating One Too," is how the narrator describes the experience. He makes the following confession to his psychiatrist:

> "What I'm saying, Doctor, is that I don't seem to stick my dick up these girls, as much as I stick it up their backgrounds—as though through fucking I will discover America. Conquer America—maybe that's more like it."

For Roth/Portnoy, "America is a *shiksa* nestling under your arm whispering love love love love love!"[21] Roth is not the only

19. Josh Lambert, *Unclean Lips: Obscenity, Jews, and American Culture*, New York UP, 2013. I quote from his original doctoral dissertation, on deepblue.lib.umich.edu
20. Joshua Lambert, *Unclean Lips, op. cit.,* pp. viii, 67-68, 166, 20.
21. Philip Roth, *Portnoy's Complaint,* Random House, 1969, p. 235, 146, quoted in Lambert, *Unclean Lips, op. cit.,* pp. 190-192.

American-Jewish novelist sharing this vision of American society as the *shiksa,* in other words, a sexual object to be screwed.[22]

And this should not be mistaken as the traditional Jewish resentment against Christianity. It is not "Christian values" that are attacked with extreme violence by hollywoodism, pornography, psychoanalysis, feminism, and homosexualism (not forgetting modern art); it is the Western tradition of love, the miracle of our civilization. This cultural assault is the enduring manifestation of Yahweh's ancient rage against the Queen of Heaven. Blessed are those Jews who turned their back on Jeremiah's sociopathic god and found comfort in the Goddess instead. We need them more than ever.

---

22. Leslie Fiedler, "The Jew in the American Novel," quoted in John Murray Cuddihy, *The Ordeal of Civility, op. cit.,* p. 62.

7 - THE LEVITICAL TERROR
Is Yahweh an Anti-Semite?

Jewish blood for Zion

Holocaust is a term taken from the Hebrew Bible (in the Greek translation), designating the sacrifice of animals that are burned completely on an altar. The first holocaust recorded in the Bible is performed by Noah in Genesis 8. In a fit of rage, Yahweh has said to himself: "I shall rid the surface of the earth of the human beings whom I created, [...] for I regret having made them" (6:7). But after drowning almost all his creatures in a flood, Yahweh regrets having regretted, when Noah offers him a huge holocaust. "Yahweh smelt the pleasing smell and said to himself, 'Never again will I curse the earth because of human beings, because their heart contrives evil from their infancy" (8:21). Yahweh has been addicted to the "sweet smell" of carbonized flesh ever since. According to the Book of Ezra, a gigantic holocaust was offered to Yahweh by the Judeo-Babylonians who (re)colonized Palestine, in preparation for the (re)building of the Temple (Ezra 7:12-17).

Why, then, was the name "Holocaust" chosen to designate the destruction of "six million" European Jews during World War II? Everything of importance in the history of Israel gets a biblical name, even Israel's nuclear deterrence policy (the "Samson Option"). But why "holocaust"? In what sense is the Holocaust a holocaust? The obvious implication is that the death of millions of European Jews pleased Yahweh, and, by consequence, hastened the fulfillment of his messianic promise. As evident as it is, that implication is of course unspeakable in explicit terms. It will only be whispered cryptically by theologians such as Irving Greenberg, or written only in Hebrew, as when Lubabitcher Rabbi Menachem Schneerson compared God to a surgeon who amputates a patient's limb in order to save his life.[1] Or it can be veiled in more conventional theology: "The State of Israel is God's answer to Auschwitz," in Abraham Herschel's Trinitarian formula linking

---

1. Yehuda Bauer, "God as Surgeon," June 01, 2007, on www.haaretz.com/1.4823447

Yahweh (the Father), Israel (the Son), and the Holocaust (the Holy Ghost?).[2]

But in his book *The Holocaust Victims Accuse,* anti-Zionist rabbi Moshe Shonfeld comes close to the outrageous claim that the Zionists needed six millions cremated Jews for the foundation of the Jewish State: "The Zionist leaders saw the spilt Jewish blood of the holocaust as grease for the wheels of the Jewish national state."[3]

Are there any facts to back the theory that the Zionist elites willingly sacrificed the German Jews on the altar of Zionism? We can start with the declaration of war published on the front page of the British *Daily Express,* March 24, 1933, at the initiative of Zionist Wall Street lawyer Samuel Untermeyer: "the Israeli people around the world declare economic and financial war against Germany." The words were carefully chosen to implicate the 600,000 Jews living in Germany among the conspirators against the German State and the German people: "Jews of All the World Unite in Action," read the headline, while the article insisted: "Fourteen million Jews dispersed throughout the world have banded as one man [...] to stand by the 600,000 Jews of Germany." This declaration, heard loud and clear in Germany, was a provocation intended to put the German Jews in danger, at a time when "not a hair on a Jew's head had been touched," as Goebbels protested.

Many Jews, it must be said, protested at the irresponsibility of the Jewish financial elites' call for boycott. American rabbi Harry Waton would write in 1939 in his *Program for the Jews*:

> "by this stupid boycott they aggravate the position of the Jews in Germany. In their vanity and stupidity the Jews in this country do not realize how inhuman and cruel it is to sacrifice the Jews in Germany in order to satisfy a stupid, and insane vanity. [...] Six years passed since the Jews outside of Germany declared war against Nazi Germany and Fascist Italy. The Jews will never admit that the recent pogroms had much to do with their stupid boycott."[4]

Neither would the Zionists admit, of course, that the pogroms were the intended outcome of the boycott, as the necessary pretext

---

2. Abraham Herschel, *Israel: An Echo of Eternity*, Doubleday, 1969, p. 115.

3. Read Lewis Brandon's review on www.unz.com, or download the book on www.truetorahjews.org/images/holocaustvictims.pdf

4. Harry Waton, *A Program for the Jews,* 1939 (archive.org), p. 48.

needed to escalate the economic war into a military one, which would in turn bring hell down upon the German Jews.

How Hitler was trapped by his own prophecy

Predictably, five days after the declaration of the boycott, Hitler announced a counter-boycott of Jewish businesses in Germany as "defensive measure." At the same time, he warned that, "Jewry must recognize that a Jewish war against Germany will lead to sharp measures against Jewry in Germany."[5]

On January 30, 1939, in an ultimate attempt to deter England from declaring war on Germany, Hitler sent her a warning from the Reichstag tribune. After recalling that he had often been a prophet, as when he predicted his own rise to power, Hitler added:

> "I want once again to be a prophet. If the international Finance-Jewry inside and outside of Europe should succeed in plunging the peoples of the earth once again into a world war, the result will be not the Bolshevization of earth, and thus a Jewish victory, but the destruction [*Vernichtung*] of the Jewish race in Europe."

This "prophetic warning to Jewry!" as the headline of *Völkische Beobachter* put it the following day, was widely distributed and discussed. As if in response to it, England declared war on September 3, 1939. The World Jewish Congress (founded in 1936 to rally world Jewry against Hitler) immediately stated that it stood wholeheartedly by Britain.

Hitler repeated his prophecy on January 30, 1941, this time at the address of the United States. The *New York Times* responded with an article that was tantamount to challenging him to act on his word: "there is not a single precedent to prove he will either keep a promise or fulfill a threat. If there is any guarantee in his record, in fact, it is that the one thing he will not do is the thing he says he will do."[6]

The United States entered the war in December 1941. A few days later, during the Reich Chancellery meeting of 12 December 1941, according to Goebbels' diary, Hitler declared that his prophecy "was not just a phrase. The world war is here, and the destruction [*Vernichtung*] of the Jews must be the necessary

---

5. Jeffrey Herf, *The Jewish Enemy: Nazi Propaganda During World War II and the Holocaust,* Harvard UP, 2006, p. 39.
6. Jeffrey Herf, *The Jewish Enemy, op. cit.,* p. 78.

consequence." Again, Hitler should have considered the obvious: he was being pushed to act on his prophecy.

That same year of 1941, in response to a plea for rescuing the Jews of Europe, Nathan Schwalb, head of the Jewish Agency in Switzerland, declined with the following justification: "if we do not bring sacrifices, with what will we achieve the right to sit at the table when they make the distribution of nations and territories after the war? [...] only through blood will the land be ours."[7]

Already in 1938, the Anglo-American Zionists had sabotaged the Evian *International Conference on Political and Economic Problems Caused by the Expulsion of Jews from the Reich,* and the resolution of Western democracies to open their borders to the Jews that Germany was happy to get rid of, because, said David Ben-Gurion, this "will endanger the existence of Zionism."[8] German Jews were either to be forcibly converted to Zionism and emigrate to Palestine—but the British only allowed limited quotas—or be left to die in Nazi concentration camps—in either case, for the ultimate benefit of Zionism. When war broke out, there remained in Germany about 275,000 Jews who, for want of a visa granted by a foreign country, were unable to emigrate. This had been planned by the Anglo-American Zionists.

Everything possible was done to intensify German rage against Jews. In early 1941 appeared the 96–page booklet by Jewish American businessman Theodore Kaufman, *Germany Must Perish,* advocating "the extinction of the German nation and the total eradication from the earth, of all her people," by sterilizing all German males under sixty, and females under forty-five, which could be done in less than a month by about twenty thousand surgeons. "Accordingly in the span of two generations, [...] the elimination of Germanism and its carriers, will have been an accomplished fact."[9] Interviewed by the *Canadian Jewish Chronicle,* Kaufman speaks of the Jews' "mission" to guide humankind toward "perpetual peace"; thanks to them, "slowly but surely the world will develop into a paradise"; but for the moment, "let us sterilize all Germans and wars of world domination will

---

7. Reb Moshe Shonfeld, *The Holocaust Victims Accuse: Documents and Testimony of Jewish War Criminals*, Bnei Yeshivos, 1977, p. 24.

8. Alan Hart, *Zionism: The Real Enemy of the Jews*, vol. 1: *The False Messiah*, Clarity Press, 2009, p. 164.

9. Theodore Kaufman, *Germany Must Perish,* Argyle Press, 1941 (archive.org), p. 30.

come to an end!"[10] Kaufman's book was reviewed in the *New York Times* and the *Washington Post*. In 1944, it would be commented upon by Louis Nizer in his influential book *What to Do with Germany?* (highly praised by Harry Truman). Nizer rejected Kaufman's solution as exaggerated, but recommended the death penalty for 150,000 Germans, and "labor battalions" for hundreds of thousands more.[11]

Louis Marschalko, in *The World Conquerors: The Real War Criminals* (1958), cites a few more well-published Jewish authors advocating a "final solution" for the "German question": Leon Dodd, who in *How Many World Wars* (New York, 1942), proclaims that no Germany and no German race must be left after the war; Charles Heartman, who in *There Must Be No Germany After This War* (New York, 1942), also demands the physical extermination of the German people; Einzig Palil, who in *Can We Win the Peace?* (London, 1942), demanded the dismembering of Germany and the total demolition of German industry; Ivor Duncan, who in the March, 1942, issue of *Zentral Europa Observer,* demanded the sterilization of forty million Germans, estimating the total cost at five million pounds sterling.[12]

Shortly after the Normandy landings, Roosevelt and Churchill discussed the future of Germany at the Second Quebec Conference of September 11, 1944, and signed a project developed under the leadership of Jewish-Americans Henry Morgenthau Jr., the Secretary of the Treasury, and his assistant Harry Dexter White. This project, titled *Suggested Post-Surrender Program for Germany, or Program to Prevent Germany from Starting a World War III,* "is looking forward to converting Germany into a country primarily agricultural and pastoral in its character," by dismantling and transporting to Allied nations "all industrial plants and equipment not destroyed by military action," while calling for "forced German labor outside Germany." The revelation of this insane Morgenthau Plan by the *Wall Street Journal* (September 23), and its German translation in *Volkische Beobachter,* pushed

---

10. "'Hitler Will Be Nothing But a Rosebud,'" *The Canadian Jewish Chronicle,* September 26, 1941, on m.forocoches.com/foro/showthread.php?t=6048156 and quoted in Brandon Martinez, *Grand Deceptions: Zionist Intrigue in the 20th and 21st Centuries,* Progressive Press, 2014.
11. Louis Nizer, *What to do with Germany?* Brentano's, 1944 (archive.org), pp. 98-107.
12. Louis Marschalko, *The World Conquerors: The Real War Criminals,* 1958 (archive.org), p. 105.

the Nazis into a desperate fight-to-the-death mentality, and a murderous rage against Jews.[13]

Meanwhile, in 1944, a new effort by the Roosevelt administration for opening the borders of allied countries to Jewish refugees was again aborted by American Zionists. When Morris Ernst, sent by Roosevelt to London to discuss the project, returned with a British agreement to welcome 150,000 refugees, Roosevelt was satisfied: "150,000 to England—150,000 to match that in the United States—pick up 200,000 or 300,000 elsewhere and we can start with half a million of these oppressed people." But a week later, Roosevelt announced to Ernst the cancellation of the project "because the dominant vocal Jewish leadership of America won't stand for it." The Zionists, said Roosevelt, "know they can raise vast sums for Palestine by saying to donors, 'There is no other place for this poor Jew to go.' But if there is a world political asylum, they cannot raise their money." Incredulous, Ernst made the rounds of his Jewish contacts. He wrote in his memoirs that, "active Jewish leaders decried, sneered and then attacked me as if I were a traitor. At one dinner party I was openly accused of furthering this plan of freer immigration [into the US] in order to undermine political Zionism."[14]

The same Jews who had lobbied so hard until the 1930s in favor of unrestricted Jewish immigration in the US now wanted Jews to remain trapped in Germany, until the survivors could be forced into Palestine.

How, otherwise, could they be able to capitalize on a death toll of "six million" Jews? Six million is the number they had settled on long ago for Israel's founding holocaust, it seems. On October 31, 1919, for example, in an article titled "The Crucifixion of Jews Must Stop!" *The American Hebrew* had warned of "this threatened holocaust of human life" on "six millions" European Jews (a figure repeated seven times in one page) who "are being whirled toward the grave [...] through the awful tyranny of war and a bigoted lust for Jewish blood," and concluded that "Israel is entitled to a place in the sun." "Jewish blood" referred in this case to the pogroms by Russian and Ukrainian counter-revolutionaries, which made 6,000 victims that year.[15]

---

13. Quoted in David Irving, *Nuremberg: The Last Battle,* Focal Point, 1996, p. 20.

14. John Mulhall, *America and the Founding of Israel,* Deshon, 1995, p. 109.

15. Martin H. Glynn, "The Crucifixion of Jews Must Stop!" *The American Hebrew,* October 31, 1919, on www.jrbooksonline.com

Ever since Theodor Herzl used the Dreyfus Affair as a springboard for Zionism, it was understood that "Anti-Semitism is a propelling force which, like the wave of the future, will bring Jews into the promised land," as Herzl wrote in his dairy. "Anti-Semitism has grown and continues to grow—and so do I."[16] Logically, the propelling force will be proportional to the violence of the anti-Semitism, that is, to the reported number of its victims and the graphic horror of their doom. And naturally, anti-Semitism must be faked if the Goyim don't show enough of it. In 1952, a columnist for *Davar,* the official organ of *Mapai,* the Israeli ruling party, wrote:

> "I shall not be ashamed to confess that, if I had power, as I have the will, I would select a score of efficient young men— intelligent, decent, devoted to our ideal and burning with the desire to help redeem Jews, and I would send them to the countries where Jews are absorbed in sinful self-satisfaction. The task of these young men would be to disguise themselves as non-Jews, and, acting upon the brutal Zionism, plague these Jews with anti-Semitic slogans, such as 'Bloody Jew', 'Jews go to Palestine', and similar 'intimacies'. I can vouch that the results, in terms of a considerable immigration to Israel from these countries, would be ten thousand times larger than the results brought by thousands of emissaries who have been preaching for decades to deaf ears."[17]

The Nazis' good Jews

The Jews who suffered the most under Nazi Germany were not the Zionists. The German Zionist Jews were regarded by the Nazis as the good Jews.[18] And for good reasons: they applauded the 1933 Nuremberg laws, and they protested against the economic boycott imposed by American Jews. The Zionist Federation of Germany addressed a memorandum to "the New German State" (dated June 21, 1933) condemning the boycott, and expressing sympathy for the Nazi ideology:

> "Our acknowledgment of Jewish nationality provides for a clear and sincere relationship to the German people and its national and racial realities. Precisely because we do not wish to falsify these fundamentals, because we, too, are against mixed marriage and

---

16. *Complete Diaries of Theodore Herzl* (1960), vol. 2, p. 581, quoted in Alan Hart, *Zionism,* vol. 1, *op. cit.,* p. 163. The 5 volumes of Herzl's diairies are on archive.org
17. Alfred Lilienthal, *What Price Israel ?* (1953), Infinity Publishing, 2003, p. 157.
18. Lenni Brenner, *Zionism in the Age of Dictators,* Lawrence Hill & Co., 1983.

are for maintaining the purity of the Jewish group and reject any trespasses in the cultural domain." "The realization of Zionism could only be hurt by resentment of Jews abroad against the German development. Boycott propaganda—such as is currently being carried on against Germany in many ways—is in essence un-Zionist."[19]

A prominent leader of German Jewry, Joachim Prinz, future president of the *American Jewish Congress,* wrote in his book *Wir Juden* ("We the Jews") published in Berlin in 1934:

> "We want assimilation to be replaced by a new law: the decla-ration of belonging to the Jewish nation and the Jewish race. A state built upon the principle of the purity of nation and race can only be honored and respected by a Jew who declares his belonging to his own kind."[20]

This was not just opportunism. There had always been sympathy between Jewish and German brands of racialism, to the point that rabbi Waton (quoted above) claimed that, "Nazism is an imitation of Judaism."[21] It was not Hitler, but Zeev Jabotinsky who wrote in his *Letter on Autonomy,* some twenty years before *Mein Kampf*:

> "A Jew brought up among Germans may assume German custom, German words. He may be wholly imbued with that German fluid but the nucleus of his spiritual structure will always remain Jewish, because his blood, his body, his physical-racial type are Jewish. [...] A preservation of national integrity is impossible except by a preservation of racial purity."[22]

So it was logical for Reinhardt Heydrich, chief of the SS Security Service, to write in 1935 in *Das Schwarze Korps,* the SS journal:

> "We must separate Jewry into two categories: the Zionists and those who favour being assimilated. The Zionists adhere to a strict racial position and by emigrating to Palestine they are helping to build their own Jewish state. [...] The time cannot be far distant when Palestine will again be able to accept its sons who have been

---

19. Lucy Dawidowicz, *A Holocaust Reader,* Behrman House, 1976, pp. 150-155.
20. Quoted in Israel Shahak, *Jewish History, Jewish Religion: The Weight of Three Thousand Years,* Pluto Press, 1994, p. 86.
21. Harry Waton, *A Program for the Jews, op. cit.,* p. 54.
22. Lenni Brenner, *51 Documents: Zionist Collaboration with the Nazis,* Barricade Books, 2002, pp. 7-20.

lost to it for over a thousand years. Our good wishes together with our official good will go with them."[23]

Sixty thousand wealthy German Zionists were allowed to settle with their fortune in Palestine under the *Haavara Agreement* signed with the Jewish Agency, a decisive contribution to the Jewish colonization of Palestine.[24] As Hannah Arendt reminded in 1963, "all leading positions in the Nazi-appointed 'Reichsvereinigung' [compulsory organization of all Jews in Nazi Germany, who selected Jews for emigration] were held by Zionists." This created "a situation in which the non-selected majority of Jews inevitably found themselves confronted with two enemies—the Nazi authorities and the Jewish authorities."[25] The Zionists and the Nazis were united against the very notion of assimilation and the abomination of intermarriage.

To say that Hitler was a Zionist would be exaggerated, for he wrote in 1923:

"For while Zionism tries to make the other part of the world believe that the national self-consciousness of the Jew finds satisfaction in the creation of a Palestinian State, the Jews again most slyly dupe the stupid goyim. They have no thought of building up a Jewish State in Palestine, so that they might inhabit it, but they only want a central organization of their international world cheating, endowed with prerogatives, withdrawn from the seizure of others: a refuge for convicted rascals and a high school for future rogues."[26]

Yet from 1933 to 1938, Hitler regarded German Zionists as ideological and strategic allies in his desire to rid Germany of its Jews. As a consequence, most Jews who died under Nazism were among the assimilationist Jews, those who had no sympathy for Zionism, and whom Zionists regarded as apostates and traitors to their race.

That, I believe, explains why the Holocaust is called the Holocaust: the notion that assimilationist Jews must perish is consistently biblical. It comes straight from Deuteronomy:

---

23. Quoted in Heinz Höhne, *The Order of the Death's Head: The Story of Hitler's SS*, Penguin Books, 2001, p. 133.

24. Tom Segev, *The Seventh Million: The Israelis and the Holocaust*, Hill&Wang, 1993.

25. Hannah Arendt, *Eichmann in Jerusalem: A Report on the Banality of Evil*, Penguin, 2006, pp. 136-138.

26. Adolf Hitler, *Mein Kampf*, Reynal & Hitchcock, 1941 (archive.org), pp. 447-448.

"If your brother, the son of your father or of your mother, or your
son or daughter, or the spouse whom you embrace, or your most
intimate friend, tries secretly to seduce you, saying, 'Let us go and
serve other gods,' […], you must stone him to death, since he has
tried to divert you from Yahweh your God. […] All Israel, hearing
of this, will be afraid, and none of you will do such a wicked thing
again." (Deuteronomy 13:7-12)

And if in one town, "scoundrels from your own stock […] have
led their fellow-citizens astray, saying, 'Let us go and serve other
gods,'" then

"you must put the inhabitants of that town to the sword; you must
lay it under the curse of destruction—the town and everything in
it. You must pile up all its loot in the public square and burn the
town and all its loot, offering it all to Yahweh your God. It is to be
a ruin for all time, and never rebuilt." (Deuteronomy 13:13-17)

Or, according to another translation: "the entire town must be
put to the torch as a burnt offering to Yahweh your God."

The Levites' rule of terror

In biblical terms, assimilation means "serving other gods." The
Jews who seek assimilation deserve death, and their death will
serve as an example to the rest. When, in the second century BC,
some Israelites thought, "let us ally ourselves with the gentiles
surrounding us, for since we separated ourselves from them many
misfortunes have overtaken us," the Maccabees stirred a civil war
against them, "striking down the sinners in their anger, and the
renegades in their fury" (1Maccabees 1-2).[27] The *Book of Jubilees,*
dating from this period, proclaims:

"And if there is any man who wishes in Israel to give his daughter
or his sister to any man who is of the seed of the Gentiles he shall
surely die, and they shall stone him with stones; for he has
wrought shame in Israel; and they shall burn the woman with fire,
because she has dishonored the name of the house of her father,
and she shall be rooted out of Israel." (30:7)

Terrorizing the Jews into strict separateness and endogamy is
the essence of the Yahwist covenant. The Torah shows that
Yahweh's rule of terror rests on the sacrifice of assimilationist and
rebellious Jews. In the Book of Numbers, when an Israelite had the

---

27. Norman Cantor, *The Sacred Chain: The History of the Jews,* Harper Perennial,
1995, pp. 55-61.

gall to appear before Moses with his Midianite wife, Phinehas, grandson of Aaron, "seized a lance, followed the Israelite into the alcove, and there ran them both through, the Israelite and the woman, through the stomach." Yahweh congratulated Phinehas for having "the same zeal as I have," and, as a reward, gave "to him and his descendants after him, […] the priesthood for ever" that is, "the right to perform the ritual of expiation for the Israelites" (Numbers 25:11-13). Let us ponder the fact that, according to the Bible, the Aaronite priesthood was a reward for the double murder of an assimilationist Israelite and his non-Jewish wife.

Even more revealing is the story in Exodus 32. After the episode of the Golden Calf, Moses conspires with the sons of Levi who rallied around him:

> "He said to them, 'Yahweh, god of Israel, says this, 'Buckle on your sword, each of you, and go up and down the camp from gate to gate, every man of you slaughtering brother, friend and neighbour.' The Levites did as Moses said, and of the people about three thousand men perished that day. 'Today', Moses said, 'you have consecrated yourselves to Yahweh, one at the cost of his son, another of his brother; and so he bestows a blessing on you today.'" (Exodus 32:27-29)

As a reward for having slaughtered 30,000 Israelite "apostates", the Levites receive their privilege as the hereditary sacerdotal class, an oligarchy sustained by the other tribes. Here is how the biblical scholar Karl Budde paraphrases this episode, the founding story of the institution of the Levites: "Here we have, in fact, the very moment of Levi's origin, and this is how it must be understood. At Moses' call the faithful from *all the tribes* hasten to him and lend him their arm even against their own kindred. Those thus tested and proved remained from this time on united, and formed a new tribe, 'Levi.' […] Levi is thus, as it were, the bodyguard, the pick of those faithful to Yahweh who gather about Moses, renouncing the old ties of tribe and family."[28]

In Numbers 16-17, a group of two hundred and fifty Levites led by Korah are themselves exterminated for having rebelled against Moses and Aaron. "I am going to destroy them here and now," said Yahweh, and "Fire then shot out from Yahweh and consumed the two hundred and fifty men offering incense" (16:20-35). "On the following day, the whole community of Israelites

---

28. Karl Budde, *Religion of Israel to the Exile,* New York, 1899 (archive.org), p. 82.

were muttering against Moses and Aaron and saying, 'You are responsible for killing Yahweh's people!'" Then Yahweh said "I am going to destroy them here and now," and a plague decimated fourteen thousand seven hundred of them (17:6-14).

What these episodes highlight is that the authority of Yahweh and of his elite caste of Levites is entirely founded on violence and terror against the Israelites themselves. It also shows that the Covenant is based on the permanent threat of destruction. Jews who challenge their representative elites and who socialize with their non-Jewish neighbors, who eat with them, who intermarry with them, and who, while doing all this, show respect to their gods, are the dregs of the Jewish people, traitors to Yahweh and to their race. They deserve to be eliminated without mercy, especially since they endanger the whole community by attracting Yahweh's wrath.

Yahweh teaches the Jewish people that friendship with non-Jews is a betrayal of the covenant, and will be punished by disaster, possibly extermination. Joshua, Moses' successor, said to the Israelites who had taken possession of Canaan:

"Never mix with the peoples who are still left beside you. Do not utter the names of their gods, do not swear by them, do not serve them and do not bow down to them. [...] if you make friends with the remnant of these nations still living beside you, if you intermarry with them, if you mix with them and they with you, then know for certain that Yahweh your god will stop dispossessing these nations before you, and for you they will be a snare, a pitfall, thorns in your sides and thistles in your eyes, until you vanish from this fine country given you by Yahweh your god. [...] For if you violate the covenant which Yahweh your god has imposed on you, if you go and serve other gods and bow down to them, then Yahweh's anger will be roused against you and you will quickly vanish from the fine country which he has given you." (Joshua 23:6-16)

Joshua's conquest of the Promised Land is the blueprint for the Zionist colonization, and the mentality has not changed. Zionism, the founding ideology of the Jewish State, is a secularized version of Yahwism. Its concept of Jewish nationhood is strictly biblical, and therefore intensely ethnocentric and xenophobic. And so it is natural that a Zionist like Benzion Netanyahu (Benjamin's father) would consider that for a Jew to marry a non-Jew is "even from a biological point of view, an act of suicide."[29] Golda Meir, prime minister of Israel from 1969 to 1974, reportedly formulated the same idea in more evocative terms: "To marry a non-Jew is to join the six million [exterminated Jews]."[30] In other words, those assimilationist Jews who break the endogamic covenant might as well be holocausted, as far as Israel is concerned. That is so biblical!

The psychopathic biblical paradigm

In the World War II "Holocaust", Jews were not killed by other Jews, as in the biblical episodes mentioned above. But from the biblical point of view, it makes no difference, because it is always Yahweh who hits the Israelites, whether he is using Moses (a murderer from the beginning), or sending them plagues, stones from heaven or foreign armies. To punish David for having ordered a national census (for some reason, counting living Jews is not allowed), Yahweh gives him the choice: "Which do you prefer: to have three years of famine befall your country; to flee for three months before a pursuing army; or to have three days of epidemic in your country?" David chose the epidemic, which made seventy thousand dead (2Samuel 24:13), but Yahweh could just as well use a foreign army.

Whenever Israelites are attacked, it is because Yahweh wants to punish them for their rebelliousness and idolatry. It is Yahweh who sent the Assyrians against the northern kingdom of Israel to punish the Israelites for their "idolatry" (2Kings 17; Amos 3:14), and it is Yahweh who moved the Babylonian army to destroy the towns of Judah, "because of the wicked deeds they committed to provoke my anger, by going and offering incense and serving other gods" (Jeremiah 44:3).

The real cause-effect relationship between religious pluralism and the Babylonian campaign against Jerusalem was, in fact, exactly the opposite of what the Bible claims. In the ancient world, international diplomacy was closely related to religious tolerance: nations showed respect to each other by respecting each other's gods. The Judean king Manasseh is blamed by the biblical scribes for having done "what is displeasing to Yahweh, copying the disgusting practices of the nations whom Yahweh had dispos-

---

29. Benzion Netanyahu, *The Founding Fathers of Zionism* (1938), Balfour Books, 2012.
30. Quoted in Edgar Morin, *Le Monde moderne et la question juive,* Seuil, 2006.

sessed for the Israelites" by worshipping "the whole array of heaven" (2 Kings 21:2-3). But his reign was a long period of exceptional peace and prosperity. By contrast, his grandson Josiah, who is praised for removing from the temple "all the cult objects which had been made for Baal, Asherah and the whole array of heaven," and for exterminating all the priests "who offered sacrifice to Baal, to the sun, the moon, the constellations and the whole array of heaven" (2Kings 23:4-5), brought disaster to his kingdom by his arrogant policy of exclusivism and provocation toward Babylon.

But the lessons of history are lost on the biblical scribes. Their teaching is not only historically deceptive; it is an insult to common sense and moral sense, which teaches that conviviality (sharing meals, occasionally intermarrying...) fosters trust and civil peace, while separateness creates mistrust and conflict. Yahweh's message is a recipe for catastrophe (*shoah* in Hebrew). It amounts to telling the Jews: "Do not socialize with your neighbors, but despise their traditions, and, if possible, dispossess them or exterminate them. If, after that, they violate you, it is your fault: you have not obeyed scrupulously enough." Such is the insane "wisdom" internalized by Jews for a hundred generations.

With their minds framed by the biblical paradigm, Jews are not easily persuaded that they may bear some collective responsibility for the persecution that befalls them. After all, even Gentiles now tell them that, "the Jew, that object of so much hatred, is perfectly innocent, nay harmless" (Jean-Paul Sartre, *Réflexions sur la question juive,* 1946). [31] Assured by their tradition and their leadership of the perfect innocence of their community, Jews naturally view their critics as irrational and pathological. It is, it seems to them, in the nature of non-Jews to hate Jews. "Judeophobia is a variety of demonopathy," wrote Leon Pinsker (a medical doctor). "As a psychic aberration it is hereditary, and as a disease transmitted for two thousand years it is incurable." [32] What the Jews have to do, then, is to protect themselves, even preventively, from the hatred of non-Jews, and whatever form of deception or coercion they have to employ in doing so is mere self-

---

31. Jean-Paul Sartre, *Réflexions sur la question juive* (1946), Gallimard, 1985, p. 183.
32. Leon Pinsker, *Auto-Emancipation,* 1882, on www.jewishvirtuallibrary.org.

defense. "For the Jew the world is a cage filled with wild beasts," wrote Henry Miller.[33]

Like most traits of Jewish collective psychology, the inability to examine oneself critically and take any responsibility for the hostility of others, is a cognitive pattern learned from the Bible. A good illustration is the black-out in the causal chain of events between, on the one hand, the end of Genesis, when Joseph ruined the peasants of Egypt, forced them into debt and finally into bondage, while enriching his tribesmen, and, on the other hand, the beginning of Exodus, when a king of Egypt "who had never heard of Joseph", seeing that the Israelites had become "more numerous and stronger than we are," decided to take measures "to stop them from increasing any further, or if war should break out, they might join the ranks of our enemies" (Exodus 1:9-10). Considering the parasitic activity of Jacob's tribe, the king's qualms and his decision to tax the Israelites with forced labor may seem entirely justified; but because Joseph the stockjobber is Yahweh's saint, acting for the prosperity of Yahweh's chosen people, his behavior is beyond reproach, and Pharaoh is therefore presented as unredeemably evil. Come to think of it, it is perfectly appropriate that Pharaoh be seen as the biblical prototype of Hitler, who wanted to curtail Jewish influence in Germany and had reasons to fear that Jews might "join the ranks of his enemies."

The Holocaust cult

History is a study of causes and effects in human decisions and actions. But Israel sees its own history through the biblical prism of its chosenness, which makes it blind to its own responsibility in Gentile hostility. History is replaced by memory, the substance of legends and myths. That is why Yosef Yerushalmi argues in his book *Zakhor: Jewish History and Jewish Memory,* that Israel "chose myth over history." That applies to the Holocaust: "its image is being shaped, not at the historian's anvil, but in the novelist's crucible."[34]

When a historical tragedy cannot be put into a cause-effect perspective, it enters the realm of mythology. If it cannot be

---

33. Henry Miller, *Tropic of Cancer,* quoted in Josh Lambert, *Unclean Lips: Obscenity, Jews, and American Culture,* New York UP, 2013, p. 125.
34. Yosef Hayim Yerushalmi, *Zakhor: Jewish History and Jewish Memory* (1982), University of Washington Press, 2011, pp. 96-98.

analyzed on a rational mode, it is fantasized on a religious mode. And so Elie Wiesel can declare that the Holocaust "defies both knowledge and description," "cannot be explained nor visualized," is "never to be comprehended or transmitted," is "'noncommunicable".[35] "Whoever has not lived through the event can never know it. And whoever has lived through the event can never fully reveal it."[36]

Those who control Jewish public discourse forbid anyone to voice the possibility that Nazi persecution may have some causes in Jewish deeds (such as pushing England and America into war). Since the Jews are, by definition, blameless, Nazi violence against them is gratuitous and therefore a manifestation of pure, metaphysical evil: Hitler's hair lock and his moustache have replaced the devil's horns and tail in popular iconography.

In the realm of mythology, everything is possible. The mythographs' imagination is the limit. With the Holocaust, even the unimaginable, the absurd, the impossible, the miraculous must be believed. Here is, for example, how renowned professor Simon Baron-Cohen—a serious man compared to his cousin, actor Sacha Baron Cohen—starts his book *The Science of Evil: On Empathy and the Origins of Cruelty,* published in 2011 by Basic Books:

> "When I was seven years old, my father told me the Nazis had turned Jews into lampshades. Just one of those comments that you hear once, and the thought never goes away. To a child's mind (even to an adult's) these two types of things just don't belong together. He also told me the Nazis turned Jews into bars of soap. It sounds so unbelievable, yet it is actually true. I knew our family was Jewish, so this image of turning people into objects felt a bit close to home. My father also told me about one of his former girlfriends, Ruth Goldblatt, whose mother had survived a concentration camp. He had been introduced to the mother and was shocked to discover that her hands were reversed. Nazi scientists had severed Mrs. Goldblatt's hands, switched them around, and sewn them on again so that if she put her hands out palms down, her thumbs were on the outside and her little fingers were on the inside. Just one of the many 'experiments' they had conducted. I realized there was a paradox at the heart of human nature—people could objectify others—that my young mind was not yet ready to figure out. [...] Today, almost half a century after my father's revelations to me about the extremes of human

---

35. Norman Finkelstein, *The Holocaust Industry,* Verso, 2014, p. 47.
36. Quoted in Tim Cole, *Selling the Holocaust,* Routledge, 1999, p. 16.

behavior, my mind is still exercised by the same, single question: How can we understand human cruelty?"[37]

Against those who dare raise issues of credibility, Primo Levi, whose memoir *If this is a man* (1947) is "considered a pillar of Holocaust literature, alongside Elie Wiesel's *Night* and Anne Frank's Diary" (French Wikipedia), has provided an unbeatable answer. He wrote in *The Drowned and the Saved* (1988) how "The SS militiamen cynically enjoyed admonishing the prisoners" with such cynicism:

> "However this war may end, we have won the war against you; none of you will be left to bear witness, but even if someone were to survive, the world would not believe him. There will perhaps be suspicions, discussions, research by historians, but there will be no certainties, because we will destroy the evidence together with you. And even if some proof should remain and some of you survive, people will say that the events you describe are too monstrous to be believed: they will say that they are the exaggerations of Allied propaganda and will believe us, who will deny everything, and not you. We will be the ones to dictate the history of the Lagers."[38]

The Holocaust is now a world religion, requiring faith and banning critical inquiry. For the Jews, it is an efficient substitute for the cult of Yahweh. "The Jewish religion died 200 years ago. Now there is nothing that unifies the Jews around the world apart from the Holocaust," once remarked Yeshayahu Leibowitz.[39] A 2013 Pew Research poll on the theme "A Portrait of Jewish Americans" shows that, to the question "What's essential to being Jewish?" "Remembering the Holocaust" comes first for 73 percent of respondents, before "Caring about Israel," and "Observing Jewish laws."[40]

The Holocaust is a jealous god. There is no museum of the Vietnam War in the United States. To the Ukrainians who wished to commemorate "Holodomor"—the death of 7 to 8 millions of

37. Simon Baron-Cohen, *The Science of Evil: On Empathy and the Origins of Cruelty,* Basic Books, 2011. This passage is from the kindle édition, also on archive.org. The author has modified it in a 2012 edition by Basic Books, deleting the sentence "It sounds so unbelievable, yet it is actually true", and requalifying the soap and lampshade stories as "rumors". Yet he sticks to his belief in the surgical miracle of the reversed hands.

38. Primo Levi, *The Drowned and the Saved* (1988), 2013, Abacus, p. 2.

39. Reported by Uri Avnery in 2005, quoted in Gilad Atzmon, *The Wandering Who?* Zero Books, 2011, pp. 161-162.

40. "A Portrait of Jewish Americans," on www.pewforum.org.

them in 1932–1933 by a deliberately provoked famine against the kulaks resisting collectivization—Israeli president Shimon Peres advised, during a visit to Kiev on November 25, 2010: "Forget History."[41]

The Holocaust is eternal. "Today we are facing, plain and simple, a danger of annihilation. [...] People think that the Shoah [Holocaust] is over but it's not. It is continuing all the time," proclaimed Benzion Netanyahu, father of the Israeli Prime minister.[42] In Israel, explains Idith Zertal, "Auschwitz is not a past event but a threatening present and a constant option."[43]

The Holocaust is not just a religion for the Jews. In some European countries like France, it is becoming a State religion: worship is compulsory at school, blasphemy and heresy are severely punished. But even though the whole world is now "remembering the Holocaust" almost daily, not all men are equal in this cult. Just as Yahweh separated the chosen people from the rest of humankind, the Holocaust draws a line between the victims—"the people chosen for universal hatred," in Pinsker's words[44]—and their tormentors—virtually the rest of the world. And so the Holocaust cult turns out to be functionally interchangeable with ancient Yahwism: its primary function is to alienate the Jews from humankind, exile them into their morbid exceptionality, and at the same time terrorize them into submission to their elites. While Jews were told in the Tanakh to "fear Yahweh," they are now urged to fear the Holocaust.

---

41. Alexander Motyl, "Ukrainians and Jews...," April 15, 2011, worldaffairsjournal.org.
42. Quoted in Alan Hart, *Zionism: The Real Enemy of the Jews*, vol. 3: *Conflict Without End?* Clarity Press, 2010, p. 364.
43. Idith Zertal, *Israel's Holocaust and the Politics of Nationhood*, Cambridge UP, 2010, p. 4.
44. Leon Pinsker, *Auto-Emancipation, op. cit.*

8 - THE DEVIL'S TRICK
Unmasking the Psychopathic God of Israel

"The finest trick of the devil is to persuade you that he does not exist," wrote Charles Baudelaire (*Paris Spleen*). He was wrong: the devil's finest trick is to persuade you that he is God.

Do I believe in the existence of the devil? It depends on the definition. I believe that humans are under the influence of spiritual forces that they have engendered over the ages. Call it the "collective unconscious" if you will, or "egregores" if you care for such terminology. My argument in this essay does not require any metaphysical presupposition. It is about group psychology. From that standpoint, I regard Yahweh's impersonation of the Divine Creator as the greatest and most devastating deception ever played on the human race, a crime against humanity, if not against divinity. Yahweh's obscenity has not only atrophied billions of people's spiritual senses and philosophical insight; it has ultimately ruined God's reputation and led to Western godlessness. Still today, for example, Darwinian high priest Richard Dawkins can only make his dogmatic atheism sound plausible by first professing, correctly: "The God of the Old Testament is arguably the most unpleasant character in all fiction: jealous and proud of it; a petty, unjust, unforgiving control-freak; a vindictive, bloodthirsty ethnic cleanser; a misogynistic, homophobic, racist, infanticidal, genocidal, filicidal, pestilential, megalomaniacal, sadomasochistic, capriciously malevolent bully."[1]

I am neither a Darwinian nor an atheist. Simply, I have reached the conclusion that the Old Testament has nothing of any worth to tell about the origin and purpose of the universe, of life and of humanity, nor any useful guidance to provide in our search for truth, beauty and justice. I am not a gnostic either: if we are to believe their detractors, the early Gnostics taught that the God of the Old Testament was the evil demiurge that created the world from which Christ came to free us. I do not take Yahweh that seriously. On the contrary, I lament that he has been taken seriously by billions of people, Jews, Christians and Muslims.

---

1. Richard Dawkins, *The God Delusion,* Houghton Mifflin, 2006, p. 51.

I assume that Yahweh is, from the start, a character of fiction, but one that has gained tremendous influence over a huge portion of mankind, either directly or indirectly. Yahweh is a *persona* (a mask) invented by those who first pretended to speak in his name. Whether they believed in their own fiction is irrelevant. Yahweh is the voice of his self-proclaimed priests and prophets. By extension, Yahweh can designate this voice as it has been internalized collectively in the Jewish mind and, to a lesser degree, in the Christian and Islamic minds. I therefore name Yahweh both the essence of biblical ideology, and the symbol of Jewish Power. Being the essence of biblical ideology, Yahweh is also the essence of Jewishness. For the Jewish tradition is like a tree with many branches, some of them grafted from other trees; but the common root of all branches is the Tanakh. That is why understanding Yahweh is essential for understanding Jewishness, and Zionism in particular.

Yahweh has the character and the attributes of the devil as any decent person can imagine him. Although most Jews will not see it this way, that is the truth that can set them free. I could quote the Fourth Gospel's Jesus telling them: "You are of the devil, your father, and it is the desires of your father you want to accomplish. He was a murderer from the beginning" (John 8:44). But I am not arguing from a Christian viewpoint, for although I see the Gospel story as a kind of vaccine against the civilizational virus of the Tanakh, I also consider that, unless it could vomit the Old Testament, Christianity will remain forever infected by the virus it was meant to combat.

The Covenant with the Prince of this world

To examine the Bible without prejudice, we need to strip it of its religious aura. The category of "religion" fails to account for its strong grip on non-religious Jews. Most Israeli leaders, from Ben-Gurion to Netanyahu, are non-religious, but their worldview is profoundly biblical nonetheless. The most appropriate category to understand both the Tanakh and Jewishness is not "religion" but "covenant" (*berit* in Hebrew, meaning also "oath of allegiance"). Religious Jews think of Jewishness as a covenant between Jews and God, but the majority of the Jewish political, economic, cultural or criminal elites—members of B'nai B'rith, for example—think of it as a covenant between Jews.

The deal is simple: what the Jews must do is stick to themselves and never befriend or marry the Goyim—except to dupe them. If the Jews follow Yahweh's command of alienating themselves from the rest of humankind, in return, Yahweh promises to make them rule over humankind: "follow his ways, keep his statutes, his commandments, his customs, and listen to his voice," and Yahweh "will raise you higher than every other nation he has made"; "You will make many nations your subjects, yet you will be subject to none" (Deuteronomy 26:17-19 and 28:12). Yahweh's pledge, repeated by the prophets, is to submit all nations to the domination of Israel, and destroy those that resist. "Kings will fall prostrate before you, faces to the ground, and lick the dust at your feet," whereas "the nation and kingdom that will not serve you will perish" (Isaiah 49:23 and 60:12).

Christian societies have never come to the realization that the Mosaic covenant is nothing but a program for world domination by the Jewish nation. That is because it is written right under their nose, in a book whose malice they cannot recognize because they have been told it is the Word of God. It takes a free-thinker like H. G. Wells to see the biblical idea of the Chosen People for what it is: "a conspiracy against the rest of the world." In the books of the Bible, "you have the conspiracy plain and clear, [...] an aggressive and vindictive conspiracy. [...] It is not tolerance but stupidity to shut our eyes to their quality."[2]

Christians have always failed to see the biblical god's utter contempt for their own cherished nations, although it is repeated again and again: "All the nations are as nothing before him, for him they count as nothingness and emptiness" (Isaiah 40:17). The vulnerability of Christian societies to Israel's psychopathy is directly related to the Christians' self-inflicted blindness to the nature of the biblical god and of his project. The message conveyed by the Israelites to the Gentiles through the Old Testament is: "Our god is your god too, but he loves us and he hates you." Christians read that message, but repress it and convince themselves that Yahweh's hatred for the nations is really love. For their own misfortune, Christians worship a deity who hates them.

Because of their blindness to the Torah's conspiratorial project of world domination, Christians have also been duped by the

---

2. Herbert George Wells, *The Fate of Homo Sapiens*, 1939 (archive.org), p. 128.

Zionists' alleged nationalism, which in reality was an imperial project of *Pax Judaica* from the start. No one seemed to worry when, in 1962, David Ben-Gurion predicted that, within 25 years, Jerusalem "will be the seat of the Supreme Court of Mankind, to settle all controversies among the federated continents, as prophesied by Isaiah."[3] If Ben-Gurion wants to fulfill Isaiah, God bless him, thought the stupid Goyim, always ready to bite at the Holy Hook. After all, Christians have always seen Jerusalem at the center of the world.

Christian exegetes also never seem to have noticed that Yahweh's covenant—domination over the nations of the world in exchange for exclusive worship—is basically identical to the pact that the devil tried to tempt Jesus into:

> "the devil showed him all the kingdoms of the world and their splendor. And he said to him, 'I will give you all these, if you fall at my feet and do me homage.' Then Jesus replied, 'Away with you, Satan!'" (Matthew 4:8-10)

As a matter of fact, Satan is hardly distinguished from Yahweh in the Tanakh. He is called an "angel of Yahweh" in Numbers 22 and 32. In 2Samuel 24, Yahweh incites David to do evil, while the role is given to Satan in the same episode told in 1Chronicles 21, where Yahweh, "the angel of Yahweh", and Satan are used interchangeably.

Christ's teaching to "store up treasures in heaven" (Matthew 6:20) is alien to Yahweh. He is the Greedy One, who wants "the treasures of all the nations" amassed into his Jerusalem residence: "Mine is the silver, mine the gold!" (Haggai 2:8). "The wealth of all the surrounding nations will be heaped together: gold, silver, clothing, in vast quantity" (Zechariah 14:14). Interestingly, according to 1Kings 10:14, the amount of gold hoarded each year into Salomon's temple was "666 talents of gold"—the "number of the Beast" in Revelation 13:18! Make of it what you want.

The Mosaic covenant functions like a classic pact with the devil: Israel will get wealth and power in exchange for becoming Yahweh's "personal possession" (Exodus 19:5). The notion of a pact with the devil is especially relevant since, as I have shown in "Israel as One Man", Yahweh denies his worshippers an individual immortal soul, which is tantamount to claiming their souls for

---

3. David Ben-Gurion and Amram Ducovny, *David Ben-Gurion, In His Own Words*, Fleet Press Corp., 1969, p. 116.

himself. As Voltaire once noted, Yahweh forbade the Jews to screw their goats (Exodus 22:18), he instructed them on how to defecate in a hole (Deuteronomy 23:14), but he didn't give them "that most useful creed in a future life."[4]

Materialism is the most fundamental aspect of the Tanakh's anthropological model, and, although it has been superficially amended in later Judaic developments (the grafted branches), its sap runs very deep in Jewishness. According to the Jewish Virtual Library, the afterlife "is rarely discussed in Jewish life, be it among Reform, Conservative, or Orthodox Jews, [...] in marked contrast to the religious traditions of the people among whom the Jews have lived. [...] The Torah, the most important Jewish text, has no clear reference to afterlife at all."[5]

Jewish materialism is such a common stereotype that I need not insist. Rather, I want to suggest that the denial of—or lack of interest for—an other world is correlated to the oft-noted Jewish lack of reverence for truth: if there is no transcendent reality, no realm of Platonic Ideas, then truth means nothing, and the quest for it is pointless. Hence post-modernism The same reasoning applies to the search for beauty, art being also a quest for truth (*aletheia*) according to Heidegger, or for the Ideas behind the phenomena according to Schopenhauer: the artist's vocation is to idealize, whereas the Jewish impulse—derived from the Torah's commandment to destroy idols—is to desecrate ideals. Hence "modern art".

The prohibition of the knowledge of good and evil

Metaphysical materialism is also incompatible with the notion of good and evil and, ultimately, with the cultivation of moral standards. And so it is consistent that there is no trace in the Tanakh of a mythic struggle between Good and Evil, as in Persian monotheism, for instance. Happiness and misfortune, peace and war, health and sickness, abundance and famine, fertility and infertility, all have their unique and direct source in the capricious will of Yahweh. In his own words, "I form the light and I create the darkness, I make well-being, and I create disaster, I, Yahweh, do all these things" (Isaiah 45:7). Yahweh is not even good for Israel: he strikes alternately Israel and the enemies of Israel. He uses the nations to hit Israel, and Israel to destroy the nations.

---

4. Félix Niesche, *Voltaire antisémite,* KontreKulture, 2019.

5. www.jewishvirtuallibrary.org/afterlife-in-judaism

Machiavellian Yahweh even "hardens the hearts of [Israel's enemies], so that they would engage Israel in battle and thus come under the curse of destruction and so receive no quarter but be exterminated" (Joshua 11:20).

The relationship between Yahweh and his people is not moral, but strictly contractual and legalistic. According to Jewish scholar Yeshayahu Leibowitz, "The Torah does not recognize moral imperatives stemming from knowledge of natural reality or from awareness of man's duty to his fellow man. All it recognizes are Mitzvot, divine imperatives."[6] The hundreds of commandments are ends in themselves, not means to a higher moral consciousness. Such Jewish legalism stifles moral consciousness, as Gilad Atzmon pointed out.[7]

Naturally, there are moral precepts here and there in the Bible. But on the whole, it is a misunderstanding to believe that Yahweh expects from his people a moral superiority. The only criterion for approval by Yahweh is obedience to his arbitrary laws and to his antisocial or genocidal commands. To slaughter treacherously hundreds of prophets of Baal is good, because it is the will of Yahweh (1Kings 18). To show mercy to the king of the Amalekites is bad, because when Yahweh says, "kill everyone," he means "everyone" (1Samuel 15). How can we expect from a people whose mentality has been shaped by these narratives and their Talmudic commentaries, that they share the sense of good and evil that most other peoples regard as inherent to humanity? It is totally consistent for a future Israeli Prime Minister like Yitzhak Shamir (1986-1992) to declare (in 1943):

> "Neither Jewish ethics nor Jewish tradition can disqualify terrorism as a means of combat. We are very far from having any moral qualms as far as our national war goes. We have before us the command of the Torah, whose morality surpasses that of any other body of laws in the world: 'Ye shall blot them out to the last man.'"[8]

Our capacity to distinguish good from evil, right from wrong, in any particular situation is our moral conscience. But in the

---

6. Yeshayahu Leibowitz, *Judaism, Human Values and the Jewish State,* Harvard UP, 1995, p. 18.
7. Gilad Atzmon, "On IDF's Failure And Jewish Ethics," August 6, 2014, on www.gilad.online
8. "Document: Shamir on Terrorism (1943)," *Middle East Report* 152 (May/June 1988), on merip.org/1988/05/shamir-on-terrorism-1943/

Garden of Eden allegory, Yahweh forbids man access to "the tree of the knowledge of good and evil" (Genesis 2:17). The Hebrew word for "knowledge", *daat*, translates in Greek as *gnosis*, meaning inner awareness or insight rather than intellectual knowledge, so that "knowledge of good and evil" can be accurately translated as "moral conscience".

To contextualize that Genesis story, we must recall that Egyptian and Persian religions taught that immortality is the reward for the blameless life. Since immortality was synonymous with divinity, being immortal could be expressed as "being among the gods", or "being like the gods". But in the Hebrew Bible, it is the serpent, a liar and deceiver, who tempts Adam and Eve into eating from the tree of the knowledge of good and evil with the guarantee that, "the day you eat it you will not die," but "your eyes will open and you will be like gods, who know good and evil" (Genesis 3:5). The serpent speaks like the religious wisdom of the great religions. The Hebrew scribes can present him as a liar because, for them, immortality ("not dying") only makes sense physically: Yahweh, they claim, intended Adam and Eve to be physically immortal on earth, and provided no otherworld for their afterlife. From this materialistic standpoint, the scribes denounce the promise of immortality through knowledge of good and evil as deceptive, and implicitly portray the Babylonian, Persian and Egyptian gods as liars.

We have been educated for so many generations by this story, and are so used to assume that the serpent of Genesis is the satanic deceiver, that it is hard to see the Torah's message for what it really was: a direct attack against the higher religions and their teaching that knowledge and practice of good and evil is the way to the blessed afterlife. But, I ask, if trying to become like gods is a Luciferian impulse, why did the Greek Fathers of the Christian Church stress man's potential for deification (*theosis*) under the logic that "*God became man* so that *man* might become God"?

Lucifer, by the way, is the Latin translation of the Greek *Phosphoros* (light-bearer), traditionally applied to the Morning Star, the planet Venus. In Isaiah 14:12-17, the prophet blames the Babylonian king Nabuchodonosor II (605-562) for having tried to "rival the Most High," and sarcastically asks: "How did you come to fall from the heavens, *Daystar, son of Dawn* [Lucifer in the Latin Vulgate]?" Discarding the reference to the Babylonian king, Christian exegetes conflated "Lucifer" with the serpent of Genesis, and declared him the chief of the fallen angels, cast away from heaven because of his rebellious pride. Yet, if we look at Yahwism from the revisionist perspective I am advocating, Yahweh, the tribal god who usurped the majesty of the Supreme God, fits the Luciferian archetype. Yahweh is the infernal demon who wanted to be God instead of God.

As I explained earlier, there is a widely shared assumption among scholars that Yahweh was originally the volcano god of a nomadic people from Midian in northwestern Arabia, perhaps specialized in ironwork, and known as the Kenites. The Kenites (*Qayn*) bore the name of their ancestor Cain, and believed that, as a result of a curse upon their fratricidal ancestor, they must live as restless wanderers, but inspire fear to the people among whom they dwell by their Yahweh-given law of sevenfold vengeance—revised as seventy-sevenfold by Cain's descendant Lamek (Genesis 4:15-24). Such a tribe will inevitable develop, together with their vengeful spirit, a fear of being exterminated.

The jealous and murderous god

Yahweh is "the Jealous One" (Exodus 34:14). Although he is supposed to be the father of all national gods (Deuteronomy 32:8-9), he feels for them a murderous hatred, manifested in this command:

> "You must completely destroy all the places where the nations you dispossess have served their gods, on high mountains, on hills, under any spreading tree; you must tear down their altars, smash their sacred stones, burn their sacred poles, hack to bits the statues of their gods and obliterate their name from that place" (Deuteronomy 12:2-3).

Yahweh's pathological jealousy is demonstrated in his struggle with Baal, which I have mentioned in "Cryptic Jewishness." But it seems to have emerged as a permanent personality trait during his struggle with Assur, the national god of Assyria. In the oldest strata of the book of Isaiah, composed soon after the destruction of Israel by Assyria, Yahweh appears unable to cope with the frustration and humiliation, and consumed with the lust for revenge:

> "Yahweh Sabaoth has sworn it, 'Yes, what I have planned will take place, what I have decided will be so: I shall break Assyria [Assur] in my country, I shall trample on him on my mountains. Then his yoke will slip off them, his burden will slip from their

shoulders. This is the decision taken in defiance of the whole
world; this, the hand outstretched in defiance of all nations. Once
Yahweh Sabaoth has decided, who will stop him? Once he
stretches out his hand, who can withdraw it?'" (Isaiah 14:24-27).

Listen to Yahweh fuming after his defeat, and you hear a
dangerous narcissistic megalomaniac: "By my own self I swear it;
what comes from my mouth is saving justice, it is an irrevocable
word: All shall bend the knee to me, by me every tongue shall
swear" (Isaiah 45:23).

For the Egyptians, wrote German Egyptologist Jan Assmann,
"the gods are social beings, living and acting in 'constellations'."[9]
The peaceful cooperation of the gods warrants the harmonious
functioning of the universe. That is because the gods form the
organic body of the world. Such a conception, which Assmann
calls "cosmotheism", fosters a form of inclusive or convergent
monotheism: all gods are one, as the cosmos is one. By contrast,
the Bible's exclusive monotheism is the expression of Yahweh's
narcissistic sociopathy. That is why some Egyptians, according to
Plutarch (*Isis and Osiris,* 31), believed the god of the Jews to be
Seth, the donkey-headed god of the desert, famine, disorder and
war, expelled from the council of the gods for having murdered his
elder brother Osiris out of jealousy. Identifying the Jewish god
with Seth was their way of accounting for the aggressive
exclusiveness of Jewish religion.

Since the polytheisms of all great civilizations were cosmo-
theisms, they were translatable into one another. This was of
practical importance, because, Assmann writes, "contracts with
other states had to be sealed by oath, and the gods to whom this
oath was sworn had to be compatible. Tables of divine equiva-
lences were thus drawn up that eventually correlated up to six
different pantheons." And so, from the third millennium BC, the
translatability of various pantheons was crucial to international
diplomacy as well as trade. But Yahweh cannot be matched with
any other god; Yahwism "blocked intercultural translatability."[10]
And when Yahweh instructed his people, "You will make no pact
with them or with their gods" (Exodus 23:32 and 33:12), or "Do
not utter the names of their gods, do not swear by them, do not

---

9. Jan Assmann, *Of God and Gods: Egypt, Israel, and the Rise of Monotheism,*
University of Wisconsin Press, 2008, p. 47.
10. Jan Assmann, *Moses the Egyptian: The Memory of Egypt in Western
Monotheism,* Harvard UP, 1998, p. 3.

serve them and do not bow down to them" (Joshua 23:7), he was in effect preventing any relationship of trust with the neighboring peoples. The Jews must place their entire trust in Yahweh alone. Dietary laws are meant to prevent any socialization outside the tribe: "I shall set you apart from all these peoples, for you to be mine" (Leviticus 20:26).

What Israelites are asked, in fact, is to reproduce toward other nations Yahweh's murderous sociopathy toward other gods. The war code of Deuteronomy 20 commands to exterminate "any living thing" in the conquered cities of Canaan. In practice, the rule is extended to all people who resist the Israelites in their conquest. It was applied by Moses to the Midianites, save their young virgin girls (Numbers 31), as mentioned earlier ("The Crucifixion of the Goddess"). It was applied by Joshua to the Canaanite city of Jericho, where the Israelites "enforced the curse of destruction on everyone in the city: men and women, young and old, including the oxen, the sheep and the donkeys, slaughtering them all" (Joshua 6:21). In the city of Ai, the inhabitants were all slaughtered, twelve thousand of them, "until not one was left alive and none to flee. [...] When Israel had finished killing all the inhabitants of Ai in the open ground, and in the desert where they had pursued them, and when every single one had fallen to the sword, all Israel returned to Ai and slaughtered its remaining population." Women were not spared. "For booty, Israel took only the cattle and the spoils of this town" (Joshua 8:22-27). Then came the turns of the cities of Makkedah, Libnah, Lachish, Eglon, Hebron, Debir, and Hazor. In the whole land, Joshua "left not one survivor and put every living thing under the curse of destruction, as Yahweh, god of Israel, had commanded" (10:40).

A more cruel fate was reserved by King David for the Ammonites. In the city of Rabba, David gathered all the prisoners, and "cut them with saws, and with harrows of iron, and with axes," and "made them pass through the brick kiln: and thus did he unto all the cities of the children of Ammon" (2Samuel 12:31 and 1Chronicles 20:3). [11] Although it is not made explicit that dismembering and cremating the Ammonites in brick kilns was meant as a "burnt offering" to Yahweh, we are given to understand that he approved of it; he must have liked the smell.

---

11. I have conflated the two almost identical accounts of the same episode in 2Samuel 12:31 and 1Chronicles 20:3.

Yahweh's genocidal code of war was also applied by King Saul to the Amalekites. Yahweh ordered Saul to kill them all, "man and woman, babe and suckling, ox and sheep, camel and donkey," and Saul was punished for sparing their king Agag, whom Samuel had to butcher himself (1 Samuel 15). In the Jewish mind, such stories are not just half-forgotten tales of the past. Biblical history holds the keys to the present and to the future. Rabbinic exegetes have constantly referred to Israel's perceived enemies in biblical terms. Amalek, in particular, came to be associated with Rome and, from the fourth century onward, with Christians, or with the Armenians in particular. Amalek is also associated to Iran, because the villain of the Book of Esther, Haman, is said to be a descendant of the Amalekite king Agag. The hanging of Haman and his ten sons and the massacre of 75,000 Persians are often conflated in Jewish tradition with the extermination of the Amalekites and the brutal execution of their king. The Torah reading on the morning of Purim is taken from the account of the battle against the Amalekites, which ends with the conclusion that "Yahweh will be at war with Amalek generation after generation" (Exodus 17:16). [12] "Tradition holds that the Amalekites are the undying enemy of the Jews," explains Jeffrey Goldberg in a *New York Times* piece called "Israel's Fears, Amalek's Arsenal," adding: "I recently asked one of his advisers to gauge for me the depth of Mr. Netanyahu's anxiety about Iran. His answer: 'Think Amalek.'" [13]

This is just one more illustration of the Israeli leadership's biblical mind frame. Modern Israel is the son of Yahweh, and acts on the international scene in a biblical way, that is, with the same indifference and cruelty toward non-Jewish nations as Yahweh demanded of his people in the Bible.

Accusatory inversion

"The belief in a cruel god makes a cruel man," wrote Thomas Paine (*The Age of Reason*, 1794). Countless biblical stories demonstrate that Yahweh's spirit is the spirit of murder and theft. We read about the hero Samson, in Judges 14:19: "Then the spirit

---

12. Elliott Horowitz, *Reckless Rites: Purim and the Legacy of Jewish Violence,* Princeton UP, 2006, pp. 122-125, 4.
13. Jeffrey Goldberg, "Israel's Fears, Amalek's Arsenal," *New York Times,* May 16, 2009, on www.nytimes.com

of Yahweh seized on him. He went down to Ashkelon, killed thirty men there, took what they wore, [...] then burning with rage returned to his father's house."

Yahweh is the cruelest of gods, but he would have us believe that all other gods are abominations. Biblical history portrays all nations but Israel as repulsive idolaters. But they were not. The Egyptians had built the first great civilization; Herodotus believed that the Greek learned everything from them. They were a spiritual and peaceful people. The Assyrians were rather harsh, and their god Assur was no angel, yet even the Bible recognizes that they did not slaughter the defeated Israelites, but deported and resettled them. The Babylonians dealt with the Judeans the same way, even allowing them to keep their tradition and their cohesion, and to prosper on the riverbanks of the Euphrates.

Reversed accusation of genocidal intention is typical of Israel, a country with nuclear warheads pointed at Iran, whose leaders have always denied having any nuclear arsenal at all, but who hysterically urges the world to stop Iran's supposed nuclear military program and determination to erase Israel from the maps. It would be laughable if Israel were just paranoid. But Israel is the psychopath among nations, and that means a tremendous capacity to manipulate, intimidate, corrupt morally, and get what they want.

The psychopath projects his own cruelty and lust for power on others. And so he thinks that those who resist his domination are out to get him. Therefore he must destroy them. From the biblical point of view, nations must either recognize Israel's sovereignty, and their kings "fall prostrate before [Israel], faces to the ground" (Isaiah 49:23), or be destroyed. Yahweh told Israel that he has identified "seven nations greater and stronger than yourself," that "you must put under the curse of destruction," and not "show them any pity." As for their kings, "you will blot out their names under heaven" (Deuteronomy 7:1-2, 24). And we recall that, according to phony whistleblower Wesley Clark, son of Benjamin Jacob Kanne, the neocons had plans for destroying precisely seven nations—another proof that they are possessed by Yahweh.

Yahweh offers only two possible paths to Israel: domination, if Israel keeps Yahweh's Covenant of separateness, or annihilation, if Israel breaks the Covenant:

> "if you make friends with the remnant of these nations still living beside you, if you intermarry with them, if you mix with them and they with you, then know for certain that Yahweh your god will

stop dispossessing these nations before you, and for you they will
be a snare, a pitfall, thorns in your sides and thistles in your eyes,
until you vanish from this fine country given you by Yahweh your
god." (Joshua 23:12-14)

Dispossess others or be dispossessed, dominate or be
exterminated: Israel cannot think beyond that alternative. A good
illustration is David Ben-Gurion's paradoxical thinking in the early
1960s. Discussing Kennedy's determination to stop Dimona,
Avner Cohen writes in *Israel and the Bomb* (1998): "Imbued with
lessons of the Holocaust, Ben-Gurion was consumed by fears of
security [...]. Anxiety about the Holocaust reached beyond Ben-
Gurion to infuse Israel's military thinking."[14] Yet in the very same
period (1962), Ben-Gurion seriously considered that, within 25
years, Jerusalem "will be the seat of the Supreme Court of
Mankind."[15]

Yahweh Molech

To understand Yahwism—and thereby Jewishness and
Zionism—it is important to know the background of its infancy,
which has nothing to do with the birth of universal monotheism.

We are told that Yahweh is the God who abolished human
sacrifice, when after ordering Abraham to tie his son Isaac, he held
back Abraham's arm and contented himself with a ram (Genesis
22). Yet long after Abraham, some Israelite leaders seemed
unaware of that great progress, and sacrificed their own children as
burnt offering to Yahweh: Jephthah in Judges 11:29-40, Hiel in
1Kings 16:34, King Azaz in 2Kings 16:3, and King Manasseh in
2Kings 21:6. Not to mention the 32 holocausted Midianite virgins
in Numbers 31.

For his alleged abolition of human sacrifice, Yahweh has been
compared favorably with the Canaanite god Molech or Moloch, to
whom firstborn infants were ritually sacrificed. But biblical
scholars like Thomas Römer speculate that Molech was in fact
none other than Yahweh himself. One of his arguments is that the
noun *mlk*, vocalized as Molek in the Masoretic text (the ninth-
century Tanakh that introduced vowels into the Hebrew script), but
Melek in the Greek Septuagint, is identical to the Hebrew word for

---

14. Seymour Hersh, *The Samson Option: Israel's Nuclear Arsenal and American Foreign Policy*, Random House, 1991, p. 141.
15. Ben-Gurion and Ducovny, *David Ben-Gurion, In His Own Words, op. cit.*, p. 116.

"king", *melek* or *melech* (*malik* in Arabic), applied more than fifty times to Yahweh. The expression *Yahweh melech,* "Yahweh is king," is found in Psalms 10 and still in use in Jewish religious songs.

The second argument for Molek's ancient identity with Yahweh comes from the Leviticus prohibition of infant sacrifices: the prohibition proves the practice, and in this case, it proves that sacrifices were made in Yahweh's name and in Yahweh's sanctuary: "You will not allow any of your children to be sacrificed to Molech, thus *profaning the name of your God*" (18:21); "Anyone [...] who gives any of his children to Molech, will be put to death, [for] he has *defiled my sanctuary and profaned my holy name*" (20:2-5). Jeremiah 7:30-31 confirms that "the people of Judah" continued "to burn their sons and daughters [...] *in the Temple that bears my name*, to defile it." Although Yahweh declares it to be "a thing I never ordered, that had never entered my thoughts," the very fact that a scribe wrote this indicates that the people who sacrificed their children did claim that it was required by Yahweh. In fact, Yahweh is caught lying, since he admits to Ezekiel, around the same period:

> "And for this reason I gave them laws that were not good and judgements by which they could never live; and I polluted them with their own offerings, making them sacrifice every first-born son in order to fill them with revulsion, so that they would know that I am Yahweh" (Ezekiel 20:25-26).

In Exodus we learn that every first-born male, human or animal, was originally sacrificed on the eighth day after birth:

> "You will give me the first-born of your children; you will do the same with your flocks and herds. For the first seven days the first-born will stay with its mother; on the eighth day you will give it to me" (Exodus 22:28-29).

Since animals were offered to Yahweh as holocausts from time immemorial, the implication is that the first-born son of every Jewish family had once been sacrificed as a holocaust too.

According to biblical record, it is King Josiah (640-609 BC) who abolished the sacrifices of children, "so that no one could pass his son or daughter through the fire of sacrifice to Molech" (2Kings 23:10). But according to Römer, it is only in the Persian era that human sacrifices became taboo.[16] They were substituted by animal offerings, as we learn from Exodus and Leviticus:

> "All that first issues from the womb belongs to me: every male, every first-born of flock or herd. But the first-born donkey you will redeem with an animal from the flock; if you do not redeem it, you must break its neck. All the first-born of your sons you will redeem, and no one will appear before me empty-handed." (Exodus 34:19-20; also in 13:11-13 and in Leviticus 27:26)[17]

As in a palimpsest, we read here two things: in ancient Yahwism, the first-born male of humans and beasts were sacrificed to Yahweh, while in the reformed Judaism elaborated during the Exile, the first-born male of humans was "redeemed" by an animal offering.

The Lord of foreskins

It was also in Babylon that the Levites introduced the Abrahamic covenant of circumcision: "As soon as he is eight days old, every one of your males, generation after generation, must be circumcised" (Genesis 17:12).

In religious reforms, innovations are presented as the restoration of ancient and lost practices. And so the Levites introduced their new rite as a pre-Mosaic commandment. For that purpose they invented Abraham, who was unknown in pre-exilic Yahwism. As a figure born in Mesopotamia and given the Promised Land in inheritance, he is the personification of the program of the priestly caste exiled in Babylon.

In pre-exilic Yahwism, every first-born male was to be offered to Yahweh on the eighth day of his life (Exodus 22:28-29), and in post-exilic Judaism, every newborn male was to be circumcised on the eighth day. That parallel is a strong clue that circumcision was introduced as another substitute for sacrifice.

Circumcision was not a novelty. It was unknown in Mesopotamia, but was practiced in ancient Egypt on fourteen-year-old boys. Circumcision of prepubescent or adolescent males was also practiced in Syria, but not uniformly: the Philistines, an Indo-European people from the Aegean world (they gave their name to

---

16. Thomas Römer, *The Invention of God,* Harvard UP, 2015, pp. 137-138.

17. Numbers 18:15-17 declares redeemable the "first-born of an unclean animal" (unfit for consumption), but forbids to redeem "the first-born of cow, sheep and goat," which are destined for the consumption of the Levites.

Palestine), are called "the uncircumcised" in the Bible: David offered two hundred foreskins of slaughtered Philistines to Saul as bride token for his daughter (1Samuel 18).

Circumcision rites practiced in ancient Judea before the Babylonian Exile were probably consistent with the practices of neighboring peoples, which would explain why it is not even mentioned in the Mosaic covenant. According to the Book of Joshua, it is only when the Hebrews had settled in the Promised Land of Canaan that "Joshua made flint knives and circumcised the Israelites on the Hill of Foreskins" (5:3).

The Yahwist priestly caste who legislated over the Judean community in Mesopotamia may have valued circumcision as a marker of ethnic identity, in a land where nobody else practiced it. But why would they introduce the radical novelty of circumcision on newborn babies? Continuity with the ancient rite of sacrificing the first-born on the eighth day is one explanation. But I suggest a more sinister one: by eighth-day circumcision, Yahweh's covenant is not only "marked in [every Jew's] flesh as a covenant in perpetuity" (Genesis 17:13), it is impressed into the deepest and unreachable layers of their subconscious, through symbolic castration and traumatic pain. Unlike the child or teenager, the newborn baby is incapable of elaborating any positive meaning to the violence done to him, and to integrate it consciously as part of his identity. Eight days after emerging from his mother's womb—a trauma in itself, but a natural one—what he needs is to build an unshakable trust in the benevolence of those who welcomed him into this world. The trauma of circumcision alters his relationship to the world in a deep and permanent way.

Because infants cannot speak, rabbis who defend the tradition speak in their place to minimize their physical pain. But according to Professor Ronald Goldman, author of *Circumcision, the Hidden Trauma,* scientific studies prove the neurological impact of infant circumcision, for which no anesthesia is used. Behavioral changes observed after the operation, including sleep disorders and inhibition in mother-child bonding, are signs of a post-traumatic stress syndrome.[18] During the ceremony of *brit milah,* the mother is normally kept away from the scene, and the baby's shrieks of agony are partly covered by the cheers of the men—a message in itself. But when mothers happen to hear them, they suffer enduring

---

18. Ronald Goldman, *Circumcision, the Hidden Trauma,* Vanguard, 1997.

trauma themselves, as can be read on the Circumcision Resource Center web page "Mothers Who Observed Circumcision": "The screams of my baby remain embedded in my bones and haunt my mind," says Miriam Pollack. "His cry sounded like he was being butchered. I lost my milk." Nancy Wainer Cohen: "I will go to my grave hearing that horrible wail, and feeling somewhat responsible." Elizabeth Pickard-Ginsburg:

> "I don't feel I can recover from it. [...] We had this beautiful baby boy and seven beautiful days and this beautiful rhythm starting, and it was like something had been shattered! [...] When he was first born there was a tie with my young one, my newborn. And when the circumcision happened, in order to allow it I had to cut off the bond. I had to cut off my natural instincts, and in doing so I cut off a lot of feelings towards Jesse. I cut it off to repress the pain and to repress the natural instinct to stop the circumcision."[19]

It is reasonable to assume, at least as a working hypothesis, that the trauma of circumcision at the age of eight days leaves a deep psychological scar. Being abused by adults can trigger in very young children's mind a mechanism known as dissociation. The pain, the terror, the rage, and the memory of the experience, will be pushed out of ordinary consciousness, and form, so to speak, a separate personality, with a life of its own and a tendency to ooze into the normal personality. The idea of the wickedness of parental figures is so devastating that the repressed anger will be deviated away from them—in this case, away from the Jewish community as a collective parent. Is it farfetched to suppose a causal link between the trauma of eighth-day circumcision and the fact that Jews tend to be incapable of seeing the abuse perpetrated on them by their own community, and instead see the rest of the world as a constant threat?

Could it be that the trauma of eighth-day circumcision has created a special predisposition, a pre-programmed paranoia that impairs the Jews' capacity to relate and react rationally to certain situations? Was *brit milah* ("covenant by circumcision") invented some twenty-three centuries ago as a kind of ritual trauma designed to enslave mentally millions of people, an unbreakable "covenant" carved into their heart in the form of an incurable subconscious terror that can at any time be triggered by code-words such as "Holocaust" or "anti-Semitism"?

---

19. "Mothers who Observed Circumcision," on www.circumcision.org/ mothers.htm

It has been suggested that traumas can be transmitted "epigenetically". According to a study conducted under the direction of Rachel Yehuda at Mount Sinai Hospital in New York, "the trauma of the Holocaust is transmitted genetically" by "epigenetic heredity";[20] May I suggest to Professor Yehuda that he now conduct a study on the epigenetics of eighth-day circumcision?

Baruch Spinoza said that, "circumcision alone will preserve the Jewish nation for ever."[21] That explains the fierce resistance of Jewish authorities against every attempt to ban it, from Roman Emperor Hadrian (117-138) to the recent Icelandic bill successfully fought by European Jewish organizations as "anti-Semitic".[22] It must be said that opposition against infant circumcision has often come from enlightened Jews. Abraham Geiger (1810-1874), one of the founders of Reformed Judaism in Germany, advocated giving up this "barbarian and bloody rite." But, on this issue as on all others, it is always "the more ethnocentric elements—one might term them the radicals—who have determined the direction of the Jewish community and eventually won the day" (Kevin MacDonald).[23] To protect their bloody rite from criticism, Jewish activists have managed to normalize it in England and North America from the 1840s to the 1960s, under fraudulent medical reasons—an amazing demonstration of their power over Christian civilization.

20. Tori Rodrigues, "Descendants of Holocaust Survivors Have Altered Stress Hormones," *Scientific American*, March 1, 2015, on www.scientificamerican.com.
21. Spinoza, *Theological-political treatise,* 3.12, Cambridge UP, 2007, p. 55.
22. David Rosenberg, "Iceland drops proposed circumcision ban," April 30, 2018, on www.israelnationalnews.com/News/News.aspx/245193
23. Kevin MacDonald, *Cultural Insurrections,* Occidental Press, 2007, pp. 90-91.

9 – THE FREUDIAN COMPLEX
Sigmund Freud, Sexual Abuse, and Cover-Up

In the last few years, there have been lots of news reports, documentary films (e.g., Yoland Zauberman's "M"), and articles about sexual abuse of children in Orthodox Jewish communities. In March 2017, for instance, *Haaretz* reported that the Israeli police arrested 22 ultra-Orthodox Jews for sex crimes against minors and women,[1] and in July 2019 *The Times of Israel* reported that "Deputy Health Minister Yaakov Litzman was alleged to have improperly intervened to aid at least 10 sex offenders from Israel's ultra-Orthodox community."[2] In 2015, Jewish attorney Michael Lesher wrote *Sex Abuse,* Shonda *and Concealment in Orthodox Jewish Communities,* to document

> "the dismal history of how far too many of those cases have been assiduously concealed both from the public and from the police: how influential rabbis and community leaders have sided with the alleged abusers against their victims; how victims and witnesses of sexual abuse have been pressured, even threatened, not to turn to secular law enforcement for help; how autonomous Jewish 'patrols,' displacing the role of official police in some large and heavily religious Jewish neighbourhoods, have played an inglorious part in the history of cover-ups; […] how some Jewish communities have even succeeded in manipulating law enforcement officials to protect suspected abusers."[3]

This calls to mind the story of how Freud, having stumbled upon the widespread reality of child abuse among his mostly Jewish clientele, covered it up with the theory that all little girls desire their fathers' penis and all little boys dream of screwing their mothers—and named his theory after a Gentile myth.

---

1. Nir Hasson and Yair Ettinger, "Israel Police Arrest 22 ultra-Orthodox Jews for Sex Crimes Against Minors and Women," March 27, 2017, on www.haaretz.com

2. Sam Sokol, "Child advocates blast systemic failures in Israel's handling of sex abuse cases," July 3, 2019, on www.timesofisrael.com

3. Michael Lesher, *Sex Abuse,* Shonda *and Concealment in Orthodox Jewish Communities,* McFarland, 2014.

Freud's Assault on Truth

The story has been told by Jeffrey Masson in *The Assault on Truth: Freud's Suppression of the Seduction Theory* (1984).[4] In 1895 and 1896, Freud, listening to his neurotic and hysterical patients, became convinced that most of them had endured traumatic sexual abuse in their childhood. The traumatic origin of "hysteria" (an overused diagnosis in those days) had already been discussed by neurologists, including Jean-Martin Charcot, whose conferences Freud had attended in Paris, and Hermann Oppenheim, who published in Berlin in 1889 a treatise on traumatic neuroses. Yet psychological traumas of sexual nature were rarely discussed openly. On the other hand, there were medical publications, known to Freud, documenting the frequency of violence on children, including sexual assaults, but they focused on the physical consequences. In April 1896, confident to have made a major breakthrough in psychiatry, Freud presented his findings to the Society for Psychiatry and Neurology in Vienna, his first major public address to his peers. His lecture met with total silence. According to Masson, Freud was urged never to publish it, lest his reputation be damaged beyond repair. He found himself isolated, but nevertheless published his paper, "The Aetiology of hysteria."

Freud's conclusions are drawn from 18 cases studies (6 men and 12 women), all of which, he claims, bear his general thesis:

> "I therefore put forward the thesis that at the bottom of every case of hysteria there are one or more occurrences of premature sexual experience, occurrences which belong to the earliest years of childhood but which can be reproduced through the work of psycho-analysis in spite of the intervening decades. I believe that this is an important finding, the discovery of a *caput Nili* in neuropathology."

> "Sexual experiences in childhood consisting in stimulation of the genitals, coitus-like acts, and so on, must therefore be recognized, in the last analysis, as being the traumas which lead to a hysterical reaction to events at puberty and to the development of hysterical symptoms."

Freud suggests that this conclusion applies not only to hysteria but to most neuroses. He assumes that children who assault

---

4. Jeffrey Masson, *The Assault on Truth: Freud's Suppression of the Seduction Theory,* Farrar Strauss & Giroud, 1984.

sexually other children do so as a result of having been sexually abused themselves: "children cannot find their way to acts of sexual aggression unless they have been seduced previously."

However, one year after this article, Freud decided that he had made a mistake in believing his patients. He determined that what he had taken for repressed memories of sexual abuse, were in fact "phantasies." For the rest of his life, he would keep telling how he overcame his error and discovered that, "these phantasies were intended to cover up the auto-erotic activity of the first years of childhood, to embellish it and raise it to a higher plane. And now, from behind the phantasies, the whole range of a child's sexual life came to light" (*The History of the Psychoanalytic Movement,* 1919).

From the standpoint of Freud's earlier theory—which he euphemistically called the "seduction theory"—his new theory of spontaneous infantile sexual fantasies can be seen as a projection, not unlike sex offenders' tendency to blame their victims: the patients themselves are now accused of both sexual passion and murderous fantasies toward their parents. By repressing these self-generated impulses, says Freudian orthodoxy, they have created their own neuroses which may, in hysterics, take the forms of false memories of abuse.

Thirty-five years later, Freud's most gifted disciple, once president of the International Psychoanalytical Association, stumbled on the same realization that Freud had shared in "The Aetiology of hysteria." Sandor Ferenczi wrote in his diary in July 1932 that the Oedipus complex could well be "the result of real acts on the part of adults, namely violent passions directed toward the child, who then develops a fixation, not from desire [as Freud maintained], but from fear. 'My mother and father will kill me if I don't love them, and identify with their wishes.'" Overcoming his apprehension of Freud's reaction, Ferenczi presented his conclusions before the 12th International Psycho-Analytic Congress in a lecture titled "Confusion of tongues between the adults and the child." His paper contains a number of important ideas confirmed by later research, such as the victims' psychological "identification with the aggressor," or "introjection": "the aggressor disappears as external reality and becomes intrapsychic instead of extrapsychic," so that even the guilt feelings of the aggressor are introjected. Ferenczi hypothesized that helplessness causes the victim to empathize with the aggressor, a process today known as the "Stockholm syndrome".

"Extreme adversity, especially fear of death," may also trigger a premature development, for which Ferenczi uses the metaphor of "a fruit that ripens or becomes sweet prematurely when injured by the beak of a bird, or of the premature ripening of wormy fruit. Shock can cause a part of the person to mature suddenly, not only emotionally but intellectually as well." Such traumatic maturation happens at the expense of psychological integration, and Ferenczi brings in the notion of a personality split: "there can be no shock, no fright, without traces of a personality split." Reflecting on a patient who cannot remember having been raped but dreams of it ceaselessly, Ferenczi writes in his personal diary: "I know from other analyses that a part of our being can 'die' and while the remaining part of our self may survive the trauma, it awakens with a gap in its memory. Actually it is a gap in the personality, because not only is the memory of the struggle-to-the-death effaced, but all other associatively linked memories disappear... perhaps forever."

This observation is consistent with the findings of French medical doctor and psychologist Pierre Janet (1859-1947), whose work has long been overshadowed by Freudian psychology but has generated increased interest since the 1980s. Janet theorized the first model of "dissociative identity disorders," now included in the *Diagnostic and Statistical Manual of Mental Disorders.* In *Les Névroses* (1909), Janet wrote: "Just as synthesis and association are the great characteristics of all normal psychological operations, so dissociation is the essential characteristic of all diseases of the mind." Dissociation accounts for the evolution of traumatic memories, composed of physiological, sensory, affective, and cognitive experiences, which Janet calls "idées fixes." These fragmented aspects of the experience do not allow a real memory to integrate the biography of the subject, and instead develop into separate psychic entities, which nevertheless interfere with the main personality. In the most severe cases, it can develop into schizophrenia or multiple personalities.

Ferenczi's lecture "Confusion of tongues" met with the same disapproval from members of the Psycho-Analytic Association as Freud's "Aetiology of hysteria" had met from Viennese psychiatrists. Ferenczi was ostracized by Freud and his sectarian disciples, and his paper was never translated in English for the *International*

Journal of Psycho-Analysis, as was customary. He died a few years later, a broken man.

The hidden fault of the father

This story raises two questions: First, what is it that made Freud change his mind in the first place, and made him shun Ferenczi's work thirty years later? Secondly, and more importantly, why was Freud's theory so successful, despite being long proven scientifically flawed, and its therapeutic value baseless?

On the first question, Masson shares his "conviction that what Freud had uncovered in 1896—that, in many instances, children are the victims of sexual violence and abuse within their own families—became such a liability that he literally had to banish it from his consciousness." This theory has been challenged, and Masson has been criticized for exaggerating the negative reaction to Freud's seduction theory.[5] All that can be said with confidence is that his paper didn't bring him the instant fame he expected.

An important element to take into account is that false memories of sexual abuse do happen. Overwhelming evidence exist that so-called "regressive" psychotherapies can produce very vivid false memories, which can in themselves have a traumatic impact on the patient.[6] Freud had objective reasons to come to doubt the reality of his patients' childhood "recovered" memories obtained during the quasi-hypnotic therapy sessions that he originally practiced, under the influence of Charcot. He was also right to conclude that memories are always reconstructions to some extent.

Nevertheless, not all of his patients' memories of sexual traumas were produced under hypnosis, and many of them were probably based on actual scenes of abuse. Ferenczi was right to assume that sexual abuses on children are a widespread and devastating reality, and that the memories of them can be partly buried through a split in the personality. When dealing with traumatic experiences, the issue of the reliability of memories is a very delicate one that cannot be solved one way or another in a reductive and dogmatic way. What can and must be reproached to

5. Allen Esterson, "The Myth of Freud's Ostracism by the Medical Community in 1896-1905", on www.esterson.org/Myth_of_Freuds_ostracism.htm
6. Elizabeth Loftus and Katherine Ketcham, *The Myth of Repressed Memory: False Memories and Allegations of Sexual Abuses,* St. Martin's Press, 1994.

Freud is to have simply negated the problem, in his desperate search for a simple and revolutionary theory.

Masson takes other factors into account. He believes that Freud was influenced by the wacky otorhinolaryngologist Wilhelm Fliess, unhappy inventor of the "nasal reflex neuroses," with whom Freud had developed a very peculiar emotional bond (incidentally, Fliess' son Robert would later write on sexual abuse and hint of his own abuse by his father). Masson is the editor of the unexpurgated version of Freud's letters to Fliess, which provide unique information on the way Freud elaborated his theories.[7] Yet at the end of his fascinating investigation, Masson admits that the full explanation for Freud's sudden conversion eludes him.

Additional insight has been supplied by two books published almost simultaneously (1979), one in French and one in German, both translated in English in 1982: Marie Balmary, *Freud and the Hidden Fault of the Father,* and Marianne Krüll, *Freud and His Father.* Both draw extensively from Freud's letters to Fliess, which document how Freud was led to his theoretical about-face by his introspective self-analysis. Balmary and Krüll point out that Freud undertook this self-analysis just after the death of his father Jacob. On November 2, 1896, ten days after his father's death, Freud wrote to Fliess about a dream he had the night before the funeral, in which appeared a sign saying, "You are requested to close the eyes," which he interpreted as referring to "one's duty to the dead." Yet on February 11, 1897, after mentioning that forced oral sex on children can result in neurotic symptoms, he adds: "Unfortunately, my own father was one of these perverts and is responsible for the hysteria of my brother (all of whose symptoms are identifications) and those of several younger sisters. The frequency of this circumstance often makes me wonder."

The following summer, he went through a depressive episode, and wrote on July 7: "I still do not know what has been happening to me. Something from the deepest depths of my own neurosis set itself against any advance in the understanding of the neuroses, and you have somehow been involved in it." Soon after, September 21, he announced to his friend: "I want to confide in you immediately the great secret that has been slowly dawning on me in the last few months. I no longer believe in my *neurotica* [his seduction theory]." He gave as one explanation, "the surprise that in all

---

7. Most relevant excerpts are on ww3.haverford.edu/psychology/ddavis/ffliess.html

cases, the father, not excluding my own, had to be accused of being perverse." In the next letter, October 3, he wrote confidently that in the case of his own neurosis, "the old man plays no active part." Finally, October 15, he referred to the Oedipus story: "A single idea of general value dawned on me. I have found, in my own case too, [the phenomenon of] being in love with my mother and jealous of my father, and I now consider it a universal event in early childhood."

Balmary and Krüll independently build a strong case that Freud backed off from a theory that tarnished the ideal image of the father he was grieving. After his father's death, Freud felt constrained by a mandate that he was unable to resist, and hence, "dutiful son that he was, took the guilt upon his own shoulders with the help of his Oedipus theory" (Krüll 179). Balmary and Krüll introduce into the equation a recent biographical discovery of Jacob Freud's less than perfect behavior; a forgotten second wife named Rebecca, who mysteriously disappeared, possibly by suicide, at the time of Jacob's marriage with his third wife, the beautiful Amelia Nathansohn, half his age and already pregnant of Sigmund (a fact Jacob tried to conceal by falsifying Sigmund's date of birth). In light of post-Freudian developments in transgenerational depth-psychology,[8] it seems possible that Freud had from early age an intuitive sense of a "hidden fault of the father" linked to his own identity, which may have combined with memories of his father's sexual abuse on himself and his brother and sisters. During his self-analysis at the age of forty, the whole thing came knocking at the door of his consciousness, but he finally surrendered to the subconscious imperative to "close the eyes." To cover-up the menacing truth of his father's faults, Freud invented the Oedipus complex, charging children themselves of "polymorphous perversion."

Balmary points out that, in his personal identification with the hero Oedipus (who solved the riddle of the Sphinx), Freud truncated the myth. According to Greek tragedians, Oedipus' father Laius was cursed by the gods for seducing a young teenage boy and leading to his suicide. Then, frightened by the oracle's prophecy that he would be killed by his own son if he conceived one, Laius had his newborn son abandoned in the forest, "ankles pierced by the middle with iron spikes" (Euripides, *The*

---

8. Nicolas Abraham and Maria Török, *L'Écorce et le Noyau,* Aubier, 1978.

Phoenician Maidens). Thus, in the complete myth, Oedipus' predestination to kill his father and marry his mother is not determined by his own impulses, but by the fault of his father. For Balmary, Freud's ignorance of this part of the myth reveals and symbolizes his own blind spot, his failure to discover the secret guilt of the father—both his own father and, by consequence, the fathers of his neurotic and hysterical patients.

The "dark, emotional powers" of Jewishness

Neither Masson not Balmary deal with the Jewish aspect of the issue. Marianne Krüll hints that the father's mandate to "close the eyes" was a question of "filial piety on which, ultimately, the entire Jewish tradition is based" (Krüll 178), but, although Jewish herself, she does not insist on that aspect.

For an interesting reflection on the Jewish hidden background of the Oedipus complex, we can turn to the very stimulating book of John Murray Cuddihy, *The Ordeal of Civility*.[9] The author points out that Freud had been fascinated by Sophocles' play *Oedipus Rex* from his adolescence. When he saw it played in 1885, it made again a deep and mysterious impression on him. Twelve years later, he wrote to Fliess (October 15, 1897) that he has found, with his new theory of universal repressed wishes of incest and parricide, the explanation for "the gripping power of *Oedipus Rex*." In other words, comments Cuddihy, Freud "proposes a theory to explain the play's power over him and to make 'intelligible' why he should identify so deeply with its hero, Oedipus. It is in the course of that effort that the core of the theory of psychoanalysis is born."

But then, Cuddihy suggests that Freud failed to see the real origin of his fascination with *Oedipus Rex*. What had resonated deeply in him from the time he first read *Oedipus Rex* was not so much the general plot of the play (the hero killing his father and marrying his mother), as the circumstances in which Oedipus killed his father: coming down a narrow road, Oedipus was rudely ordered to step aside by the herald of the king, then was struck on the head by the king himself. Enraged, Oedipus slew the king, his herald and the rest of his retinue except one. This story—not acted but narrated in the play—bears an uncanny resemblance with

---

9. John Murray Cuddihy, *The Ordeal of Civility: Freud, Marx, Lévi-Strauss, and the Jewish Struggle with Modernity*, Delta Book, 1974 (archive.org), pp. 48-57.

another story that had made a lasting impression on Freud a few years earlier, as he explained in *The Interpretation of Dreams.* This is a story that his father, a shtetl Jew from Moravia—where Sigmund was born—, had told him when he was ten or twelve years old,

> "to show how much better things were now than they had been in his days. 'When I was a young man,' he said, 'I went for a walk one Saturday in the streets of your birthplace; I was well dressed, and had a new cap on my head. A Christian came up to me and with a single blow knocked off my cap into the mud and shouted: 'Jew! get off the pavement!' 'And what did you do?' I asked. 'I went into the roadway and picked up my cap,' was his quiet reply. This struck me as unheroic conduct on the part of the big, strong man who was holding the little boy by the hand. I had contrasted this situation with another which befitted my feelings better: the scene in which Hannibal's father, Hamilcar Barca, made his boy swear before the household altar to take vengeance on the Romans. Ever since that time Hannibal had had a place in my fantasies."

Freud, Cuddihy argues, had experienced shame of his father, and "to be ashamed of a father is a kind of 'moral parricide'"; "Freud presumably experienced not only this rage and shame, but guilt about the rage and shame. He quickly 'censored' these unacceptable feelings, unacceptable to a dutiful son ostensibly proud of his father; he 'repressed' them. Years later he encounters Sophocles' tragedy and it lays a spell on him."

Still later, after his father's death, he rationalized this spell with a universal theory that discharged him from further inquiry into his own family story. "But the *idée fixe* that Oedipus was to become for Freud," Cuddihy maintains, "hinges on a small detail (small, but structurally indispensable for the action of the story) that Freud never mentions in all the countless times he retells the 'legend': [...] a social insult, a discourtesy on the road, stemming from someone in a position of social superiority (King Laius to the unknown wayfarer, Oedipus, just as the Christian in Freiberg who forced Jacob Freud into the gutter)." According to Cuddihy, the supposedly universal "Oedipus Complex" that Freud thought he discovered was in reality the veil of a characteristically Jewish complex of his time.

Even if we judge that thesis overstrained (it is questionable how the phantasies of avenging and killing the father could merge), we can appreciate how Cuddihy draws attention to the fact that Freud's father—the father whom he felt compelled to exculpate, but toward whom he nevertheless experienced a murder wish—was a Jewish father recently immigrated from Yiddishland into the heart of European civilization.

Freud's disciple and first biographer Ernest Jones remarks that Freud "felt himself to be Jewish to the core, and evidently it meant a great deal to him."[10] Books dealing specifically with Freud's Jewishness (such as Moshe Gresser, *Dual Allegiance: Freud as a Modern Jew,* 1994) can rely on several statements made by Freud himself, either in private correspondence or in Jewish environment. In the preface for the Hebrew translation of *Totem and Taboo,* for example, asking himself rhetorically what is Jewish in his work, Freud answered: "a very great deal, and probably its very essence."[11] In a speech prepared for delivery at the B'nai B'rith Lodge in Vienna in 1926, Freud explained his motivation for joining thirty years earlier (1897):

> "Whenever I have experienced feelings of national exaltation, I have tried to suppress them as disastrous and unfair, frightened by the warning example of those nations among which we Jews live. But there remained enough to make the attraction of Judaism and the Jews irresistible, many dark emotional powers all the stronger the less they could be expressed in words, as well as the clear consciousness of an inner identity, the familiarity of the same psychological structure. [...] So I became one of you."[12]

This statement is an excellent illustration of what Cuddihy calls "the ordeal of civility," the struggle of every Jew who wishes to assimilate yet feels unable to overcome the "dark emotional powers" of his ancestral Jewishness, with its implicit imperative *not to* assimilate. Jewishness has much to do with what Ivan Boszormenyi-Nagy calls those "invisible loyalties" that bind a person to his ancestors by an irresistible system of values, obligations and debts.[13] The question is to what extent Freud's psychoanalytical theory is the result of Freud's surrender to those "dark emotional powers."

---

10. Ernest Jones, *The Life and Work of Sigmund Freud,* vol. 1, Basic Books, 1953, p. 22.

11. Richard J. Bernstein, *Freud and the Legacy of Moses,* Cambridge UP, 1998, p. 1, on assets.cambridge.org

12. Sigmund Freud, "On Being of the B'nai B'rith," quoted in Peter Homans, *The Ability to Mourn: Disillusionment and the Social Origins of Psychoanalysis,* University of Chicago Press, 1989, p. 71.

13. Ivan Boszormenyi-Nagy, *Invisible Loyalties: Reciprocity in Intergenerational Family Therapy,* Harper & Row, 1973.

We must take Freud seriously when he tells us, in *The Interpretation of Dreams,* that his own Jewishness took the form of an identification with Hannibal, and the fantasy of "taking vengeance on the Romans." He went on to say:

"I myself had walked in Hannibal's footsteps [...]. Hannibal, with whom I had achieved this point of similarity, had been my favourite hero during my years at the Gymnasium; [...] Moreover, when I finally came to realize the consequences of belonging to an alien race, and was forced by the anti-Semitic feeling among my classmates to take a definite stand, the figure of the Semitic commander assumed still greater proportions in my imagination. Hannibal and Rome symbolized, in my youthful eyes, the struggle between the tenacity of the Jews and the organization of the Catholic Church. The significance for our emotional life which the anti-Semitic movement has since assumed helped to fix the thoughts and impressions of those earlier days. Thus the desire to go to Rome has in my dream-life become the mask and symbol for a number of warmly cherished wishes, for whose realization one had to work with the tenacity and single-mindedness of the Punic general, though their fulfillment at times seemed as remote as Hannibal's life-long wish to enter Rome."

The significance of this public confession, printed in 1899 for all the world to read, cannot be overestimated. Here Freud names as the driving force in his life the fantasy of entering Rome (the Christian world) and destroying it to avenge the Phoenicians (the Jews).

If Freud was deeply influenced by his Jewish background, so were the other founding members of the psychoanalytical movement. Dennis Klein writes in *Jewish Origins of the Psychoanalytic Movement:*

"From its beginning in 1902 to 1906, all 17 members were Jewish. The full significance of this number lies again in the way their viewed themselves, for the analysts were aware of their Jewishness and frequently maintained a sense of Jewish purpose and solidarity. [...] this feeling of positive Jewish pride formed the matrix of the movement in the psychoanalytic circle: As a spur to renewed independence, it tightened the bond among the members and powered their self-image of a redemptive elite."[14]

The exception is Carl Jung, whom Freud named president of the International Psychoanalytical Association in 1910 precisely to

---

14. Dennis B Klein, *Jewish origins of the psychoanalytic movement,* The University of Chicago Press, 1985, p. xi.

deflect the reproach that psychoanalysis was a "Jewish science."[15] Interestingly, Jung is the only member who never subscribed to Freud's theory of infantile sexuality. In response to a letter by Karl Abraham, who complained that "Jung seems to be reverting to his former spiritualistic inclinations," Freud explained: "it is really easier for you than it is for Jung to follow my ideas, for [...] you stand nearer to my intellectual constitution because of racial kinship (*Rassenverwandtschaft*)." Freud asked Abraham not to antagonize Jung because "it was only by his appearance on the scene that psychoanalysis escaped the danger of becoming a Jewish national affair."[16]

In contrast to Jung, Abraham was the most zealot supporter of Freud's theory of infantile sexuality. In *The History of the Psychoanalytic Movement,* 1919, Freud wrote that, "The last word in the question of traumatic etiology was later on said by Abraham, when he drew attention to the fact that just the peculiar nature of the child's sexual constitution enables it to provoke sexual experiences of a peculiar kind, that is to say, traumas" (self-inflicted traumas, so to speak). Freud was referring to a 1907 paper by Abraham, "The Experiencing of Sexual Trauma as a Form of Sexual Activity." It is significant that Abraham, son of an Orthodox rabbi, was also the most ethnocentric of Freud's disciples. He wrote in 1913 an essay "On Neurotic Exogamy," diagnosing Jewish men who say they "could never marry a Jewess" with a neurosis resulting from "disappointed incestuous love."[17]

Denial, projection, inversion

I suggest that Freud's abandon of the seduction theory and its cover-up by the Oedipus complex were motivated, half-unconsciously at least, by Freud's loyalty, not only to his father, but to his Jewish community. In the 1890s, Freud's clientele was drawn almost exclusively from the Jewish middle class. Imagine if Freud's seduction theory had earned him the recognition he craved for: although he disguised the identity of his patients in his case

---

15. Andrew Heinze, *Jews and the American Soul,* Princeton UP, 2004.
16. Moshe Gresser, *Dual Allegiance: Freud as a Modern Jew,* State University of New York Press, 1994, p. 138; Cuddihy, *The Ordeal of Civility, op. cit.,* p. 77.
17. Karl Abraham, "On Neurotic Exogamy," in *Clinical Papers and Essays on Psycho-analysis*, ed. Hilda Abraham, Basic Books, 1955, pp. 48-50.

studies, it would not have been long before his work was attacked, not just as "Jewish science," but as evidence of the depravity of Jewish mores.

However, I don't think Freud reasoned consciously in this manner. As he was turning a blind eye on the incestuous sexuality of his patients' families, his blindness was not fake, but psychologically constrained; it is the blindness that characterizes Jewishness. At the core, Jewishness is the conviction, deeply internalized from the earliest age, of the superiority of Jews over non-Jews—"chosenness". Anything contradicting this superiority creates a cognitive dissonance which is overcome by denial.

Denial means projection: to protect the dirty secret of child abuse in Jewish families—including his own—, Freud projected an imaginary repressed infantile perversion on all mankind. Projection, in turn, means inversion: Freud's close disciple Otto Rank claimed that Jews had a more primitive, and therefore more healthy sexuality than Gentiles (Rank, "The Essence of Judaism," 1905). Freudians and Freudo-Marxists have systematically denounced Christian civilization as suffering from sexual repression. According to Wilhelm Reich, anti-Semitism is itself a symptom of sexual frustration, and could be cured by sexual liberation (*The Mass Psychology of Fascism*, 1934)—an improvement from Leo Pinsker's theory that Judeophobia was a "hereditary" and "incurable" "disease transmitted for two thousand years."[18] In order to understand the psychological background of this Reichian messianic mission to cure the Christian West, and in order to see more clearly the projective nature of the psychoanalytical theory of repression, it is helpful to know the personal story of Wilhelm Reich, which reads as a caricature of Freud's: At ten years old, when he realized that his mother was having an affair with his tutor, the young Wilhelm thought of blackmailing his mother into having sex with him. Eventually, he confided in his father about his mother's adultery. In 1910, after a period of beatings from his father, his mother committed suicide, for which Reich blamed himself.[19]

One of the most puzzling aspects of Jews' relationship with their host nations is its ambivalence—patterned on biblical "history": within Jewish thinking, saving the nations and

---

18. Leon Pinsker, *Auto-Emancipation,* 1882, on www.jewishvirtuallibrary.org
19. Myron Sharaf, *Fury on Earth: A Biography of Wilhelm Reich,* St. Martin's Press, 1983, as retold by Gilad Atzmon in *Being in Time*, Skyscraper, 2017, pp. 93-94.

destroying them are not two sides of the same coin, but one and the same, because what nations are supposed to be cured of is their very identity (their gods, in biblical terms). According to Andrew Heinze, author of *Jews and the American Soul*, Jews have shaped "American ideas about the mind and soul" with the preoccupation "to purge the evils they associated with Christian civilization."[20] It really started with Freud. In September 1909, invited to give a series of lectures in New England, Freud jokingly asked his companions, Sandor Ferenczi and Carl Jung: "Don't they know we're bringing them the plague?"[21]—an extraordinary statement for a medical doctor pretending to have found a "cure" for neurosis. And a prophetic one: Freudism became a justification for a sexual "liberation" that can be seen in retrospect as a massive sexual abuse of the youth. And although it might seem unfair, I believe it appropriate to mention that Freud's grandson Sir Clement Freud, British MP, was exposed—but only after his death—as a pedophile, rapist, and suspected murderer of a three-year-old girl.[22]

B'nai B'rith and the road to fame

By a stunning coincidence, Freud was initiated into the recently founded B'nai B'rith in September 1897, precisely the time of his conversion to the dogma of infantile sexuality. Dennis Klein writes in chapter 3 of his book ("The Prefiguring of the Psychoanalytic Movement: Freud and the B'nai B'rith") that after the bitter disappointment of being denied professorship, "Freud filled, through the B'nai B'rith, the professional as well as the social vacuum in his life." He was a very active member attending almost every meeting during the first decade, his most productive years. He recruited at least three members and in 1901 was a founding father of a second lodge in Vienna. The same year, he gave a talk on "Goals and Purposes of the B'nai B'rith Societies." Freud often presented his work to the B'nai B'rith before publishing it. In this respect, writes Klein, the Viennese B'nai

---

20. Andrew Heinze, *Jews and the American Soul, op. cit.*, pp. 3, 352.

21. George Prochnik, *Putnam Camp: Sigmund Freud, James Jackson Putnam, and the Purpose of American Psychology,* Other Press, 2006, p. 422.

22. Martin Evans, "Sir Clement Freud exposed as a paedophile as police urged to probe Madeleine McCann links," *The Telegraph,* June 15, 2016, on www.telegraph.co.uk

B'rith lodge "was a precursor of the movement of psycho-analysis."[23]

To what extent were the B'nai B'rith masonic meetings influential in Freud's swing from the seduction theory to the Oedipus theory? We don't know. However, we can hold as fairly certain that Freud's membership in the B'nai B'rith was influential in his becoming one of the major intellectual stars and gurus of modernity.

As a scientist, Freud was a failure, duped by his own unconscious and his unrealistic confidence that he could solve the human enigma by self-analysis alone. He was also an impostor who, in his published case studies, invented cures when there was none (as investigations into the real biographies of his patients have shown). [24] True, he was sometimes insightful. But the hagiographic image of Freud as the "discoverer of the unconscious" is totally unwarranted, as Henri Ellenberger has shown in his classic study, *The Discovery of the Unconscious*:

"throughout the nineteenth century there existed a well-rounded system of dynamic psychiatry. [...] The basic features of the first dynamic psychiatry were the use of hypnosis as an approach to the unconscious mind, the interest in certain specific conditions called 'magnetic diseases,' the concept of a dual model of the mind with a conscious and an unconscious ego, the belief in the psychogenesis of many emotional and physical conditions, and the use of specific psychotherapeutic procedures; the therapeutic channel was seen as being the 'rapport' between hypnotist and patient. [...] the cultural impact of the first dynamic psychiatry was far greater than is generally believed."[25]

It could easily be argued that, in matters of psychology, every sensible thing that Freud said had been said before him, and that almost everything he said that hadn't been said before has been proven wrong.

So why did Freud become so famous? The long answer is that Freud benefitted from the same kind of communication networking that produced many other Jewish intellectual "geniuses"—a system that made French novelist André Gide comment in 1914 (in his diary) about "this tendency to constantly emphasize the Jew, [...]

23. Dennis B. Klein, *Jewish Origins of the Psychoanalytic Movement, op. cit.,* p. 74.

24. Richard Webster, *Why Freud was Wrong,* Orwell Edition, 2005.

25. Henri F. Ellenberger, *The Discovery of the Unconscious: The History and Evolution of Dynamic Psychiatry,* Basic Books, 1981, p. vii.

this predisposition to recognizing in him talent, even genius."[26] The shorter answer to the question above is: B'nai B'rith. I will not suggest that the B'nai B'rith supported Freud's pestilential theory of infantile sexuality because they saw its potential for the moral corruption of Western civilization. But I do suggest that, had Freud maintained his earlier conviction in the reality of the abuses suffered by his Jewish patients, he would not have received as much support.

To clarify this point, it is appropriate to recall a memorable demonstration of power by the B'nai B'rith, which has an obvious relevance to Freud's intellectual biography. In 1913, the B'nai B'rith created the Anti-Defamation League to save the life and the reputation of Leo Frank, the wealthy young president of the Atlanta chapter of B'nai B'rith, who was convicted of the rape and murder of Mary Phagan, a thirteen-year-old girl working in his pencil factory. The evidence for Frank's guilt was overwhelming, but tremendous financial resources were deployed for his legal defense—including false testimonies—and an intense publicity was orchestrated in the news media, with the *New York Times* devoting enormous coverage to the case. I quote from Ron Unz's article on the subject:

"For almost two years, the nearly limitless funds deployed by Frank's supporters covered the costs of thirteen separate appeals on the state and federal levels, including to the U.S. Supreme Court, while the national media was used to endlessly vilify Georgia's system of justice in the harshest possible terms. Naturally, this soon generated a local reaction, and during this period outraged Georgians began denouncing the wealthy Jews who were spending such enormous sums to subvert the local criminal justice system. [...] All appeals were ultimately rejected and Frank's execution date for the rape and murder of the young girl finally drew near. But just days before he was scheduled to leave office, Georgia's outgoing governor commuted Frank's sentence, provoking an enormous storm of popular protest, especially since he was the legal partner of Frank's chief defense lawyer, an obvious conflict of interest. [...] A few weeks later, a group of Georgia citizens stormed Frank's prison farm, abducting and hanging him."[27]

---

26. André Gide, *Œuvres complètes,* Gallimard, 1933, tome VIII, p. 571.
27. Ron Unz, "American Pravda: the ADL in American Society," October 15, 2018, on unz.com

Thanks to the mobilization of the Jewish power elite, united as one man, Leo Frank, the first and only Jew lynched in American history, was turned from a convicted pedophile and child murderer into a martyr of anti-Semitism. We don't know what Freud thought of the case, but there is an obvious resonance between his "assault on truth" and the B'nai B'rith's. If young Mary Phagan had visited a Freudian psychoanalyst before her atrocious death, and complained of her boss' sexual overtures, she probably would have been told about her own "penis envy"; had she protested, she would have been told that her protest proved her sexual repression—exactly as happened to Freud's patient Dora, Ida Bauer by her real name, an eighteen-year-old girl suffering from hysterical symptoms.[28]

The Isaac complex

The son's repressed wish to murder his father is perhaps Freud's most fertile intuition. The problem is with Freud's abusive generalization. Only the neurotic son of a destructive and manipulative father has a repressed wish to "kill the father." Freud discovered this impulse in himself and, confounding his self-analysis for a scientific quest of universal laws, projected it on all mankind. But the fact that Freud's Jewish disciples all discovered the same impulse, and that Freudism became so widely accepted by Jews, suggests that Freud's generalization was not without merit. It only suffered from the tendency of Jewish intellectuals to project Jewish issues on all humankind. The child's repressed wish to kill his father is not universally human, but may be characteristically Jewish. The Jewish father is the guardian of Jewishness and the representative of the Jewish god. And every Jew aspires in the depth of his soul to free himself from Yahweh, the archetypal abusive and castrating Father. As Philip Roth's character Smilesburger says in *Operation Shylock*: "To appeal to a crazy, *violent* father, and for three thousand years, that is what it is to be a crazy Jew!"[29] Therefore, the secret wish to murder the Jewish father is also a secret wish for the death of the Jewish god. It is identical with the so-called "Jewish self-hatred" that Theodor Lessing saw affecting every Jew without exception: "There is not a

---

28. Kevin MacDonald, *The Culture of Critique,* Praeger, 1998, p. 124.
29. Philip Roth, *Operation Shylock: A Confession,* Simon & Schuster, 1993, p. 110.

single man of Jewish blood in whom cannot be detected at least the beginning of Jewish self-hatred."[30]

By choosing a Greek myth as a metaphor for his theory, Freud was projecting on Gentiles a Jewish problem. Had he recognized the Jewish overtone of the complex, he might have called it the "Isaac complex," since Isaac is the son that Abraham was willing to slaughter.

The expression "Isaac complex" has actually been used by French heterodox psychoanalyst Jean-Pierre Fresco, who defines it as "the overall consequences in the son's psyche of a father perceived as psychologically menacing, destroying or murderous."[31] Fresco calls such a father "Abrahamic." He draws his insight from a reading of Franz Kafka's autobiographical and posthumously published *Letter to the father,* in which Kafka describes the devastating effect on his personality of a father whose means of education were "abuse, threats, irony, spiteful laughter, and—oddly enough—self-pity." Kafka also wrote to his father: "My writing was all about you, all I did there, after all, was to bemoan what I could not bemoan upon your breast."

Kafka's major novels refer autobiographically to his relationship with his father and its deleterious psychic consequences. *The Metamorphosis* tells of Gregor Samsa's transformation into a repulsive insect chased and killed by his father, whose incestuous violence is suggested in the scene where the father attacks his son from behind with a cane, tapping his feet and "pushing out sibilants, like a wild man." After the death of Gregor appears his sister Grete, his double in the other sex, the homosexualized son. In *The Verdict,* Georg (anagram of Gregor) has just become engaged with Frieda Brandenfeld (same initials as Felice Bauer, the woman that Kafka had started dating), and announces it to his father. The father opposes a terrible prohibition to this project of marriage, accompanied by extreme narcissistic violence. The paternal prohibition of emancipation through marriage is linked to an incestuous domination that becomes clear when Georg submissively proposes to the father to exchange beds. Fresco also finds the psychic trace of the father in Kafka's novel *The Trial,* whose narrator Joseph K. was arrested without knowing who slandered him nor who will judge him. According to Fresco, this

---

30. Theodor Lessing, *La Haine de soi: ou le refus d'être juif* (1930), Pocket, 2011, p. 68.
31. Jean-Pierre Fresco, "Kafka et le complexe d'Isaac," *Le Coq-Héron,* 2003/2, pp. 108-120, on www.cairn.info

incomprehensible and omnipotent slanderer-accuser-judge is "the palimpsest of an archaic Abrahamic father unconsciously introjected as an archaic and sadistic superego, and turned into an inner persecutor."

I find it very significant that Kafka—by his own admission—drew his inspiration from his experience as the son of a psychopathic father, while his Jewish literary critics consider him quintessentially Jewish. "By common consent," wrote Harold Bloom, "Kafka is not only the strongest modern Jewish writer, but *the* Jewish writer."[32] (Hence Israel's decade-long legal battle to secure his autograph manuscripts as national treasure.) Who is right, of Kafka and his critics? Does his genius come from his being Jewish, or from his having a psychopathic father? Obviously, we cannot distinguish the two factors, because his psychopathic father happens to be Jewish; he is, in Fresco's terms, the typical "Abrahamic father." But are not all Jewish fathers Abrahamic in the measure of their Jewishness? Is not the Jewish god a psychopathic father, and the psychopathic father a Jewish god?

Kafka perceived his sadistic father as a cruel divinity, whose laws were totally arbitrary and yet unquestionable, just like the Jewish god: "for me as a child everything you called out to me was positively a heavenly commandment," he wrote in his *Letter to the Father.* "From your armchair you ruled the world. Your opinion was correct, every other was mad, wild, meshugge, not normal. Your self-confidence indeed was so great that you had no need to be consistent at all and yet never ceased to be in the right."

> "Hence the world was for me divided into three parts: one in which I, the slave, lived under laws that had been invented only for me and which I could, I did not know why, never completely comply with; then a second world, which was infinitely remote from mine, in which you lived, concerned with government, with the issuing of orders and with the annoyance about their not being obeyed; and finally a third world where everybody else lived happily and free from orders and from having to obey. I was continually in disgrace; either I obeyed your orders, and that was a disgrace, for they applied, after all, only to me; or I was defiant, and that was a disgrace too, for how could I presume to defy you; or I could not obey because I did not, for instance, have your

---

32. "Foreword" in Yosef Hayim Yerushalmi, *Zakhor: Jewish History and Jewish Memory* (1982), University of Washington Press, 2011.

strength, your appetite, your skill, although you expected it of me
as a matter of course; this was the greatest disgrace of all."

Freud on circumcision

Above all, the Abrahamic father is the executioner of the
commandment given to Abraham: "As soon as he is eight days old,
every one of your males, generation after generation, must be
circumcised" (Genesis 17:12). Had Freud preserved his original
insight into the psychological damage of sexual abuse on children,
he might have eventually reflected on the impact of neonatal
circumcision. But he has been rather discreet on the subject—
though he didn't have his own sons circumcised. He broaches it in
his latest books, but only in the context of anthropological
speculations. In *New Introductory Lectures on Psychoanalysis,* he
speculated that "during the human family's primeval period,
castration used to be carried out by a jealous and cruel father upon
growing boys," and that "circumcision, which so frequently plays a
part in puberty rites among primitive people, is a clearly
recognizable relic of it." [33] Freud went further in *Moses and
Monotheism*:

> "Circumcision is a symbolical substitute of castration, a punish-
> ment which the primeval father dealt his sons long ago out of the
> awfulness of his power, and whosoever accepted this symbol
> showed by so doing that he was ready to submit to his father's
> will, although it was at the cost of a painful sacrifice." [34]

Interestingly, Freud originally got that idea from Sandor
Ferenczi, who had written in an article that greatly impressed
Freud, that circumcision is "a means of inspiring terror, a symbol
of castration by the father." [35]

But we note that in the above quotations Freud isn't referring
to Jewish circumcision of eight-day-old children, only to circumcision of adolescent boys. Given the Jewish undercurrent in Freud's
intellectual biography, it is reasonable to assume that his inability
to deal with the issue of Jewish neonatal circumcision is connected
to his refusal to face the devastating reality of child abuse. Isn't
circumcision on the eighth day the first abuse suffered by every

---

33. Sigmund Freud, *New Introductory Lectures* (1933), Hogarth Press, 1964, p. 86.

34. Sigmund Freud, *Moses and Monotheism*, Hogarth Press, 1939, p. 192.

35. Sandor Ferenczi, *Further Contributions to the Theory and Technique of Psycho-
Analysis* (1926), Hogart Press, 1999, p. 228.

Jewish male from the part of his parents and community? It physically impresses on every Jew, and on all Jews collectively, the traumatic domination of Yahweh and his Covenant.

The unnatural incestuous wish that Freud and his Jewish male disciples discovered in their repressed unconscious could perhaps be explained as a result of the inhibition in mother-child bonding caused by the trauma of neonatal circumcision. A trauma caused at this age has little chance to ever be brought back into consciousness and be healed. More research is perhaps needed on the possible link between Jewish circumcision and the fact that, according to the 1906 *Jewish Encyclopedia*, "the Jews are more subject to diseases of the nervous system than the other races and peoples among which they dwell."[36] Research done by sociologist Leo Srole in 1962 showed that the rate of neuroses and character disorders among Jews was about three times as high as among Catholics and Protestants.[37]

In *The Future of an Illusion*, Sigmund Freud describes "religion"—meaning essentially Christianity—as a "universal obsessional neurosis" which has for believers the merit that "their acceptance of the universal neurosis spares them the task of constructing a personal one."[38] With a similar approach, Judaism can be described as a "collective sociopathy." This does not mean that "the Jews" are sociopaths, but rather that, in proportion to the degree of their identification as Jews, they are victims of a sociopathic mindset patterned from the Tanakh, "marked in their flesh" (impressed traumatically in their subconscious) by circumcision, and fueled by their elites with the paranoia of anti-Semitism. The difference between collective sociopathy and individual sociopathy is the same as between collective neurosis and individual neurosis according to Freud: participation in a collective sociopathic mentality allows members of the community to channel sociopathic tendencies toward the outside of the community, and to maintain inside a high degree of sociability.

---

36. "Nervous diseases," by J. Jacobs and M. Fishberg, on www.jewishencyclopedia.com
37. Leo Srole, *Mental Health in the Metropolis*, McGraw-Hill, 1962, New York UP, 1978; Nathan Agi, "The Neurotic Jew," *The Beacon*, December 5, 2011.
38. Sigmund Freud, *The Future of an Illusion*, Hogarth Press, 1928, p. 76.

10 - THE MARXIAN COVENANT
Karl Marx in Yahweh's Plan for Mankind

In the preceding essay, I explored the influence of Freud's Jewishness on the formation, reception and propagation of his psychoanalytical theory. I wish now to do the same for Karl Marx (1818-1883). In contrast to Freud's, Marx's Jewishness is seldom considered an important factor. If you type "Freud Jewish" as keywords on Amazon, you will be suggested a dozen books dealing specifically with Freud's Jewishness, whereas "Marx Jewish" will yield no result except Marx's own essays "On the Jewish Question", and a discussion of them, with precious little about Marx's own Jewish background and connections.

Even within the literature exposing the role of Jews in the Russian Bolshevik revolution and in other revolutionary movements of the twentieth century, such as Alexander Solzhenitsyn's two-volume *200 Years Together*, a contextualized analysis of Marx's Jewishness is lacking.[1]

One obvious reason is that Marx was not Jewish: he had been baptized a Lutheran at the age of six. Yet to claim that baptism had washed away all traces of Jewishness would be absurd, and particularly ironic in the case of a person who insisted that religion was an inessential part of Jewishness (as we shall see).

My purpose here is to examine Marx's contribution to Jewish empowerment, and, ultimately, to the historical movement toward Jewish global domination that made a major breakthrough a century exactly after the *Communist Manifesto* (1848).

I must insist in preamble that the question is not: Did Marx deliberately conspire with other Jews to advance the Jewish global agenda, while pretending to emancipate Gentile proletarians? Jewishness doesn't necessarily work that way. It could be defined as the inability to distinguish between the interest of peoples, and the interest of the chosen people, between what is good for mankind and what is good for the Jews. As a rule, Jews who believe they are working for the salvation of the world while thinking Jewishly are advancing Jewish power one way or another.

---

1. Solzhenitsyn's book has only been partially translated in English, on archive.org

This applies to Jewish thinkers who believe that Jews have a mission to guide mankind toward perpetual peace, like Theodore Kaufman, who in 1941 believed that the first step to that goal was to "sterilize all Germans".[2] But it also applies to Jewish thinkers who do not publicly identify as Jews and are even critical of Jews, yet whose worldview is profoundly biblical, that is, both materialistic and prophetic. It is a question of inherited cognitive pattern, rather than deliberate intention. That being said, in Marx's case, there is evidence of intellectual dishonesty, concealment and deception.

Marx's prophecy and Bakunin's foresight

According to Karl Popper, "the heart of the Marxian argument [...] consists of a historical prophecy, combined with an implicit appeal to the following moral law: *Help to bring about the inevitable!*"[3] There is no doubt that Marx's prophecy of a messianic transformation of the world was profoundly Jewish in inspiration. What distinguishes Marx's prophetic vision from the biblical project is that its explicit goal is the international dictatorship of a cosmopolitan proletariat, not of Jewry. Yet, as Mikhail Bakunin warned in *Statism and Anarchy* (1873), Marx's proletarian state "is a lie behind which the despotism of a ruling minority is concealed." Behind the expression "scientific socialism", Marx could only mean "the highly despotic government of the masses by a new and very small aristocracy of real or pretended scientists."[4] That centralized state, according to Marxist doxa, will be a transitional stage before true socialism; it will "wither away", according to Engels' expression. To this, Bakunin replies "that no dictatorship can have any other objective than to perpetuate itself, and that it can engender and nurture only slavery in the people who endure it." Bakunin suspected that if Marx had his way, German Jews like him would end up ruling the Communist state.

Indeed, Marx's revolutionary prophecy appealed particularly to non-proletarian German Jews. Fritz Kahn hailed him as more than

---

2. *Canadian Jewish Chronicle,* September 26, 1941, on m.forocoches.com/foro/showthread.php?t=6048156
3. Karl Popper, *Unended Quest: An Intellectual Autobiography* (1976), Routledge, 2002, books.google.com
4. Mikhail Bakunin, *Statism and Anarchy,* Cambridge UP, 1990, pp. 538-545.

a prophet in *Die Juden als Rasse und Kulturvolk* (1920): "in 1848, for the second time, the star of Bethlehem was raised to the firmament […] and it rose again above the rooftops of Judea: Marx."[5]

If Marx was the Messiah in 1848, then Benjamin Disraeli could be called his prophet. In his novel *Coningsby*, published in 1844, the Jewish character Sidonia—"a cross between Lionel de Rothschild and Disraeli himself," according to Disraeli's biographer[6]—declared: "That mighty revolution which is at this moment preparing in Germany, and which will be, in fact, a second and greater Reformation, and of which so little is as yet known in England, is entirely developing under the auspices of Jews, who almost monopolize the professorial chairs of Germany."

Four years after these words were written, the *Communist Manifesto* was published and, almost simultaneously, the revolution broke out in Germany, as Disraeli had predicted. Jews did play a major role in the 1848 revolution, as Amos Elon has shown in his book *The Pity of It All: A History of Jews in Germany 1743-1933.* "80 percent of all Jewish journalists, doctors, and other professionals" supported the revolution. The most prominent were Ludwig Bamberger in Mainz, Ferdinand Lassalle in Dusseldorf, Gabriel Riesser in Hamburg, Johan Jacoby in Koeningsberg, Aron Bernstein in Berlin, Herman Jellinek in Vienna, Moritz Harmann in Prague, and Sigismund Asch in Breslau. "All over the country," Elon writes, "rabbis in their sermons greeted the revolution as a truly messianic event." The Jewish magazine *Der Orient* praised "the heroic Maccabean battle of our brethren on the barricades of Berlin," and raved, "The savior from whom we have prayed has appeared. The fatherland has given him to us. The messiah is freedom." The Jewish scholar Leopold Zunz, founder of academic Judaic Studies (*Wissenschaft des Judentums*), "described what was happening in specifically biblical terms shot through with the Messianic political view which saw revolutionary politics as the fulfillment of biblical promise. Haranguing the Berlin students from the barricades, Zunz portrayed Metternich [Chancellor of the Austrian Empire] as Haman and hoped that 'perhaps by Purim,

---

5. Quoted in Alexandre Soljénitsyne, *Deux siècles ensemble (1795–1995),* tome I: *Juifs et Russes avant la Révolution,* Fayard, 2003, p. 269.
6. Robert Blake, *Disraeli* (1966), Faber Finds, 2010, p. 202.

Amalek [meaning the Prussian king Friedrich Wilhelm IV] will be beaten.'"[7]

After the failure of the revolution, many revolutionaries (known as Forty-Eighters) exiled themselves to London. Marx settled there for the rest of his life, "living encased in his own, largely German, world, formed by his family and a small group of intimate friends and political associates," according to Isaac Berlin.[8] Apart from Engels, Marx's friends and associates were, in fact, almost all Jewish. Marx's influence, which had been small in the 1848 revolution, would then develop, thanks to what Bakunin called in 1872, in an unpublished "Lettre au Journal *La Liberté* de Bruxelles," his "remarkable genius of intrigue." Bakunin added: "he also has in his service a numerous corps of agents, hierarchically organized and acting secretly under his direct orders; a kind of socialist and literary freemasonry in which his compatriots, the German Jews and others, occupy a considerable place and deploy a zeal worthy of a better cause."[9]

Bakunin was particularly intrigued by Marx's insistence on the centralization of all banking activity. The *Communist Manifesto* not only proclaims the abolition of private banks, but "Centralisation of credit in the hands of the State, by means of a national bank with State capital and an exclusive monopoly." In another unpublished editorial of 1872, Bakunin wrote:

> "this Jewish world is today, for the most part, at the disposal of Marx on the one hand, and of Rothschild on the other. I am convinced that the Rothschilds, on their side, appreciate the merits of Marx and that Marx, on his side, feels an instinctual attraction and a great respect for the Rothschilds. / This may seem strange. What can there be in common between socialism and a major bank? The point is that Marx's communism wants a strong centralization of the state, and where there is centralisation of the state, there must necessarily be a central bank, and where such a bank exists, the parasitic nation of the Jews, speculating with the Labour of the people, will always thrive."[10]

Having succeeded in getting Bakunin and his "anti-authoritarian" followers expelled from the International Working-

---

7. Amos Elon, *The Pity of It All: A History of Jews in Germany 1743-1933,* Metropolitan Books, 2002, pp. 153, 157, 163-164.

8. Isaac Berlin, *Karl Marx: His Life and Environment,* 1939, 2nd ed, 1948, p. 17.

9. www.marxists.org/reference/archive/bakunin/works/1872/la-liberte.htm

10. *Aux compagnons de la Fédération des sections internationales du Jura*, quoted in Henri Arvon, *Les Juifs et l'Idéologie,* PUF, 1978, p. 50.

men's Association (the First International), Marx transferred its General Council from London to New York—the city that would soon become the Western capital of Jewry, where another German Jew, Leon Braunstein aka Trotsky, would be preparing the Bolshevik revolution, with the financial support of Wall Street Jewish bankers like Jacob Schiff.[11]

The Jewish Question in nineteenth-century Germany

In order to understand Marx's hidden agenda, the best is to start with his first two significant articles, published in 1844 in the *Deutsch-Französische Jahrbücher,* four years before the *Communist Manifesto.* Their topic was the "Jewish Question". Before we present what Marx had to say about it, we must recall the context.

The "Jewish Question" is the question of the possibility and means of Jewish assimilation. The problem, as it was commonly formulated from the end of the eighteenth century, was that Jews considered themselves, and were considered, as aliens in the European nations among which they lived. One solution was to transform Jewishness from a nationality into a religion compatible with the secular values of modern nations. Moses Mendelssohn (1729–1786) paved the way in Germany for a "Reform Judaism" that defined itself as purely religious and renounced nationalist aspirations. On the basis of this new pact, Napoleon granted political emancipation to the Jews in France, and was hailed as a liberator by German Jews when he invaded the German principalities. Although Jewish emancipation underwent a setback in Prussia when he withdrew in defeat, it was complete by 1848.

However, the assumption that Jewishness was a matter of private religion created a new problem for the Jewish community, aggravated by residual forms of segregation: for many secular and educated Jews, Judaism had little appeal as a religion, and converting to Christianity seemed the logical continuation of their conversion to the Enlightenment. Half the Jews of Berlin converted to Protestantism or Catholicism in the late eighteenth and early nineteenth century.

Karl Marx's family falls in that category. His father Herschel Levi, though the son and brother of rabbis, became a Lutheran in order to practice law in the Prussian courts, and had his six

---

11. Antony Sutton, *Wall Street and the Bolshevik Revolution,* Arlington House, 1974 (archive.org).

children and his wife baptized in 1824, when Karl was six years old. Another famous Jewish convert is Heinrich Heine (1797-1856), who conceived of his baptism in 1825 (one year after Marx) as the "entrance ticket to European civilization." [12] Marx met Heine, a generation his elder, shortly after his arrival in Paris in 1843, and the two men met frequently until Marx moved to London in 1849. It is believed that their conversations had a formative influence on both men. Heine may in fact have introduced Communism to Marx, for he wrote in 1842, one year before meeting Marx:

> "Though Communism is at present little talked about, vegetating in forgotten attics on miserable straw pallets, it is nevertheless the dismal hero destined to play a great, if transitory role in the modern tragedy. [...] There will then be only one shepherd with an iron crook and one identically shorn, identically bleating human herd." [13]

The dissolution of Jewish identity into a religious faith led to a reaction in the form of a Jewish nationalist movement that would ultimately morph into Zionism. It was the German Jewish historian Heinrich Graetz (1817-1891), almost the same age as Marx, who gave the first impetus to a new Jewish national consciousness with his multivolume *History of the Jewish People,* published in 1853. Marx first met Heinrich Graetz in the summer 1874 while "taking the waters" at Carlsbad in Bohemia. The two following summers, they coordinated they vacations there. We do not know what they talked about, but as Shlomo Avineri comments, "a more dramatic prefiguration of the encounter between Zion and Kremlin could not be imagined." [14]

Graetz reawakened the national consciousness of European Jews such as Moses Hess (1812-1875), author in 1862 of *Rome and Jerusalem: The Last National Question,* which in turn impressed Theodor Herzl. According to Hess, the efforts of the Jews to merge with a nationality other than their own are doomed to failure. "We shall always remain strangers among the nations," for "the Jews are something more than mere 'followers of a religion,' namely, they are a race brotherhood, a nation." [15]

---

12. Quoted in Kevin MacDonald, *Separation and Its Discontents,* Praeger, 2013.
13. Amos Elon, *The Pity of It All, op. cit.,* p. 146.
14. Shlomo Avineri, *Karl Marx: Philosophy and Revolution,* Yale UP, 2019, pp. 171-172.
15. Moses Hess, *Rome and Jerusalem,* 1918 (archive.org).

Interestingly, before his conversion to Jewish nationalism, Moses Hess (originally Moritz) was a pre-Marxist communist. He was the founder of the *Rheinische Zeitung,* for which Marx served as Paris correspondent in 1842-43. Hess had a strong influence on both Engels and Marx.[16] Marx borrowed from Hess' 1845 essay on "The Essence of Money" his concept of economic alienation.[17] Hess always remained close to Marx; in 1869, at Marx's request, he even penned an article slandering Bakunin, accusing him to be an "agent provocateur" of the Russian government.[18]

Marx's response to Bruno Bauer

Marx's essays on the Jewish Question were critical reviews of two works by Bruno Bauer (1809-1882), a leading figure of the Young Hegelians: a book titled *Die Judenfrage* (1842), and a follow-up article on "The Capacity of Present-day Jews and Christians to Become Free."[19]

Bauer's approach to the question of Jewish assimilation was innovative. For him, the religious nature of Judaism is the problem, not the solution. He argued that Jews cannot be emancipated politically without first being emancipated religiously, because the Jews' resistance to assimilation is based on the commandment of the Torah to live permanently in separation from other people. The essence of their religion is their claim to be the chosen people, and that prevents them from even respecting other peoples. "Jews as such can not amalgamate with peoples and associate their fate with theirs. As Jews, they must wait for a particular future, allotted to them alone, the chosen people, and assuring them the dominion of the world." Therefore, there can be no emancipation of the Jews. A Jew can emancipate himself only by ceasing to be a Jew, because his true alienation is his Jewishness.

Bauer was the first since Voltaire to point at the toxic influence of the Tanakh as the key to the Jewish Question. Christians could obviously never reach that conclusion, but even secular thinkers who subscribed to the new science of "higher criticism" (pioneered by David Strauss' *Life of Jesus,* 1835) generally looked away from

---

16. Sydney Hook, "Karl Marx and Moses Hess," 1934, on www.marxists.org
17. Shlomo Avineri, *Moses Hess: Prophet of Communism and Zionism*, New York UP, 1985.
18. Bakunin's response, "Aux citoyens rédacteurs du *Réveil*," on fr.wikisource.org
19. French translation: Bruno Bauer, *La Question juive* (1843), Union générale d'Éditions, 1968, on dissibooks.files.wordpress.com/2013/09/question_juive.pdf

the xenophobia of the Tanakh. "One even screams at betrayal of the human race when the critics try to examine the essence of the Jew as a Jew," remarked Bauer.

In his critical reviews,[20] Marx does not argue against Bauer's point that Jewish religion is opposed to assimilation. Rather, he denies altogether that Jewishness is a matter of religion. He writes: "Let us consider the actual, worldly Jew—not the *Sabbath Jew,* as Bauer does, but the *everyday Jew.* Let us not look for the secret of the Jew in his religion, but let us look for the secret of his religion in the real Jew." Since Marx downplays the religious definition of Jewishness, it would be expected that he opt for the second term of the alternative and define Jewishness as a nationality, as will his friend Hess twenty years later. But he doesn't. Instead, Marx posits, for the first time, his dogma that religion belongs to the cultural "superstructure" of society, while the real "infrastructure" is economic. The essence of the Jew, he writes, is not his religion, but his love of money: "What is the secular basis of Judaism? *Practical* need, *self-interest.* What is the worldly religion of the Jew? *Huckstering.* What is his worldly God? *Money.*"

Marx redefines Jewish religion as the cult of money: "Money is the jealous god of Israel, in face of which no other god may exist." He does the same for Jewish nationality, in one short sentence: "The chimerical nationality of the Jew is the nationality of the merchant, of the man of money in general." It follows naturally, according to Marx, that if you abolish money you will solve the Jewish question:

> "Very well then! Emancipation from *huckstering* and *money,* consequently from practical, real Judaism, would be the self-emancipation of our time. An organization of society which would abolish the preconditions for huckstering, and therefore the possibility of huckstering, would make the Jew impossible. His religious consciousness would be dissipated like a thin haze in the real, vital air of society."

Jews will be emancipated when all men will be emancipated, for there is no other emancipation than emancipation from money.

Marx makes the radical claim that love of money and economic alienation came to the world from the Jews. He equates economic alienation to Jewish influence:

---

20. www.marxists.org/archive/marx/works/download/pdf/On The Jewish Question.pdf

"the practical Jewish spirit has become the practical spirit of the Christian nations. The Jews have emancipated themselves insofar as the Christians have become Jews. [...] The Jew is perpetually created by civil society from its own entrails. [...] The god of the Jews has become secularized and has become the god of the world"

And so, "In the final analysis, the *emancipation of the Jews* is the emancipation of mankind from *Judaism.*" That sounds terribly anti-Semitic, from today's standards. Because of these essays on the Jewish Question, Marx's biographers have been more concerned by the question, "Was Marx an anti-Semite?" (the title of a 1949 book by Edmund Silberner) than by the issue of his Jewish background, environment, and mindset. Michael Ezra speaks of "Karl Marx's Radical Antisemitism."[21]

But in the context of the time, Marx's view of the Jews as money worshippers was rather banal. It was almost unanimously shared among socialists, as Hal Draper reminds us in "Marx and the Economic-Jew Stereotype."[22] It was especially common among revolutionary Jews as well as among Zionists who were generally socialists. Moses Hess himself, for instance, wrote in "The Essence of Money": "The *Jews*, who in the natural history of the social animal-world had the *world-historic* mission of developing the *beast of prey* out of humanity have now finally completed *their mission's work.*"

What Marx did was to push the stereotype to its limit: he made the love of money not just an *attribute* of *some* Jews, but the very *essence* of *the* Jews. By doing so, he was in effect dissolving the Jewish question into a socio-economic question: the Jew becomes the archetypal bourgeois. By this sleight of hand, Marx eliminated the Jewish question once and for all. He would never return to it.[23]

In fact, never again would Marx target specifically Jewish financiers. Nesta Webster draws attention to that anomaly in her *World Revolution: The Plot Against Civilization* (1921):

---

21. Michael Ezra, "Karl Marx's Radical Antisemitism," March 23, 2015, on www.philosophersmag.com

22. Hal Draper, "Marx and the Economic-Jew Stereotype," from *Karl Marx's Theory of Revolution*, Vol.1, 1977, on www.marxists.org.

23. Another "anti-Semitic" article, unsigned and titled "The Russian Loan" (*New York Daily Tribune,* January 4, 1856), has been attributed to Marx by his daughter, but I find Marx's authorship dubious (read "Karl Marx and the Authorship of 'The Russian Loan'" by Karl Radl on thepurityspiral.com).

"The period of 1820 onwards became, as Sombart [Werner Sombart, *The Jews and Modern Capitalism,* 1911] calls it, 'the age of the Rothschilds,' so that by the middle of the century it was a common dictum, 'There is only one power in Europe, and that is Rothschild.' Now how is it conceivable that a man who set out honestly to denounce Capitalism should have avoided all reference to its principal authors? Yet even in the section of his book dealing with the origins of Industrial Capitalism, where Marx refers to the great financiers, the stock-jobbing and speculation in shares, and what he describes as 'the modern sovereignty of finance,' he never once indicates the Jews as the leading financiers, or the Rothschilds as the super-capitalists of the world."[24]

By reducing Jewishness to capitalism, Marx was also overlooking another side of Jewish influence in the world: the revolution. The strong involvement of Jews in revolutionary movements would not become fully apparent to the world before 1848, but Marx, being himself a German Jewish revolutionary, could not be unaware of it. Jewish revolutionary activity is one form of resistance to assimilation, especially when it calls for the destruction of the nations in the name of internationalism. By simply ignoring it, Marx was, at the very least, concealing the role of his own Jewishness in his revolutionary enterprise, while at the same time removing in advance all suspicion of his Jewish sympathies.

I believe Marx's treatment of the Jewish question set the standard of his subsequent method. First, Marx misrepresents the arguments of his adversaries, often turning them upside down before proceeding to criticize them. For example Marx pretends that Bauer sees Jewishness as a religious faith, but that was not Bauer's point. Rather, Bauer showed that defining Jewishness as a religion or ethnicity makes no big difference, because either way, the essence of Jewishness is separateness. Being religious only worsens the xenophobic nature of Jewishness, because it makes separateness a divine commandment rather than simply an ancestral habit. Secondly, Marx dismisses the complexity of things, in order to focus exclusively on a single and often secondary aspect of reality, making it look two-dimensional. Defining Jewishness as the love of money is obviously inadequate

---

24 . Nesta Webster, *World Revolution: The Plot Against Civilization,* 1921 (archive.org), pp. 95-96.

for anyone who has reflected even superficially on the question. Either Marx believes what he says, and that tells a lot about his intellectual limits, or he doesn't—which is more likely—, and that tells a lot about his intellectual dishonesty.

With the same reductionism Marx will claim in 1848, in the *Communist Manifesto* (Engels credited this insight to Marx alone), that, "The history of all hitherto existing society is the history of class struggles." It is obvious to any (non-Marxist) historian that class struggles fall far behind ethnic struggles in the list of forces shaping history, even in modern times. Even an internationalist socialist like Mikhail Bakunin could only be puzzled by Marx's total ignorance of this fact:

> "Marx completely ignores a most important element in the historic development of humanity, that is, the temperament and particular character of each race and each people, a temperament and a character which are themselves the natural product of a multitude of ethnological, climatological, economic, and historic causes, but which exercise, even apart from and independent of the economic conditions of each country, a considerable influence on its destinies and even on the development of its economic forces."[25]

Marx's ignorance is all the stranger that discussions on "national geniuses" was central to the German Romantic movement in the mid-nineteenth century. Moreover, coming from someone who grew up in a Jewish home and, despite his baptism, evolved in a mostly Jewish circle, counting among his friends zealot Jewish nationalists, I find it unbelievable that Marx's ignorance of the national factor was sincere. Or perhaps, it must be considered very typical of Jewish discourse targeted at Gentiles. In that sense, Marx's internationalism confirms Bauer's remark that Jews consider only their own nationality as real:

> "According to their fundamental representation, they wanted to be absolutely *the* people, the unique people, that is to say the people beside whom other peoples did not have the right to be a people. Any other people was, in comparison with them, not really a people; as the chosen people they were the only true people, the people who were to be All and take the world."

---

25. Bakunine, "Lettre au Journal *La Liberté* de Bruxelles," October 5, 1872, on www.fondation-besnard.org

Proudhon and the socialist movement before Marx

Having examined how Marx positioned himself on the background of the Jewish question, we can now do the same with the social question that occupied socialist thinkers.

At the time when Marx and Engels joined the movement, the most influential socialist theorist was Pierre-Joseph Proudhon (1809-1865), of nine years Marx's elder. There is no better way to understand the originality of Marx's economic ideas than by comparing them to Proudhon's. (Proudhon's work is accessible to English readers through Iain McKay's anthology: *Property is Theft! A Pierre-Joseph Proudhon Anthology,* AK Press, 2011. McKay's 82-page introductory chapters, including one on "Proudhon and Marx," can be read online).[26]

Proudhon's book *Qu'est-ce que la propriété?* (*What is Property? An Inquiry into the Principle of Right and of Government*) published in 1840, had a huge echo and became a cornerstone of the European socialist movement. Proudhon was the first to use the expression "scientific socialism", meaning a society ruled by a scientific government, one whose sovereignty rests upon justice and reason, rather than sheer will. His book was a critic of previous theories of economy (then called "political economy") developed in Great Britain by Adam Smith (1723-1790) and David Ricardo (1772-1823). As explained by McKay, "It was Proudhon who first located surplus value production within the workplace, recognizing that the worker was hired by a capitalist who then appropriates their product in return for a less than equivalent amount of wages" (McKay 66).

Proudhon's thought was in constant evolution, and therefore not totally consistent from beginning to end, even in terminology. Nevertheless, if we want to summarize it, we shall say that Proudhon advocated a decentralized, self-managed, federal, bottom-up socialism, which he called "anarchism". His vision was based on an organic model of society, the basic cell of which was the patriarchal family, while the "commune" was the fundamental unit of democratic sovereignty. In contrast, "governmental power is mechanical" and fundamentally inhuman (*Confession of a Revolutionary,* McKay 404).

Proudhon consistently spoke against projects of state socialism. For him, state ownership of the means of production was the

---

26. anarchism.pageabode.com/pjproudhon/introduction-contents

continuation of capitalism with the state as the new boss. Nationalization would simply make a nation of wage-workers, and Proudhon viewed the condition of the wage-worker as little better than slavery. State control also kills competition, and Proudhon considered that "competition is as essential to labour as division"; it is "the vital force which animates the collective being" (*System of Economic Contradictions,* McKay 197 and 207).

Although he called himself a revolutionary, Proudhon was a reformist and a democrat. He recommended that workers gain political and economic emancipation by organizing themselves in "clubs", cooperatives and associations for mutual credit, by electing representatives, and by exercising pressure and influence onto the state.

Proudhon's central formula, "Property is theft," is often misunderstood. Proudhon was attacking the capitalistic property of the means of production. Whereas the French constitution of 1793 defined property as "the right to enjoy the fruit of one's labor," capitalist property is, according to Proudhon, "the right to enjoy and dispose at will of another's goods—the fruit of another's industry and labour" (*What is Property?* McKay 124). In fact, Proudhon formulates a thesis and an antithesis. While claiming that "property is theft," he devotes long pages to the apology of the small owner, whether artisan or peasant, whose property is based on use, what he calls "possession". "Individual *possession* is the condition of social life. [...] Suppress property while maintaining possession, and, by this simple modification of the principle, you will revolutionize law, government, economy, and institutions" (*What is Property?* McKay 137). Proudhon encouraged mutualist forms of possession, but he condemned communism, which called for the complete abolition of private property: "Communism is oppression and slavery" (*What is Property?* McKay 132). Proudhon's ideal was less the abolition of private property than its fair distribution.

Marx's hijacking of the Proudhonian legacy

In *The Holy Family,* published in 1845, Marx and Engels praised Proudhon's book *What is Property?*

> "Proudhon makes a critical investigation—the first resolute, ruthless, and at the same time scientific investigation—of the basis of political economy, *private property.* This is the great scientific advance he made, an advance which revolutionizes political

economy and for the first time makes a real science of political economy possible."

"Proudhon was the first to draw attention to the fact that the sum of the wages of the individual workers, even if each individual labour be paid for completely, does not pay for the collective power objectified in its product, that therefore the worker is not paid as a part of the collective labour power."[27]

But the praises of Marx and Engels for Proudhon suddenly ceased in 1846. Two reasons can be conjectured. First, in May 1846, Proudhon rejected Marx's invitation to become his correspondent in Paris. In his answer, Proudhon criticizes Marx's will to forge a unifying dogma:

"Let us seek together, if you will, for the laws of society, the manner in which these laws are manifested, the progress of our efforts to discover them. But for God's sake, after having demolished all *a priori* dogmatisms, let us not in turn dream of making our own, of indoctrinating the people; [...] let us show the world an example of learned and insightful tolerance, but since we are in the lead, let us not set ourselves up as leaders of a new intolerance; let us not be the apostles of a new religion..."

Proudhon also expressed reservations on the idea of violent revolution: "Our proletariat has a great thirst for science, which would be very poorly served if you only brought them blood to drink" ("Letter to Karl Marx," McKay 163-165).[28]

The second reason for Marx's about-face regarding Proudhon was the Frenchman's publication of *Philosophie de la Misère* (or *System of Economic Contradictions*), in which he developed new conceptual tools to understand the structure of the capitalist world. Marx, who had announced in 1846 a book of economy, was taken by surprise. He responded with a pamphlet in French, *Misère de la philosophie,* which Proudhon described as "a tissue of vulgarity, of calumny, of falsification and of plagiarism," written by "the tapeworm of socialism" (McKay 70). Iain McKay agrees:

"While, undoubtedly, Marx makes some valid criticisms of Proudhon, the book is full of distortions. His aim was to dismiss Proudhon as being the ideologist of the petit-bourgeois and he obviously thought all means were applicable to achieve that goal. So we find Marx arbitrarily arranging quotations from Proudhon's book, often out of context and even tampered with, to confirm his

27. chapter 4, on www.marxists.org/archive/marx/works/1845/holy-family/ch04.htm
28. www.marxists.org/reference/subject/economics/proudhon/letters/46_05_17.htm

own views. This allows him to impute to Proudhon ideas the Frenchman did not hold (often explicitly rejects!) in order to attack him. Marx even suggests that his own opinion is the opposite of Proudhon's when, in fact, he is simply repeating the Frenchman's thoughts. He takes the Frenchman's sarcastic comments at face value, his metaphors and abstractions literally. And, above all else, Marx seeks to ridicule him."

Twenty years later, and two years after Proudhon's death, the most essential concepts of Marx's *Capital: A Critique of Political Economy*, would be borrowed from Proudhon, without any credit given him. When Marx writes that, "property turns out to be the right, on the part of the capitalist, to appropriate the unpaid labour of others or its product, and the impossibility, on the part of the worker, of appropriating his own product" (*Capital*, vol. 1, quoted in McKay 66), he is repeating what Proudhon wrote 27 years earlier in *What is Property?*

In 1867, when Marx published the first volume of *Das Kapital*, Proudhon's notoriety and influence still far exceeded Marx's in Europe. The International Workingmen's Association (the First International) had been founded in 1864 by Proudhon's followers, who called themselves mutualists and anti-authoritarians. Mikhail Bakunin (1814-1876), who became Marx's strongest opponent within the International after Proudhon's death, considered his own ideas as "Proudhonism widely developed and pushed right to its final consequences" (McKay 46), although he criticized the Proudhonians' attachment to hereditary property. At the Geneva Congress of 1866, the Proudhonians prevailed and convinced the Congress to vote unanimously in favor of working toward the suppression of salaried status through the development of co-operatives. Marxism had almost no influence on the French Commune of 1871, which was predominantly inspired by Proudhon's ideas of decentralized federations of communes and workers' associations.

The intensity of Marx's resolve to supplant Proudhon can be grasped from a letter he wrote to Engels on July 20, 1870, at the dawn of the Franco-Prussian War, a war which Marx saw as the opportunity to get the upper hand over his rival:

"The French need a thrashing. If the Prussians win, the centralisation of the state power will be useful for the centralisation of the German working class. German predominance would also shift the centre of gravity of the workers' movement in Western Europe from France to Germany, and one has only to compare the movement in the two countries from 1866 till now to see that the German working class is superior to the French both theoretically and organisationally. Their predominance over the French on the world stage would also mean the predominance of our theory over Proudhon's, etc."[29]

The outcome of the war gave entire satisfaction to Marx.

The Communist Manifesto, a monopolist's dream

Although Marx's economic theory is largely plagiarized from Proudhon, his solutions are the exact opposite. That is because Marx's project doesn't proceed from his economic theories. According to Karl Jaspers, Marx's approach "is one of vindication, not investigation, but it is a vindication of something proclaimed as the perfect truth with the conviction not of the scientist but of the believer." British historian Paul Johnson concurs and, after quoting from the apocalyptic and "Luciferian" poetry of Marx's youth, he concludes that, "Marx's concept of a Doomsday [...] was always in Marx's mind, and as a political economist he worked backwards from it, seeking the evidence that made it inevitable, rather than forward to it, from objectively examined data."[30]

Therefore, Marx's theoretical sum published in 1867, *Das Kapital,* is almost irrelevant to understand his program, laid out in 1848 with Friedrich Engels in the *Manifesto of the Communist Party*. "The theory of the Communists," we read there, "may be summed up in the single sentence: Abolition of private property." As if responding to protests by the informed Proudhonians, they add:

> "We Communists have been reproached with the desire of abolishing the right of personally acquiring property as the fruit of a man's own labour, which property is alleged to be the groundwork of all personal freedom, activity and independence. / Hard-won, self-acquired, self-earned property! Do you mean the property of the petty artisan and of the small peasant, a form of property that preceded the bourgeois form? There is no need to abolish that; the development of industry has to a great extent already destroyed it, and is still destroying it daily."

Abolition of private property naturally includes "abolition of all rights of inheritance," especially since the *Manifesto* also

29. www.marxists.org/archive/marx/works/1870/letters/70_07_20.htm

30. Paul Johnson, *Intellectuals: From Marx and Tolstoy to Sartre and Chomsky* (1990), HarperCollins, 2007.

proclaims the "abolition of the family," seen as a bourgeois institution "based [...] on capital, on private gain." Nations will disappear too, because "the working men have no country"; capitalism "has stripped him of every trace of national character."

The current epoch "has simplified class antagonisms. Society as a whole is more and more splitting up into two great hostile camps, into two great classes directly facing each other—Bourgeoisie and Proletariat." Engels adds in a footnote to the 1888 English edition that, "By bourgeoisie is meant the class of modern capitalists, owners of the means of social production and employers of wage labour." Marx and Engels await the complete disappearance of "the lower strata of the middle class—the small tradespeople, shopkeepers, and retired tradesmen generally, the handicraftsmen and peasants—all these sink gradually into the proletariat." The bourgeoisie, on the other hand, "has concentrated property in a few hands."

Marx and Engels predict that this concentration of wealth in ever fewer hands, and the corresponding increase in misery among the growing working class, will intensify class warfare, and lead inevitably to the violent revolution of the proletariat. The Communists "openly proclaim that their goals cannot be reached except through the violent overthrow of the entire social order of the past." After the failure of the 1848 revolution in Germany, Marx wrote that, "there is only one way in which the murderous death agonies of the old society and the bloody birth throes of the new society can be shortened, simplified and concentrated, and that way is revolutionary terror."[31]

The goal of the revolution is to establish the "dictatorship of the proletariat," as a transition toward the abolition of all classes. This stage is necessary for the proletariat to defend itself against a counter-revolution and to bring about the classless society. Although the expression "dictatorship of the proletariat" doesn't appear until 1852, the idea is clearly stated in the *Manifesto*:

> "The proletariat will use its political supremacy to wrest, by degree, all capital from the bourgeoisie, to centralise all instruments of production in the hands of the State, *i.e.*, of the proletariat organised as the ruling class; and to increase the total productive forces as rapidly as possible."

---

31. Karl Marx, "The Victory over the Counter-Revolution in Vienna," on www.marxists.org

The first thing to note is that Marx and Engels have no intention to appease the antagonism between the proletarians and the bourgeois, by improving the condition of workingmen. On the contrary, they hope that the conflict will intensify to the point of turning into a bloody civil war. For that, the misery of the working class must increase. We should remember here that tearing apart the social fabric of nations by exacerbating social, racial, generational or gender tensions is a strategy that Jewish intellectuals have used to this day.

Secondly, Marx and Engels have no intention to stop or even resist the progress of capitalism. On the contrary, they call for the total disappearance of the social and economic structures that preceded it, and look forward to its most extreme development, when all the means of production have fallen into a few hands. For only then, they claim, the new world can be born. Capitalism contains the seeds of its own destruction, but capitalism must first reach its full maturity, which is the monopoly of a few billionaires.

Obviously, monopolists can support wholeheartedly that goal. Should they fear the next step, the revolution and the appropriation of all capitals and all means of production by the state? Not necessarily, as Bakunin argued in 1872, and as Antony Sutton explained in more detail in *Wall Street and the Bolshevik Revolution* (2001):

"one barrier to mature understanding of recent history is the notion that all capitalists are the bitter and unswerving enemies of all Marxists and socialists. This erroneous idea originated with Karl Marx and was undoubtedly useful to his purposes. In fact, the idea is nonsense. There has been a continuing, albeit concealed, alliance between international political capitalists and international revolutionary socialists—to their mutual benefit. This alliance has gone unobserved largely because historians—with a few notable exceptions—have an unconscious Marxian bias and are thus locked into the impossibility of any such alliance existing. The open-minded reader should bear two clues in mind: monopoly capitalists are the bitter enemies of laissez-faire entrepreneurs; and, given the weaknesses of socialist central planning, the totalitarian socialist state is a perfect captive market for monopoly capitalists, if an alliance can be made with the socialist powerbrokers. Suppose—and it is only hypothesis at this point—that American monopoly capitalists were able to reduce a planned socialist Russia [or Germany] to the status of a captive technical colony? Would not this be the logical twentieth-century internationalist extension of the Morgan railroad monopolies and the Rockefeller petroleum trust of the late nineteenth century?"[32]

Sutton sees no Jewish conspiracy in this collusion between the Bank and the Revolution. But documents relative to the failed Russian revolution of 1905 show that there is another dimension to that unnatural alliance, as explained in an article by Alexandros Papagoergiou.[33] In 1904, Russian Prime Minister Sergei Witte was tasked to secure a huge foreign loan to stabilize Russian public finances. He tells in his memoirs that, after turning down the offer of the Jewish banks headed by the Rothschilds, because it was conditioned on "legal measures tending to improve the conditions of the Jews in Russia," he was able to raise the enormous amount of 2,250,000,000 francs via "Christian Banks".[34] Revolutionary riots started soon after. A report of the Russian Foreign Minister to Tsar Nicholas II notes that it happened "just at the time when our government tried to realize a considerable foreign loan without the participation of the Rothschilds and just in time for preventing the carrying out of this financial operation; the panic provoked among the buyers and holders of Russian loans could not fail to give additional advantages to the Jewish bankers and capitalists who openly and knowingly speculated upon the fall of the Russian rates." According to the report, the revolutionaries "are in possession of great quantities of arms which are imported from abroad, and of very considerable financial means," which had been collected by Anglo-Jewish capitalists "under the leadership of Lord Rothschild, [...] for the officially alleged purpose of helping Russian Jews who suffered from pogroms."[35]

Marxism vs. Zionism: the dialectical pliers

Jewish movements seem to be working history through dialectical antagonisms that ultimately advance Zion's Great Game. The capacity of the Jewish community to present itself either as a religion or as a nationality, depending on the circumstances, is the prime example. As I recalled in "Cryptic Jewishness," after gaining political emancipation in the name of

---

32. Antony Sutton, *Wall Street and the Bolshevik Revolution, op. cit.*
33. Alexandros Papagoergiou, "The Bloody Rehearsal: Russia's 1905 Revolution," October 24, 2019, on russia-insider.com
34. *The Memoirs of Count Witte*, Doubleday, 1921 (archive.org), pp. 292-294.
35. Boris Brasol, *The World at the Cross Roads,* 1923 (archive.org), pp. 74-78.

religious freedom in the first part of the nineteenth century, European Jews were in the position to reclaim their special nationhood. For a few decades, reformed rabbis would ostensibly oppose Jewish nationalism, proclaiming in the 1885 Pittsburgh Conference: "We consider ourselves no longer a nation, but a religion community."[36] Yet the same Pittsburgh Conference saw no contradiction in adopting the theory of German rabbi Kaufmann Kohler, that "Israel, the suffering Messiah of the centuries, shall at the end of days become the triumphant Messiah of the nations,"[37] which amounts to say that Israel is not an ordinary nation, but *the* super-nation. In the twentieth century, any trace of a contradiction between Reformed Judaism and Zionism was removed.

The early collaboration between Marx and Hess and the late encounter between Marx and Graetz both prefigure another dialectical opposition between Communism (the International revolution aimed at destroying Christian nations) and Zionism (the national project aimed at building the Jewish nation). Both movements developed simultaneously. Chaim Weizmann recounts in his autobiography (*Trial and Error*, 1949) that in early twentieth-century Russia, revolutionary communists and revolutionary Zionists belonged to the same milieu. Weizmann's brother Schmuel was a communist, and that was not a source of family discord. These divisions were relative and changeable; many Zionists were Marxists, and *vice versa*. The borderline was all the more vague that the Communist Bund, born the same year as Zionism (1897), inscribed in its revolutionary agenda the right of the Jews to found a secular Yiddish-speaking nation. As Gilad Atzmon wrote, the Bund was "also an attempt to prevent Jews from joining the 'Hellenic' route by offering Jews a tribal path within the context of a future Soviet revolution."[38]

But the most important thing to note is that, from the early days, Jewish revolutionary activity provided Zionists with a diplomatic argument in favor of their alternative program for the Jews. Herzl mentions in his diary (June 4, 1900) that "intensifying Jewish Socialist activities" was a way to "stir up the desire among the European governments to exert pressure on Turkey to take in the Jews" (Palestine was then under Ottoman control). He hawked Zionism as a solution to the problem of Jewish revolutionary

36. Alfred Lilienthal, *What Price Israel?* (1953), Infinity Publishing, 2003, p. 14.

37. Kaufmann Kohler, *Jewish Theology,* Macmillan, 1918 (www.gutenberg.org), p. 290.

38. Gilad Atzmon, "Impeachment and Antisemitism," January 7, 2020, on unz.com

subversion when meeting Kaiser Wilhelm II in 1898, and again when meeting Russian ministers in St. Petersburg in 1903.[39] The next generation of Zionists continued the stratagem. Churchill, who spoke with one voice with Chaim Weizmann,[40] dramatized the opposition between the "good Jews" (Zionists) and the "bad Jews" (communists) in his 1920 article "Zionism versus Bolshevism: A struggle for the soul of the Jewish people." He referred to Bolshevism as "this world-wide conspiracy for the overthrow of civilization" and to Zionism as the solution "especially in harmony with the truest interests of the British Empire."[41] (Churchill's later alliance with Stalin proves that his Zionism was stronger than his anti-communism.)

In the aftermath of World War II, the rivalry between the Communist and the Capitalist worlds remained the indispensable context for the creation and expansion of Israel. That explains why Roosevelt's administration, largely controlled by Jews, helped Stalin conquer half of Europe and thwarted all attempts to stop him. Curtis Dall, Roosevelt's son-in-law, has revealed a secret diplomatic channel demonstrating that the White House went out of its way to give the USSR all the time and the armament necessary to invade Central Europe.[42] Thus the Second World War was completed with the determined aim of laying the foundations for the Cold War, that is, a highly explosive polarization of the world that would prove crucial for Project Zion. In fact, during this whole period, it is almost impossible to distinguish, among the Jewish advisors of Roosevelt and Truman on foreign policy, the pro-Communists from the pro-Zionists, as David Martin remarks in *The Assassination of James Forrestal.* A case in point is David Niles, who was guilty of spying for the Soviets while advising Roosevelt, but then played a key role in Truman's support of the U.N. Partition Plan and the recognition of Israel.[43]

The Cold War proved instrumental when Nasser, Israel's most formidable enemy, was pushed into the communist camp in 1955, setting off an intense Zionist campaign to present him as a danger

---

39. *The Complete Diaries of Theodor Herzl,* 1960, vol. 1, pp. 362–379, and vol. 3, p. 960.
40. Martin Gilbert, *Churchill and the Jews*, Henry Holt & Company, 2007.
41. Published on *Illustrated Sunday Herald,* January 8, 1920, on en.wikisource.org
42. Curtis Dall, *FDR: My Exploited Father-in-Law,* Christian Crusade Publications, 1968, pp. 146–157.
43. David Martin, *The Assassination of James Forrestal,* McCabe Publishing, 2017, pp. 57-65.

to the stability of the Middle East, and to present Israel, by contrast, as the only reliable ally in the region. The Cold War was also the crucial context for Israel's defeat of Egypt in 1967 and Israel's annexation of territories stolen to Egypt, Syria and Lebanon.

Made in the USA
Monee, IL
02 November 2020

46595632R00132